INFORMATION AND COMMUNICATION TECHNOLOGIES: CONSIDERATIONS OF CURRENT PRACTICE FOR TEACHERS AND TEACHER EDUCATORS

The *Yearbook of the National Society for the Study of Education* (ISSN 0077-5762, online ISSN 1744-7984) is published in April and September by Blackwell Publishing, Inc. with offices at (US) 350 Main Street, Malden, MA 02148-5020, (UK) 9600 Garsington Road, Oxford OX4 2ZG, and (Asia) PO Box 378, Carlton South 3053 Victoria, Australia.

Society and Membership Office:
The *Yearbook* is published on behalf of the National Society for the Study of Education, with offices at University of Illinois at Chicago, College of Education (M/C 147) 1040 W. Harrison Street Chicago, IL 60607-7133. For membership information, please visit www.nsse-chicago.org.

Subscription Rates for Volume 106, 2007

	The Americas[†]	Rest of World[‡]
Institutional Standard Rate*	$146	£90
Institutional Premium Rate	$161	£99

*Includes print plus online access to the current and previous volume. [†]Customers in Canada should add 7% GST or provide evidence of entitlement to exemption.
[‡]Customers in the UK should add VAT at 5%; customers in the EU should also add VAT at 5%, or provide a VAT registration number or evidence of entitlement to exemption.
For more information about Blackwell Publishing journals, including online access information, terms and conditions, and other pricing options, please visit www.blackwellpublishing.com.
All orders must be paid by check, money order, or credit card. Checks should be made payable to Blackwell. Checks in US dollars must be drawn on a US bank. Checks in Sterling must be drawn on a UK bank.

Each volume of the 106th Yearbook is available from the publisher for $40 a copy. For earlier volumes please contact Periodical Service Company, L. P., 11 Main Street, Germantown, NY 12526-5635 USA. Tel: (+518) 537-4700, Fax: (+518) 537-5899, Email: Psc@backsets.com or http://www.backsets.com.

For new orders, renewals, sample copy requests, claims, changes of address and all other subscription correspondence please contact the Journals Department at your nearest Blackwell office (address details listed above). US office phone 800-835-6770 or 781-388-8206, Fax 781-388-8232, Email customerservices@blackwellpublishing.com; UK office phone +44 (0) 1865-778315, Fax +44 (0) 1865-471775, Email customerservices@blackwellpublishing.com; Asia office phone +65 6511 8000, Fax +44 (0) 1865 471775, Email customerservices@blackwellpublishing.com.

MAILING: Journal is mailed Standard Rate. Mailing to rest of world by IMEX (International Mail Express). Canadian mail is sent by Canadian publications mail agreement number 40573520. **POSTMASTER:** Send all address changes to *Yearbook of the National Society for the Study of Education*, Blackwell Publishing Inc., Journals Subscription Department, 350 Main St., Malden, MA 02148-5020.

Blackwell Synergy

Sign up to receive Blackwell *Synergy* free e-mail alerts with complete *Yearbook* tables of contents and quick links to article abstracts from the most current issue. Simply go to www.blackwell-synergy.com, select the journal from the list of journals, and click on "Sign-up" for FREE email table of contents alerts.

Disclaimer: The Publisher, the National Society for the Study of Education and Editor(s) cannot be held responsible for errors or any consequences arising from the use of information contained in this journal; the views and opinions expressed do not necessarily reflect those of the Publisher, Society or Editor(s).

INFORMATION AND COMMUNICATION TECHNOLOGIES: CONSIDERATIONS OF CURRENT PRACTICE FOR TEACHERS AND TEACHER EDUCATORS

106th Yearbook of the
National Society for the Study of Education

PART II

Edited by
LOUANNE SMOLIN AND KIMBERLY LAWLESS OF THE UNIVERSITY
OF ILLINOIS AT CHICAGO AND NICHOLAS C. BURBULES OF THE
UNIVERSITY OF ILLINOIS AT CHAMPAIGN-URBANA

20 07

Distributed by BLACKWELL PUBLISHING MALDEN, MASSACHUSETTS

National Society for the Study of Education

The National Society for the Study of Education was founded in 1901 as successor to the National Herbart Society. It publishes an annual two-volume Yearbook, each volume dealing with a separate topic of concern to educators. The Society's yearbook series, now in its one hundred and sixth year, presents articles by scholars and practitioners who are noted for their significant work in critical areas of education.

The Society welcomes as members all individuals who wish to receive its publications and take part in Society activities. Current membership includes educators in the United States, Canada, and elsewhere throughout the world—professors and graduate students in colleges and universities; teachers, administrators, supervisors, and curriculum specialists in elementary and secondary schools; policymakers and researchers at all levels; and any others with an interest in teaching and learning.

Members of the Society elect a Board of Directors. The Board's responsibilities include reviewing proposals for Yearbooks and authorizing their preparation based on accepted proposals, along with guiding the other activities of the Society, including presentations and forums.

Current dues (for 2007) are a modest $40 ($35 for retired members and for students in their first year of membership; $45 for international membership). Members whose dues are paid for the current calendar year receive the Society's Yearbook and are eligible for election to the Board of Directors.

Each year the Society arranges for meetings to be held in conjunction with the annual conferences of one or more of the national educational organizations. All members are urged to attend these meetings, at which the current Yearbook is presented and critiqued. Members are encouraged to submit proposals for future Yearbooks.

Information and Communication Technologies: Considerations of Current Practice for Teachers and Teacher Educators is Part II of the 106th Yearbook. Part I is *Evidence and Decision Making*.

For further information, write to the Secretary, NSSE, University of Illinois at Chicago, College of Education M/C 147, 1040 W. Harrison St., Chicago, Illinois 60607-7133 or see http://www.nsse-chicago.org

v

Table of Contents

Kenneth J. Rehage
1910-2007

The 106th Yearbook of the National Society for the Study of Education is dedicated to Ken Rehage, who served as NSSE's Secretary-Treasurer from 1975–1999.
He will be missed by many.

Technologies in Schools: Stimulating a Dialogue

LOUANNE SMOLIN AND KIMBERLY LAWLESS

There is little dispute that technology has transformed our everyday lives. We shop online, download news in our iPods, communicate via text and video, take digital photos, and conduct all manner of personal and professional business via the Internet. While these technologies have afforded new opportunities to improve efficiency, exponentially increase access to information, and expand the notion of global citizenship, they have also caused many researchers and educators to rethink what it means to be literate in this post-typographic world (Leu & Kinzer, 2000). It is not enough for citizens in the 21st century to know how to decode and comprehend information as they have in the past. They are also now responsible for efficiently and effectively finding and evaluating information as well as quickly adapting personal learning goals in response to the varied structures and complexities of these technology-enhanced environments (Alexander & Fox, 2004; Dieberger, 1997; Grabinger, Dunlap, & Duffield, 1997). As argued by Dede (this volume), these differences are nontrivial and demand critical reform of our current educational approaches at all levels.

Still, the infusion of technology in schools has not yet transformed everyday lives and learning in our nations' schools. Its progression has been slow and labored. Early pressure for integrating technology in schools came from contexts external to the school—most notably from the business sector (Scott, Cole, & Engel, 1992). The American business community became distressed about what was widely perceived as the inadequate preparation of their future workforce when "by the 1980s it began to appear that highly educated workers were needed to run high-technology machinery and that such workers were in increasing demand" (Sherman, 1985). Schools responded to this pressure, but

Louanne Smolin is currently an adjunct faculty member at National Louis University. Prior to that, she was a Clinical Assistant Professor of Curriculum and Instruction in the Department of Education at the University of Illinois at Chicago. Kimberly Lawless is an Associate Professor of Educational Psychology and Language, Literacy, and Culture at the University of Illinois at Chicago.

because business and school contexts are quite distinct, technology became added *to* the school curriculum rather than integrated *within* it.

Students were enrolled in specialized computer classes implemented by a computer teacher who focused on developing students' programming skills. Teachers often used this time as a prep period, and were rarely meaningfully involved in this innovation. Increased accessibility of personal computers and falling hardware prices in the late 1980s and early 1990s prompted a shift in the focus of technology within the schools away from computer programming and toward a more "functional computer literacy" approach (Scott et al., 1992). Software tools like word processors and drill-and-practice software resembling entertainment outlets were incorporated into content area curriculum. Although technology was being used within classrooms, it was still employed as a separate productivity tool, often replicating older forms of information transfer. However, as many have argued, the potential of technology can and should go beyond this (Coiro, Knobel, Lankshear, & Leu, in press; Kozma, 1991; Unsworth, 2002). Technology can be more than a tool. It can also be a medium for reshaping the way in which we access information, communicate with one another, and learn in school.

Although it is clear that efforts to align teaching and learning to the new affordances of information and communication technologies (ICT) are necessary in order to realize their full pedagogical potential, such reform efforts are extremely challenging, particularly for the teachers and teacher educators who must implement them. Technology-based reform is especially challenging because it is a multifaceted endeavor. Not only must we determine what and how technology should be integrated into the schools, we must also attend to local and national policy issues that impinge upon matters of infrastructure, the preparation of teachers to help all students meet technology standards, and assessment. Additionally, there are multiple groups involved, multiple perspectives through which to analyze technology-based reform efforts, and multiple domains in which to integrate technology. We believe that, to move forward and to more closely align the reality of technology with its potential, teachers and teacher educators must take the lead in sorting through the complexities of this important effort.

Multiple Professional Communities

One dimension of this multifaceted endeavor is the number of different professionals—representing different discourse communities and often working within metaphorical "silos," insulated from one another—who are involved. Computer scientists create new technologies and applications such as gaming software or multimedia authoring tools. These are often designed in idyllic laboratory settings without the school curriculum in mind. As a result, these products are not immediately applicable in real-school contexts. Researchers explore relationships between technology and learning, including the contexts surrounding technology and student outcomes. While recent research indicates a positive relationship between technology and student is the outcome when technology is part of a larger reform agenda (Ringstaff & Kelley, 2002; Zhao & Frank, 2003), researchers do not always describe the process or strategies for achieving these outcomes. Therefore, it is difficult for teachers to apply what has been learned within the dynamic realities of their unique classrooms (National Research Council [NRC], 1999). Another professional group, school administrators and policy makers, develops policies and procedures for allocating technology resources and technical support into and within schools. While they emphasize the "hardware and wire" aspects of technology integration, their decisions are often made far removed from classroom practice. Yet these decisions dictate how technology gets integrated within the classroom, oftentimes more than the curriculum does. For example, teachers may not be able to incorporate curriculum projects that rely on intensive Internet research or communication when their only Internet access points are in a lab setting that is devoted to computer literacy instruction. As a result of this professional isolation, few reforms based upon research or policy "noted the workplaces within which teachers labored, involved teachers in the design itself, allocated sufficient resources to develop teachers' capacity to implement the desired changes, or provided sustained support to insure those changes become part of teachers' daily routines" (Cuban, Kirkpatrick, & Peck, 2001, p. 816). In reality, teachers often rely on their beliefs and personal experiences, rather than documented research or policy, to guide whether and how they incorporate technology in their classrooms (Waxman, Lin, & Michko, 2003).

Multiple Theoretical Perspectives

Multiple theoretical perspectives inform the impact of ICT on educational practice. One such perspective is *sociocultural*, which emphasizes learning as a social practice through which the learner plays a central role (Vygotsky, 1978; Wells, 1999; Wenger, 1999). Through this lens, practitioners are encouraged to understand and incorporate students' prior knowledge of technology into instruction, as well as actively inquire how their race, gender, ethnicity, and social class have and will continue to impact their technology-based learning experiences. A *curriculum studies* perspective raises the question of what is important for students to understand and be able to do (Bruner, 2004; Wraga, 2002), as well as other questions about the role technology should play in 21st-century learning, why this role is important, and how should we plan and implement instruction accordingly. *Teacher education* provides another perspective. As noted by Pellegrino, Goldman, Bertenthal, and Lawless (this volume), we all recognize the importance of preparing teachers to implement technology. Yet pre-service and in-service teachers are rarely exposed to technology use in university coursework, nor do they often gain technology experiences in the natural contexts that field-based courses provide (Moursund & Bielefeldt, 1999).

Multiple Strategies

Finally, multiple disciplines contribute to technology integration strategies. For example, a scientist uses technology differently than a historian. A scientist might use virtual labs to simulate real-life contexts, while an historian uses primary source documents to construct historical arguments (Unsworth, 2002). Technology can afford students the possibility of thinking like a disciplinarian, "becoming multi-literate" across disciplines, and working like disciplinarians, in contexts reflective of these communities of practice. Yet a clear articulation of what technologies are important for any particular discipline and how these technologies are appropriated differentially across domains has not yet been afforded at the curricular level.

Therefore, while teachers and teacher educators are called upon to meet the challenge of educating students to be independent learners and informed consumers of ICT, it is difficult to sort through all of the information and diverse perspectives which contribute to our success (or lack of success) at accomplishing these goals. As a result, when technology is used in classrooms, it is often poorly integrated with other classroom activities (Gewertz, 2007). Word processing and basic skills practice remain the most frequent uses of computers at all levels. For example, a survey investigating teachers' current uses of technology conducted by the National Center of Education Statistics (NCES, 2000) states that "Forty-one percent of teachers reported assigning students work that involved computer applications such as word processing and spreadsheets to a moderate or large extent; 31 percent of teachers reported assigning practice drills and 30 percent reported assigning research using the Internet to a moderate or large extent." Rather than using technology to transform classroom pedagogies and engage students in a knowledge-based world, it is often used to merely replicate the traditional curriculum (Cuban et al., 2001). It seems that a gap exists between the promise of ICT and its current reality in classrooms.

What has become clear is that we are neither harnessing the power of technology nor appropriately leveraging it to meet the needs of 21st-century students. We contend that technology integration is not a unilateral endeavor, and that what is missing is an *overall picture* of what constitutes transformative practices for technology integration. Information emerges from a variety of academic communities, including those involved in teacher education, professional development, the academic disciplines, educational psychology, and educational technology. Whatever our academic perspective, changes in one area impact the others, and we must start bridging these gaps as an entire community. We believe that dialog across multiple groups, perspectives, and domains is key to successful reform efforts in the future. This volume is an attempt to stimulate discussion across a variety of academic perspectives and to be inclusive of the researchers, policymakers, and practitioners who work within them.

How might technology be used for *transformative* efforts aimed at developing alternative models of education that reinvent many aspects of teaching, learning and schooling in order to prepare students for the 21st century? To start the dialogue, we invited Chris Dede to contribute a vision. In his chapter, Dede highlights several trends that support the contention that technology should be used for educational reform. For example, the world in which we are preparing our students is shifting, and requires that we emphasize different literacies, habits of mind, and skills than are traditionally targeted in schools. In fact, the revised National Educational Technology Standards for Students reflects this change in focus, from preparing students to be proficient with technology tools to an emphasis on creativity, innovation, and critical thinking (International Society for Technology in Education [ISTE], 2007). Dede also argues that new interactive media can support new forms of pedagogy, and he maintains that the technologies that have transformed our day-to-day lives are also changing our students' learning profiles, including their learning styles, strengths, and preferences. The opportunity for new educational paradigms made possible by technology has been advocated before (November, 2001; Schank & Cleary, 1995; Thornburg, 2002), but we believe it bears further consideration. In particular, we think a deeper examination of four themes can help us move beyond advocacy to a realization of positive change. These four themes are technology use in and out of school contexts, educational technology policy, diversity, and teacher development. How these themes are discussed in this volume is described below.

Technology In and Out of School

The first theme examines use of technology in and out of school contexts. As pointed out by Gewertz (2007), today's students typically use technology more outside school than in. In this same article, Mark Prensky discusses students' fluency with ICT and is quoted as saying that ". . . school represents the past. After school is where they are training themselves for the future." Our students' technology practice outside of school represents a unique "fund of knowledge" (Moll, Amanti, Neff, & Gonzalez, 1992) that we must explore to meet their educational needs and better understand what their futures might be. If we do not soften the boundaries between technology use in and out of school, we run the risk of "school becoming less and less relevant [to students' lives]" (Prensky, in Gewertz).

Both Olga Vásquez's and Steve Jones's chapters explore "outside interests" related to technology. In "The Internet Landscape In and Out of School," Steve Jones helps us gain a sense of what students know. His research for Pew Internet describes college students' Internet habits, indicating that they are using technology to create and deepen their support network. They are seeking mentorship and assistance. Through their initiative, they are using technology to extend their classroom walls, although more as "activities that are basically *supplements* to the classroom curriculum" as Burbules (this volume, p. 212) notes. In "Technology Out of School: What Schools Can Learn From Community-based Technology," Olga Vásquez reminds us that "the skills privileged in a globalized world are very different from those being promoted by the schools" (p. 186). Based upon her work in after-school settings, she provides insights into why these programs are successful and discusses their promise for those working inside schools. Developing a better understanding of these outside contexts and interests can serve as fertile ground for generating transformative practices *in* school.

Policy Making

The policy context exerts enormous influence on how technology is used in schools. Geneva Haertel, Barbara Means, and Bill Penuel, in "Technology Tools for Collecting, Managing, and Using Assessment Data to Inform Instruction and Improve Achievement," discuss how this policy context has impacted the nature of technology adoptions in schools. While the policies they discuss created pockets of innovation, the resulting initiatives did not occur in a cohesive manner, contributing to slow adoptions and lack of widespread change. In "Educational Technology Policy: Educators Influencing the Process," Hilary Goldmann uses her vantage point as a lobbyist to argue that the education community's participation in the policy process can improve this situation. She considers several federal initiatives, such as No Child Left Behind, and their associated technology implications. She also provides suggestions for advocacy that teachers, teacher educators, and administrators can engage in.

Diversity

Many of our authors address the multiple dimensions associated with technology and diversity. The varied technology experiences of teachers and students represent one aspect of diversity noted in Jones' chapter. Students' cultural diversity is another dimension. The relationship between cultural diversity and technology has often been discussed as a deficit labeled the "digital divide." This divide has been characterized as a singular issue: differential access to technologies across socioeconomic groups. In "A Teacher's Place in the Digital Divide," Mark Warschauer first challenges this assumption and then focuses our attention on using technology to incorporate student diversity as an asset. He begins by defining the multiple, interconnected digital divides that exist in school settings. For example, he shows that students in low-income schools are more likely to have teachers inexperienced in the educational uses of ICT. He also discusses the experiential divide between students and teachers, with students often having more frequent and creative experiences with ICT than their teachers. Warschauer deconstructs how these multiple divides function in actual classrooms through an analysis of differential patterns of technology usage. He then offers examples of school curriculum that use technology *to build upon* student diversity, using sociocultural learning theory and critical literacy practices as the foundation for this approach.

In "Reconsidering the Digital Divide: Using Online Content to Understand Teaching and Learning," Tettegah, Whang, Collins, and Taylor argue for technology as a means of *confronting* diversity issues. They discuss new media, such as social simulation software, that can provide opportunities for educators to rethink their assumptions about "multiculturalism, diversity, and equity." Their research describes how technology facilitates the analysis and dialog necessary for teachers to not only understand the intersection of cultural diversity and classroom dynamics, but to also explore how their beliefs and attitudes affect student achievement, self-esteem and academic performance.

Teacher Development

If we are to use technology to reinvent schooling, then we must prepare teachers to assume an active role. Teacher educators acknowledge the important role that teachers play in technology and education reform, but we do not necessarily know what constitutes the effective teacher preparation or professional development that could support them in their roles as change agents. In "Teaching Teachers to Use Technology: What Works and Why," Pellegrino et al. discuss ICT as related to teacher preparation. They assert that while there is agreement within the educational community that preparing teachers to integrate technologies in classrooms is desirable, there is no systematic evidence concerning what constitutes effective practice. In this chapter, the authors maintain that the "inherently dynamic and complex context that juxtaposes teacher education, educational technology, and the practice of teaching demands a multi-faceted approach to building a knowledge base sufficient to address issues of what works, for whom, and why" (p. 52). Following Pellegrino et al., Vrasidas and Glass address in-service teacher learning in their chapter "Teacher Professional Development and ICT: Strategies and Models," discussing the common themes and unique issues of ICT-related professional development and providing illustrative examples. From these examples, they describe key strategies for effective ICT-related professional development.

Assessment

A persistent gap exists between the ways in which technologies are used for assessment and for instruction. Haertel et al. acknowledge that technology holds great promise as a catalyst for improving the depth and breadth of teacher and student learning when it is used to link assessment and instruction. They describe categories of technology applications for assessment, highlight findings from available research as to how these applications impact student achievement, and propose a framework for integrating these assessment applications so that teachers can make informed instructional choices tailored to their students' needs.

Finally, Nick Burbules, in "E-Lessons Learned," provides a summary commentary and synthesizes the issues raised by authors, anchored by his description of the "ubiquitous learning" opportunities of the 21st century. He underscores authors' contributions in presenting the obstacles to "e-learning" technologies having a truly transformative effect on the classroom and reinforces the importance of seeing this problem as a "systemic one: schools, higher education and professional development programs, national policy, all reinforc[ing] in each other a resistance to change" (p. 207).

Dede argues that "to be achieved, a transformative vision must generate the professional commitment and political will to realize a major shift in education" (p. 12). In this volume, our authors identify and explore issues that have challenged our commitment and will, clouding the promise of technology. We hope that this volume will lead teachers and teacher educators to examine their own roles in planning and implementing uses of ICT with students in mind. We maintain that stimulating discussion across academic perspectives about these four themes—technology in and out of school, policy making, diversity, and teacher development—can empower us and sustain us as we take an active stance toward using ICT for transformative purposes.

ACKNOWLEDGEMENT

Coordinating a publication devoted to multiple perspectives and dialogue is a considerable undertaking that requires thoughtfulness and constant communication. Kimberly, Nick and I gratefully acknowledge the incredible support of Deb Miretzky. Over the past two years her wisdom, wit and finely tuned editorial eye ensured this volume would be accessible to the many audiences we hope to reach.

REFERENCES

Alexander, P.A., & Fox, E. (2004). A historical perspective on reading research and practice. In R.B. Ruddell & N.J. Unrau (Eds.), *Theoretical models and processes of reading* (5th ed., pp. 33–68). Newark, DE: International Reading Association.

Bruner, J. (2004). *Toward a theory of instruction*. Cambridge, MA: Belknap Press.

Coiro, J., Knobel, M., Lankshear, C., & Leu, D.J. (in press). *Handbook of research on new literacies*. Mahwah, NJ: Lawrence Erlbaum.

Cuban, L., Kirkpatrick, H., & Peck, C. (2001). High access and low use of technologies in high school classrooms: Explaining an apparent paradox. *American Educational Research Journal*, *38*(4), 813–834.

Dieberger, A. (1997). Supporting social navigation on the World Wide Web. *International Journal of Human-Computer Studies, 46,* 805–825.

Gewertz, C. (2007, March 29). Outside interests: Young people typically plug in to new technology far more often on their own time than in school. *Education Week, Technology Counts 2007.* Retrieved October 6, 2007, from http://www.edweek.org/ew/articles/2007/03/29/30tcstudent.h26.html.

Grabinger, R.S., Dunlap, J.C., & Duffield, J.A. (1997). Rich environments for active learning in action: Problem-based learning. *Association for Learning Technology Journal, 5*(2), 5–17.

International Society for Technology in Education (2007). *National educational technology standards for students: The next generation.* Washington, DC: ISTE. Retrieved October 6, 2007, from http://www.iste.org/AM/Template.cfm?Section=NETS

Kozma, R. (1991). *Learning with media. Review of Educational Research, 61*(2), 179–211.

Leu, D.J., Jr., & Kinzer, C.K. (2000). The convergence of literacy instruction with networked technologies for information and communication. *Reading Research Quarterly, 35*(1), 108–127.

Moll, L., Amanti, C., Neff, D., & Gonzalez, N. (1992). Funds of knowledge for teaching: Using a qualitative approach to connect homes and classrooms. *Theory into Practice, 31*(2), 132–141.

Moursund, D., & Bielefeldt, T. (1999). *Will new teachers be prepared to teach in the digital age: A national survey on information technology in teacher education.* Santa Monica, CA: Milken Exchange on Information Technology.

National Center For Education Statistics. (2000). *Teacher use of computers and the Internet in public schools.* Institute of Educational Sciences. Retrieved October 1, 2007, from http://nces.ed.gov/surveys/frss/publications/2000090/index.asp?sectionID=2.

National Research Council. (1999). *Improving student learning: A strategic plan for education research and its utilization.* Washington, DC: National Academy Press.

November, A. (2001). *Empowering students with technology.* Thousand Oaks, CA: Corwin Press.

Ringstaff, C., & Kelley, L. (2002). *The learning return on our educational investment.* San Francisco: WestEd RTEC.

Schank, R., & Cleary, C. (1995). *Engines for education.* Mahwah, NJ: Lawrence Erlbaum Associates.

Scott, T., Cole, M., & Engel, M. (1992). Computers and education: A cultural constructivist perspective. *Review of Research in Education, 10,* 191–251.

Sherman, B. (1985). *The new revolution: The impact of computing on society.* New York: Wiley.

Thornburg, D. (2002). *The new basics: Education and the future of work in the telematic age.* Washington DC: Association for Supervision and Curriculum Development.

Unsworth, L. (2002). *Teaching multiliteracies across the curriculum: Changing contexts of text and image in classroom practice.* New York: Open University Press.

Vygotsky, L. (1978). *Mind in society.* Cambridge, MA: Harvard University Press.

Waxman, H.C., Lin, M., & Michko, G. (2003). *A meta-analysis of the effectiveness of teaching and learning with technology on student outcomes.* Naperville, IL: Learning Point Associates.

Wells, G. (1999). *Dialogic inquiry: Toward a sociocultural practice and theory of education.* Cambridge, UK: Cambridge University Press.

Wenger, E. (1999). *Communities of practice: Learning, meaning, and identity.* Cambridge, UK: Cambridge University Press.

Wraga, W. (2002). Recovering curriculum practice: Continuing the conversation. *Educational Researcher, 31*(6), 17–19.

Zhao, Y., & Frank, K. (2003). Factors affecting technology uses in schools: An ecological perspective. *American Educational Research Journal, 40*(4), 807–840.

Reinventing the Role of Information and Communications Technologies in Education

CHRIS DEDE

This is a pivotal time for reinventing the role of information and communications technologies (ICT) in teaching and learning, because emerging tools, applications, media, and infrastructures are reshaping three aspects of education simultaneously:

- The knowledge and skills society wants from the graduates of education are shifting as a result of the evolution of a global, knowledge-based economy and a "flat" world (Friedman, 2005).
- Methods of research, teaching, and learning are expanding, as new interactive media support innovative forms of pedagogy (Dede, in press-a).
- The characteristics of students are changing, as their usage of technology outside of academic settings shapes their learning styles, strengths, and preferences (Dede, 2005).

Combined, these trends suggest that—beyond implementing at scale the types of educational computers and telecommunications research and experience that have been proven effective—we should also develop alternative models of education that use emerging technologies to reinvent many aspects of teaching, learning, and schooling.

This chapter attempts to answer the question: If we were to redesign education not to make historic models of schooling more efficient, but instead to prepare students for the 21st century—simultaneously transforming teaching in light of our current knowledge about the mind—what types of learning environments might sophisticated ICT enable us to create? In framing a possible answer to this question, we must consider that the primary barriers to altering curricular, pedagogical, and assessment practices towards any ICT-based transformative vision are not conceptual, technical, or economic, but instead psychological,

Chris Dede is the Timothy E. Wirth Professor in Learning Technologies at Harvard's Graduate School of Education. His fields of scholarship include emerging technologies, policy, and leadership.

11

political, and cultural. The largest challenges in changing schooling are people's emotions and their almost unconscious beliefs, assumptions, and values. To be achieved, a transformative vision must generate the professional commitment and political will to realize a major shift in educational practice.

Implications for Education of the Impacts ICT Are Having on Society

The rethinking of conventional educational models I advocate in this chapter is based on three fundamental observations about the impact of ICT on society. The first observation is that the definition of what computers and related technologies can accomplish has repeatedly expanded since these devices were first developed in the 1940s: from numerical calculators to data processors, to productivity enhancers, to information managers, to communications channels, to pervasive media for individual and collective expression, experience, and interpretation. Past visions of technology in teaching and learning largely reflect using ICT as a means of increasing the effectiveness of traditional instructional approaches: enhancing productivity through tools such as word processors, aiding communication through channels such as email and threaded asynchronous discussions, and expanding access to information via web browsers and streaming video. All these have proven worthy in conventional schooling; however, as discussed later, none draw on the full power of ICT for individual and collective expression, experience, and interpretation—core life-skills for the 21st century.

The second observation about the impact of ICT on society is that cognition is now distributed across human minds, tools/media, groups of people, and space/time (Dede, in press-b; Engeström & Middleton, 1996; Hutchins, 1995; Salomon 1993). As one illustration, I do my income taxes in cognitive partnership with a tax preparation tool that understands part of the thinking involved (e.g., multiplication, on which line to list a number). As another example, when I have an asynchronous threaded discussion in my courses, my students and I think collectively though we are distributed across distance and time. Because of sophisticated computers and telecommunications, the process of individual and collective thought in civilization is increasingly dispersed symbolically, socially, and physically.

For better or for worse, entertainment and human interaction are delocalizing as well. People who share the same dwelling may have very different personal communities as their major sources of sociability, support, information, sense of belonging, and social identity, as contrasted to the historic pattern of lifestyles centered on face-to-face groups interacting with local resources (Rheingold, 2002). Our great-grandparents would see our lifestyle as bizarre—"electronic nomads wandering among virtual campfires" (Mitchell, 2003)—yet in counterpoint many youth today see prior generations as hapless prisoners of geography, trapped in the limits of a single physical location. Given that distributed thought, action, and sociability show no signs of receding, formal education should prepare people to achieve their full potential in this emerging, novel context, avoiding its weaknesses and traps while maximizing its strengths and opportunities.

The third observation about the impact of ICT on society is that the types of work done by people, as opposed to the kinds of labor done by machines, are continually shifting. Economists Frank Levy and Richard Murnane (2004) have documented a very important aspect of how the skills society needs from graduates are changing:

Declining portions of the labor force are engaged in jobs that consist primarily of routine cognitive work and routine manual labor—the types of tasks that are easiest to program computers to do. Growing proportions of the nation's labor force are engaged in jobs that emphasize expert thinking or complex communication—tasks that computers cannot do. (pp. 53–54)

These economists go on to explain that "expert thinking [involves] effective pattern matching based on detailed knowledge; and metacognition, the set of skills used by the stumped expert to decide when to give up on one strategy and what to try next" (Levy & Murnane, 2004, p. 75). They further note, "Complex communication requires the exchange of vast amounts of verbal and nonverbal information. The information flow is constantly adjusted as the communication evolves unpredictably" (Levy & Murnane, p. 94). Education should prepare students for a world in which computers do almost all types of routine cognitive tasks and in which expert thinking and complex communications are the core intellectual skills for prosperity. These higher order skills are based on fundamental knowledge about how to do simpler tasks, so the shift needed is not about removing the learning of routine cognitive performances from the curriculum. Rather, the fundamental change involves deemphasizing fluency in simple procedures as an end-goal of preparation for work and life, instead using these routine skills as a substrate for mastering complex mental performances.

Based on these three interrelated shifts, this chapter advocates that we as a field develop a new, transformative vision for the evolution of education over the next 15 years. In this enterprise of reinventing teaching, learning, and schooling, we would not need to rely on any major technological advances not yet achieved, such as a substantial leap forward in artificial intelligence. Instead, we could make full use of emerging, sophisticated technologies that are not creative or smart in comparison to humans, but are increasingly adept at accomplishing "routine" tasks. In our process of reconceptualization, we must first focus on what educational needs we are meeting with the increased power of emerging ICT, because centering new visions simply on recently expanded capabilities of computers and telecommunications will merely generate "solutions" in search of problems.

Numerous reports on the global, knowledge-based economy and the "flat" world document that tomorrow's workers must be prepared to shift jobs and careers more frequently, to be flexible and adaptable in acquiring job skills, and to integrate and focus a changing mix of job and education knowledge on business processes and problems (Friedman, 2005). The worker of the 21st century must have science and mathematics skills, creativity, fluency in information and communication technologies, and the ability to solve complex problems (Business-Higher Education Forum, 2005). And yet much of U.S. education is still based on the premise that economic processes and institutions will mirror those in the 20th century (Dede, Korte, Nelson, Valdez, & Ward, 2005). Students are prepared to be future employees of business organizations now rapidly becoming obsolete (Business Roundtable, 2005). Current trends suggest that more students will run their own businesses rather than work for others and, as adults, must constantly, quickly, and efficiently learn new skills and information to be effective entrepreneurs.

Unfortunately, at a time when sophisticated reasoning is becoming an entry-level skill for a desirable job, the rate at which high school graduates are going on to postsecondary education is falling, not rising. Our country is losing vital talent because our current educational system neither engages many students nor helps them succeed. Failure to address our dropout crisis will lead to dismal economic results in the years ahead. Why are we throwing away so much human potential? A substantial part of the explanation is that we use far too narrow a range of pedagogies in schooling students.

Learning is a human activity quite diverse in its manifestations from person to person (Dede, in press-a). Consider three activities in which all humans engage: sleeping, eating, and bonding. One can arrange these on a continuum from simple to complex, with sleeping towards the simple end of the continuum, eating in the middle, and bonding on the complex side of this scale. People sleep in roughly similar ways; if one is designing hotel rooms as settings for sleep, while styles of décor and artifacts vary somewhat, everyone needs more or less the same conditions to foster slumber.

Eating is more diverse in nature. Individuals like to eat different foods and often seek out a range of quite disparate cuisines. People also vary considerably in the conditions under which they prefer to dine, as the broad spectrum of restaurant types attests. Bonding as a human activity is more complex still. People bond to pets, to sports teams, to individuals of the same gender and of the other gender. They bond sexually or platonically, to those similar or opposite in nature, for short or long periods of time, to a single partner or to large groups. Fostering bonding and understanding its nature are incredibly complicated activities.

Educational research strongly suggests that individual learning is as diverse and as complex as bonding, or certainly as eating. Yet theories of learning and philosophies about how to use ICT for instruction tend to treat learning like sleeping, as a simple activity relatively invariant across people, subject areas, and educational objectives. Current, widely used instructional technology applications have less variety in approach than a low-end fast-food restaurant—small wonder that, even by middle school, so many children give up on our educational system and lose the belief that learning is motivating and possible for them.

As discussed earlier, a crucial challenge for U.S. education is to align curriculum and learning to a whole new economic model[1] based on an emerging global, knowledge-based workplace (Dede et al., 2005). Linking economic development, educational evolution, workforce development, and strengthened social services is essential to meeting this challenge (National Academy of Science, 2006). Given the huge loss of human capacity from dysfunctions in our current systems of schooling, to compete successfully in a "flat" world we must transform children's learning processes in and out of school and engage student interest in gaining 21st-century skills and knowledge. But what "21st-century skills" are we neglecting to teach?

21st-Century Skills

If we apply the three observations about the impact of sophisticated ICT on society (individual and collective expression, experience, and interpretation; distributed cognition and action; erosion of routine tasks in favor of expert decision making and complex communications skills) to predictions about the emerging global, knowledge-based economy, insights emerge about the 21st-century skills today's students should acquire in school (Dede, in press-c). As one illustration, in current instructional practice, a frequently neglected cluster of 21st-century skills is *collective problem resolution via mediated interaction*. In much of 21st-century work, problem *finding* (the front end of the inquiry process: making observations and inferences, developing hypotheses, and conducting experiments to test alternative interpretations of the situation) is crucial to reaching a point where the work team can do problem *solving*. Individual and collective metacognitive strategies for making meaning out of complexity (such as making judgments about the value of alternative problem formulations) are vital. Some of the time, team members communicate face-to-face; other times they communicate across barriers of distance and time using various media like videoconferencing or email (mediated interaction). Knowledge is grounded in a setting and distributed across a community, rather than abstract and isolated within individuals.

Each person involved has strong skills in effective pattern matching based on detailed knowledge and in judging when to give up on a particular problem-solving strategy and what to try next. Individuals on the work team are adept at manipulating sophisticated ICT applications and representations utilized within the complementary perspectives they bring to bear (e.g., using a spreadsheet to examine financial hypotheticals). They also are skilled in expressing core insights from their knowledge to others who have different backgrounds and experiences. Richly interactive complex communication among team members is not limited to face-to-face dialogue, but frequently relies on mediated interaction across distance during which the team co-constructs and negotiates shared interpretive understandings and a problem-resolution strategy. Collaborating across a conference table is important, but so is collaborating in a shared virtual workplace with a person half a world away that one may never meet.

For example, a school district might task a team of teachers, school administrators, parents, and local business executives to develop a plan for improving students' educational outcomes in mathematics. Potential factors leading to sub-par educational performance include individual differences in native language, gender, culture, and socioeconomic status; teachers' experience and preparation in mathematical content, subject-specific pedagogy, classroom management, and student engagement; state and district policies related to educational reform; the curricular materials used in mathematics; and the capacity of the technology infrastructure at local schools, among others. Under these circumstances, individual and collective skills in problem finding, inquiry, metacognition, collaboration, expert decision making, complex communication, and use of ICT tools, communicative media, and representations are vital to the team's success. Through mediated interaction, they may well also draw on distant experts in preparing their report.

Unfortunately, the interrelated 21st-century skills delineated earlier are largely absent in current pedagogical and assessment practices. The next section describes the strengths and limits of current ICT-based instructional design approaches in helping students attain this cluster of 21st-century knowledge and skills. The following section then delineates how emerging technologies such as multiuser virtual environments (MUVEs) and augmented realities enable new types of pedagogical strategies that meet a broader spectrum of learning styles and enable mastery of more sophisticated kinds of skills, complementing current teaching methods to more effectively prepare students for the 21st century.

Shortfalls in How Current ICT for Learning Meet 21st-Century Educational Challenges

Three competing schools of thought on how people learn—behaviorism, cognitivism, and constructivism—have strongly influenced the design of instructional technologies (Dede, in press-a). Behaviorists believe that, because learning is based on experience, pedagogy centers on manipulating environmental factors to create instructional events inculcating content and procedures in ways that alter students' behaviors. Cognitivists posit that, because learning involves both experience and thinking, instruction centers on helping learners develop interrelated, symbolic mental constructs that form the basis of knowledge and skills. Constructivists believe that, because learning involves constructing one's own knowledge in a context richly shaped by interactions with others, instruction centers on helping learners to actively invent individual meaning from experiences. At times, a collective cultural setting may influence this interpretive process.

Each school of thought is not a single, unified theory, but rather a collection of theories distinct from each other but loosely related by a common set of fundamental assumptions. Further, any given pedagogical tool, application, medium, or environment may incorporate perspectives from more than one of these intellectual positions.

Behaviorism

In the behaviorist school of thought (Dabbagh, 2006), the purpose of education is for students to acquire skills of discrimination (recalling facts), generalization (defining and illustrating concepts), association (applying explanations), and chaining (automatically performing a specified procedure). The learner must know how to execute the proper response as well as the conditions under which the response is made. Computer-assisted instruction (CAI) and drill-and-skill learning management systems (LMS) are the two types of instructional technologies most closely associated with this school of thought, although many other ICT tools and applications utilize some aspects of behaviorist design.

Behaviorist instructional technologies are limited both in what they can teach and in the types of engagement they offer to learners, but have proven useful for tasks involving learning facts and simple procedural skills (National Research Council, 2000). What the diverse subject areas taught by CAI and LMS have in common is an emphasis on factual knowledge and recipe-like procedures: material with a few correct ways of accomplishing tasks. So, for example, behaviorist instructional technologies can teach simple skills such as alternative algorithms for division, in which the number of permissible variants is small and the end result is always the same. Factual knowledge, such as the year Columbus discovered America, is similar in its cognitive attributes: one right answer and basic mental processes primarily involving assimilation into memory. A contrasting illustration of knowledge and skills not well taught by CAI and LMS is learning how to write an evocative essay on "My Summer Vacation." Behaviorist instruction can help with the spelling and grammar aspects of this task, but effective literary style is not reducible to a narrow range of "correct" rhetorical and narrative processes.

Cognitivism

In contrast to behaviorist objectives for teaching, goals for instruction characteristic of the cognitivist school of thought include (National Research Council, 2005):

- providing a deep foundation of factual knowledge and procedural skills;
- linking facts, skills, and ideas via conceptual frameworks—organizing domain knowledge as experts in that field do, in ways that facilitate retrieval and application; and

- helping students develop skills that involve improving their own thinking processes, such as setting their own learning goals and monitoring progress in reaching these.

Although a wide variety of instructional technologies incorporate some principles from cognitivism, intelligent tutoring systems (ITS) are veridical examples of pedagogical media based on this school of thought.

The Andes Physics Tutoring System illustrates the cognitivist instructional design underlying an ITS (VanLehn et al., 2005). Andes aids college students with physics homework problems. Its screen simultaneously presents each problem and provides specialized work-spaces for learners to draw vectors and coordinate axes, define variables, and enter equations. Unlike pencil and paper representations, Andes generates immediate feedback on the correctness of each step a student takes. In addition, Andes includes a mathematics package for equation solving and provides three kinds of tutorial help customized to each specific process in a task. As the student solves a problem, Andes computes and displays a score that is a complex function of degree of correctness, number of hints, and good problem-solving strategies.

Scholars disagree on how broad a range of knowledge and skills cognitivist instructional technologies can teach (Dede, in press-a). What the diverse subject areas now taught by pedagogical media like ITS have in common is well-defined content and skills, material with a few correct ways of accomplishing tasks. Proponents of cognitivist approaches believe that eventually ITS-like educational devices, coupled with human instructors, will teach most of the curriculum, including less well-defined skills such as the rhetoric of writing an evocative essay. However, three decades of work toward this ambitious goal have yielded limited progress to date.

Constructivism

The constructivist school of thought is characterized by goals for instruction that include (Dabbagh, 2006):

- instruction as a process of supporting knowledge construction rather than communicating knowledge;
- teacher's role as guide, rather than an expert transferring knowledge to novices' "blank slates";
- learning activities that are authentic and that center on learners' puzzlement as their faulty or incomplete knowledge and skills fail to predict what they are experiencing;

- encouragement for students to reflect on experiences, seek alternative viewpoints, and test the viability of ideas.

Student motivation to achieve these goals is determined by factors such as challenge, curiosity, choice, fantasy, and social recognition (Pintrich & Schunk, 2001).

Constructivist pedagogical media span a wide range. An example that illustrates many aspects of this approach is the Jasper Woodbury mathematics curriculum. Middle-school students in math class view 15-minute video adventures that embed mathematical reasoning problems in complex, engaging real-world situations. One episode depicts how architects work to solve community problems, such as designing safe places for children to play. This video ends with a challenge to spend the next week of class meetings designing a neighborhood playground:

Students in the classroom help Christina and Marcus by designing swing sets, slides, and sandboxes; then building models of their playground. As they work through this problem, they confront various issues of arithmetic, geometry, measurement, and other subjects: How do you draw to scale? How do you measure angles? How much pea gravel do we need? What are the safety requirements? (National Research Council, 2000, p. 208)

Contrasting this example to the two schools of thought described previously provides a sense of the differences in pedagogical media developed by these differing theories of learning and teaching. In particular, note that these students are learning simpler skills in the context of a complex task, in sharp contrast to behaviorist instructional design.

Constructivist approaches can potentially teach a very broad spectrum of knowledge and skills (Dede, in press-a). However, in practice, constructivist instruction has proven quite difficult to implement in conventional school settings, for a variety of reasons discussed in the other chapters in this volume. Also, the efficiency of constructivist learning technologies for material that behavioralism and cognitivism can teach is questionable. Content and skills that are relatively invariant regardless of individual perspective (e.g., arithmetic operations) are learned more quickly when taught as "truths" than when found through exploration that, in extreme unguided forms, involves students slowly reinventing civilization (Kirschner, Sweller, & Clark, 2006).

Of all the pedagogies sketched earlier, the closest to preparing students for collective problem resolution is guided social constructivism (Duffy & Cunningham, 1996; Kafai & Ching, 2001). Guided constructivism is defined as students actively constructing their knowledge with instructional support, as opposed to being passive recipients assimilating information communicated by the teacher (Jonassen, 1996). In social constructivism, students construct knowledge as a result of their interactions with their community (Edelson, Pea, & Gomez, 1996). Some scholars (Pear & Crone-Todd, 2001; Simpson, 2002) identify the scientific research community as an example of social constructivism, because researchers construct their own ideas, share those with peers, and through these interactions reformulate their knowledge.

Unfortunately, many forms of "project-based" or "problem-based" learning (frequently used synonyms for both strong and weak forms of guided social constructivist pedagogy) make little use of ICT (Krajcik & Blumenfeld, 2006). Also, as other chapters in this Yearbook describe, successfully implementing innovative curricula based on guided social constructivism in the era of No Child Left Behind is difficult for a myriad of reasons (Wiske, Franz, & Breit, 2004).

When comparing all these current uses of ICT in the design of instruction to the types of 21st-century skills graduates of schooling need, serious shortfalls are evident (Dede, in press-c). Conventional K-12 instruction, particularly behaviorist and cognitivist approaches, emphasizes manipulating predigested information to build fluency in routine problem solving, rather than filtering data derived from experiences in complex settings to develop skills in sophisticated problem finding. Also, problem-solving skills are presented in an abstract form that makes transfer to other academic disciplines (inside of schools) and real-world situations (outside of schools) difficult. In all three types of instructional designs, the ultimate objective of education is often presented as learning a specific problem-solving routine to match every work situation, rather than developing expert decision making and metacognitive strategies that indicate how to proceed when no standard approach seems applicable.

Little time is spent on building capabilities in group interpretation, negotiation of shared meaning, and co-construction of problem resolutions, particularly in behaviorist and cognitivist instructional strategies. The communication skills stressed are those of simple presentation, rather than the capacity to engage in richly structured interactions that articulate perspectives unfamiliar to the audience. As discussed earlier, ICT applications and representations are largely used to automate traditional methods of teaching and learning, rather than to model complexity and express insights to others. In all three types of learning theories, face-to-face communication and assessment based on pencil-and-paper tests are seen as the "gold standard," so students develop few skills in mediated dialogue and in shared design within a common virtual workspace.

Conventional assessments and tests focus on measuring students' fluency in various abstract, routine skills, but typically do not assess their capabilities for expert decision making when no standard approach seems applicable. Essays emphasize simple presentation rather than sophisticated forms of rhetorical interaction. Students' abilities to transfer their skills to real-world situations are not assessed, nor are capabilities related to various aspects of teamwork. The use of ICT applications and representations is generally banned from testing, rather than being used to measure students' capacities to use tools, applications, and media effectively. Abilities to effectively utilize various forms of mediated interaction are typically not assessed. In other words, the *effects from* technology usage (what one can accomplish without tools) are measured, but the *effects with* technologies essential to effective practice of a skill are not (Salomon, 1993).

None of this analysis is meant to imply that behaviorist, cognitivist, and constructivist pedagogical approaches do not play a valuable role in schooling. On the contrary, learning technologies based on all three types of instructional designs are important in developing foundational knowledge and cognitive skills that serve as a necessary substrate for mastering complex mental performances, such as collective problem resolution via mediated interaction. However, to prepare students for 21st-century work and citizenship, the usage of sophisticated ICT based on a complementary pedagogical theory, situated learning, is a vital supplement to current educational technologies. In particular, situated forms of instructional design are better suited than behaviorist, cognitivist, or constructivist approaches to teaching sophisticated "problem finding" as the front end of the inquiry process for making meaning out of complexity.

Situated Learning

The seminal works of Brown, Collins, and Duguid (1989) and Lave and Wenger (1991) define *situated learning* as embedded within and inseparable from participating in a system of activity deeply determined by a particular physical and cultural setting. The unit of analysis is neither the individual nor the setting, but instead the relationship between the two, as indicated by the student's level of participation in the setting (Barab & Plucker, 2002). Studies of apprenticeship in "communities of practice" (moving from newcomer to expert within a sociocultural structure of practices) are a central construct for situated learning (Wenger, McDermott, & Snyder, 2002).

In essence, situated learning requires authentic contexts, activities, and assessment coupled with guidance from expert modeling, situated mentoring, and legitimate peripheral participation (Lave & Wenger, 1991). Brown et al. (1989) proffer the graduate student experience as an example of apprenticeship in a community of practice. As part of their academic program, graduate students evolve from pupils to researchers through a series of learning activities embedded within a scholarly milieu. For example, graduate students may work within the laboratories of expert researchers, who model the practice of scholarship. These students will interact with experts in research as well as with other members of the research team who understand the complex processes of scholarship to varying degrees. While in these laboratories, students gradually move from novice researchers to more advanced roles, with their skills and the expectations for them evolving (legitimate peripheral participation). In contrast to coursework, students learn the knowledge and skills expected of them in their future research careers through modeling, mentoring, and legitimate peripheral participation.

While powerful and prevalent in life settings, situated instructional designs are seldom utilized in academic contexts, especially in the precollege context. Greeno and the Middle-school Mathematics Through Applications Project Group (1997) indicate that the power of situated learning is derived from a person learning to solve problems as part of a community in the authentic context confronting these challenges, a difficult environment to develop in a K-12 classroom. Previous attempts to evaluate situated theory in school settings have encountered severe limits in authenticity, legitimate peripheral participation, and developing problem-solving communities with participants at different levels, from novice through expert. For example, Griffin and Griffin (1996) conducted a research study to develop mapping skills through methods leveraging situated learning theory. However, in this study students were first taught in a school-type environment and then were provided an expert from whom to learn. This approach lacked a means to create and evaluate classroom-based situated learning because no multileveled community of learning was involved.

Fortunately, emerging ICT that enable immersive, collaborative simulation now offer the capability to implement situated learning environments in classroom settings. This potentially provides the missing piece in the puzzle of how to teach 21st-century skills of problem finding in academic contexts remote from real-world communities of practice engaging in collective problem resolution via mediated interaction.

A Vision of How Emerging ICT Can Aid in Meeting 21st-Century Educational Challenges

Three complementary technological interfaces are currently shaping how people learn, with multiple implications for K-12 education:

- The familiar *"world-to-the-desktop"* interface provides access to distributed knowledge and expertise across space and time through networked media. Sitting at their laptop or workstation, students can access distant experts and archives, communicate with peers, and participate in mentoring relationships and virtual communities of practice. This interface provides the models for learning that now underlie most tools, applications, and media in K-12 education.
- Emerging MUVE interfaces offer students an engaging "Alice in Wonderland" experience in which their digital emissaries in a graphical virtual context actively engage in experiences with the avatars (see Figure 1) of other participants and with computerized agents. MUVEs provide rich environments in which participants interact with digital objects and tools, such as historical photographs or virtual microscopes. Moreover, this interface facilitates novel forms of communication among avatars, using media such as text chat and virtual gestures. This type of "mediated immersion" (pervasive experiences within a digitally enhanced context), intermediate in complexity between the real world and paint-by-numbers exercises in K-12 classrooms, allows instructional designers to construct shared simulated experiences otherwise impossible in school settings. Researchers are exploring the affordances of such models for learning in K-12 education (Barab et al., 2004 ; Clarke, Dede, Ketelhut, Nelson, & Bowman, 2006).
- *Augmented reality (AR)* interfaces enable "ubiquitous computing" models. Students carrying mobile wireless devices through real-world contexts engage with virtual information superimposed on physical landscapes (such as a tree describing its botanical characteristics or an historic photograph offering a contrast with the present scene). This type of mediated immersion infuses digital resources throughout the real world, augmenting students' experiences and interactions. Researchers are starting to study how

FIGURE 1
AVATARS

these models for learning aid students' engagement and understanding (Klopfer & Squire, in press; Klopfer, Yoon, & Rivas, 2004).

As emerging forms of ICT for learning, MUVEs empower the creation of contexts inaccessible in the real world, while AR enables the infusion of virtual contexts within physical locations.

My colleagues and I are conducting design-based research on one such MUVE-based learning experience, *River City* (http://muve.gse.harvard.edu/rivercityproject/), a project funded by the National Science Foundation (NSF) to enhance middle-school students' educational outcomes in science (Clarke et al., 2006). Students virtually immerse themselves inside a simulated, historically accurate 19th-century city, represented by an avatar (Figure 1). Collaborating in teams of three or four participants, they try to figure out why people are getting sick and what actions can remove sources of illness. They talk to various residents in this simulated setting, such as children and adults who have fallen ill, hospital employees, merchants, and university scientists (Figure 2). Participants go to different places in the town (Figure 3) and collect data on changes over time, gradually acting in

FIGURE 2
TALKING TO COMPUTER-BASED AGENTS

more purposeful ways as they develop and test hypotheses. They help each other and also find experts and archives to guide them (Figure 4). Further, students use virtual scientific instruments, such as microscopes, to test water for bacteria (Figures 5 and 6).

This immersive simulation allows them to conduct an experiment by changing an independent variable they select, then collecting data in the city to test their hypothesis. Students not only hypothesize what would happen if, for example, a sanitation system were built—they can actually visit the city with a sanitation system added and see how this change affects the patterns of illness. Our research results indicate students are deeply engaged by this curriculum and are developing sophisticated problem-finding skills.

If we examine students' technology use outside of school, we see widespread use of MUVE interfaces occurring in their informal, voluntary educational activities. For example, while one child sitting in front of a console game is still prevalent, collaborative, mediated gameplay is rising. The latest generation of console systems (Xbox 360, PS3, and Wii) has hardware architectures that encourage "connected" playing right out of the box, encouraging interaction across distance and space. Massively multiuser online (MMO) environments, such as *Second Life* (Linden Lab), *World of Warcraft* (Blizzard Entertainment) and *Everquest* (Sony Online Entertainment), bring participants together online

FIGURE 3
MAP OF RIVER CITY

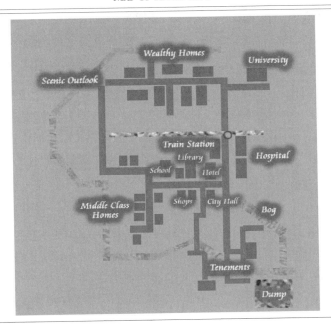

where they can interact in a virtual-collaborative context. Emerging communities such as "modding," in which users create new content for games (often contributing to a shared database of models), and "machinima," in which users create new content via video-capturing techniques, are further shaping how kids now express themselves via collaborative digital experiences. Youth are forming networked communities around games and movies, in which they share codes and strategies and build collaborative clans working together to fulfill quests.

As with MUVEs, youth also increasingly have access outside of school to a new generation of wireless handheld devices (WHDs) that combine the affordances of personal information managers, telephony, wireless Internet connectivity, and Global Positioning Systems (GPS)—all the capabilities needed to support educational AR. Two of the most common WHDs utilized by school-aged children are cell phones and handheld gaming devices. Among U.S. teenagers, as Lenhart, Madden, and Hitlin (2005) have found, almost half report owning a cell phone, with a greater percentage of older teens owning a phone (nearly three in

FIGURE 4

VIEW OF 3-D ENVIRONMENT AND WEB-BASED CONTENT ON RIGHT SIDE OF
SCREEN

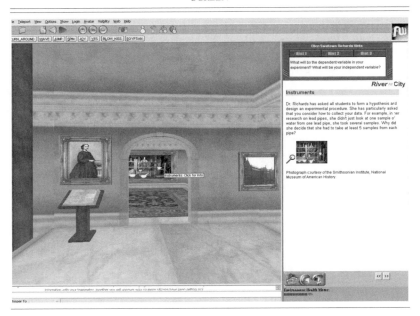

five teens aged 15–17) than younger teens (nearly one in three teens aged 12–14). Roberts, Foehr, and Rideout (2005) have found that more than half of U.S. students aged 8 to 18 years old own at least one handheld gaming device. Wireless mobile devices can support social interactivity, are sensitive to shifts in context, enable individualized scaffolding, and can facilitate cognition distributed among people, tools, and contexts (Klopfer & Squire, in press).

My colleagues and I are in the early stages of developing an AR designed to promote skills in collective problem resolution via mediated interaction (Clarke, Dede, & Dieterle, in press). *Alien Contact!* is part of a project funded by the U.S. Department of Education Star Schools program (http://education.mit.edu/arworkshop/) and is designed to teach math and literacy skills to middle school students. This immersive collaborative simulation is played on a Dell Axim X51 handheld computer and uses GPS technology (Figure 7) to correlate the students' real-world location to their virtual location in the simulation's digital world (Figures 8 and 9). As the students move around a physical loca-

FIGURE 5

TAKING A WATER SAMPLE WITH THE VIRTUAL MICROSCOPE

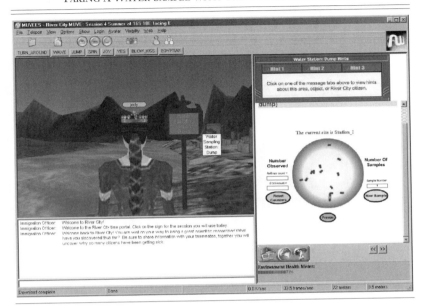

FIGURE 6

CLOSE UP OF MICROSCOPE. STUDENTS CLICK "FREEZE" AND COUNT THE
AMOUNT OF E. COLI AND ANTHRAX IN THE WATER

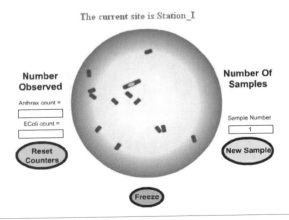

FIGURE 7
DELL AXIM & GPS RECEIVER

FIGURE 8
STUDENTS EXPLORING SCHOOL GROUNDS

tion, such as their school playground or sports fields, a map on their handheld displays digital objects and virtual people who exist in an AR world superimposed on real space.

In the *Alien Contact!* math- and literacy-focused curriculum, middle school students are presented with the following scenario: Aliens have landed on Earth and seem to be preparing for a number of possible

FIGURE 9
HANDHELD DISPLAY OF DIGITAL OBJECTS ON SCHOOL GROUNDS

Student's
physical
location

Characters
& items the
student
encounters

actions, including peaceful contact, invasion, plundering, or simply returning to their home planet. Working in teams of four, the students must explore an AR world located immediately outside of their school, interviewing virtual characters, collecting digital items, and solving mathematics and literacy puzzles to determine why the aliens have landed.

Students work in teams of four; each member of the team plays one of four complementary roles (chemist, computer expert, linguist, or FBI agent) which determines the information and experiences provided to that learner. Each team member has access to different data, so team members must collaborate to solve the problems they encounter (jigsaw pedagogy, in which each learner is provided only part of the information needed to understand the situation). Prior results from AR research indicate the promise of this instructional design strategy for teaching problem finding and for supporting a wide range of students' "neomillennial" learning styles and strengths (Dieterle, Dede, & Schrier, 2007).

In their learning processes, many of the distributed communities among youth based on AR and MUVE interfaces parallel the activities of 21st-century professionals in knowledge-based workplaces. In both MUVEs and AR, knowledge is grounded in a setting and distributed across a community rather than isolated within individuals. Contrary to conventional K-12 instruction where knowledge is decontextualized and explicit, in MUVEs and AR the learning is situated and tacit: Problem finding is central to problem solving. This parallels the nature of 21st-century work, as well as the "neomillennial" learning styles and strengths of today's digital-age students (Dede, 2005).

MUVE- and AR-immersive interfaces for collaborative simulation foster situated learning and can aid students in learning collective problem resolution via mediated interaction as a key cluster of skills in the global, knowledge-based economy. But will students have access to the types of ICT infrastructure—in and out of school—that can support this type of transformative educational model?

The Growing Availability of "Cyberinfrastructure"

In recent years, the NSF has championed a vision of the future of research that centers on "cyberinfrastructure": the integration of computing, data and networks, digitally enabled sensors, observatories and experimental facilities, and an interoperable suite of software and middleware services and tools (National Science Foundation Cyberinfrastructure Council [NSFCC], 2006). Gains in computational speed, high-bandwidth networking, software development, databases, visualization tools, and collaboration platforms are reshaping the practices of scholarship and beginning to transform teaching (Dede, in press-b). Sophisticated simulation software and distributed, wireless observation-networks are enabling the exploration of phenomena that cannot be studied through conventional experimental methods. Research in the sciences relies more and more on computational models to understand topics such as genetic decoding, weather prediction, and information security.

Cyberinfrastructures developed for research purposes also create intriguing opportunities to transform education. Scientific and educational resources can now pervade a wide variety of settings, rather than being accessible only in limited, specialized locations. Real-time data collection can enable assessing students' educational gains on a formative basis, providing insights into the microgenetics of learning knowledge and skills. Students can customize and personalize learning environments to a degree never before possible. Extensive "online" learning can complement conventional face-to-face education, and ubiquitous, pervasive computing can infuse smart-sensors and computational access throughout the physical and social environment.

Accomplishing these shifts requires more than the creation and maintenance of the cyberinfrastructure itself:

To employ the tools and capabilities of cyberinfrastructure-enabled learning environments effectively, teachers and faculty must also have continued professional development opportunities. For example, teachers and faculty must learn to use new assessment techniques and practices enabled by cyberinfrastructure, including the tailoring of feedback to the individual and the creation of personalized portfolios of student learning that capture a record of conceptual learning gains over time. These conditions permit new learning organizations to form, raising in turn new research questions about the creation, operation, and persistence of communities of practice and learning. In such cyberlearning networks people will connect to learn with each other, even as they learn to connect with each other, to exploit increasingly shared knowledge and engage in participatory inquiry (NSFCC, 2006, pp. 32–33).

Just as the invention of the microscope enabled the creation of whole new fields in biology, new disciplines may result from these emerging methods of education, fields as important as the relatively new areas of computer science, mathematical biology, genomics, environmental science, and astrophysics are today.

During 2004–05, with NSF funding, the Computing Research Association (CRA) convened four workshops attended by experts in education. The CRA report from these workshops (CRA, 2005, pp. 5–6) described the probable effects of cyberinfrastructure on the evolution of learning and teaching:

As STEM [science, technology, engineering, mathematics] research becomes increasingly collaborative, distributed, and dependent upon access to large amounts of computational power and data, students as well as teachers and educational decision makers at all levels will need to learn how to think with data—using diverse forms of data, information resources, tools, and services in many different fields of study to support making a broad range of decisions. They will need to become proficient in navigating a rich universe of data resources; in engaging with statistics, probability and evidence-based argumentation; and in discerning the authenticity, quality and reputation of these data sources. Emerging tools and frameworks for interactive and dynamic visualizations of patterns in data will be integral to these new literacies for thinking and decision making.

However, the report cautions that networked systems can create unexpected side effects, citing usage of data and usage privacy and accessibility, as well as the potential intertwining of formal schooling and assessment with ubiquitous informal learning.

In addition, the CRA report (2005) presents a vignette of a "serious game":

Learners cooperate in designing and conducting a mission to Mars, in the context of a game-based simulation. In the course of the project they carry out a variety of STEM-related learning activities, spanning physics, chemistry, biology, engineering and mathematics. These become springboards for seeking other learning resources outside the game, and collaborating with other learners in online working groups. Learners access online science and engineering data sets and models in order to compare their predictions against results from space scientists. They receive guidance in inquiry skills, metacognitive learning skills, and collaboration skills. The game itself is constructed and adapted through the collaborative efforts of the participating learners. In his earth sciences course, John, for example, studies terrain data from Mars Rover missions and creates a model of the Martian terrain to be explored by others. Manuela, in her high school engineering class, designs an autonomous rover vehicle to collect geo-logic samples and constructs a simulation of her rover design for use in the mission. She can then compare her model's performance in the simulation against records of actual Mars Rover missions. Sherry, the teacher, is assisted by virtual assistant teachers (intelligent tutors) embedded in the game that help her monitor learner progress and offer guidance and challenges. One of Sherry's virtual assistants reports that Manuela is having difficulty getting the controller of her virtual robot to work, and is not availing herself of online resources, so Sherry suggests that she discuss her design with an online community of robot enthusiasts. Data collected from learner performance within and surrounding the game provide the teacher with documentation and evidence of learning progress relating to curriculum standards and goals. In some contexts this may replace the need for standardized tests, but in others the teacher already has sufficient evidence to predict that the learners will meet the required standards (p. 7).

While not articulating the role innovative interfaces for situated learning might play, this vision resonates with teaching 21st-century skills, such as collective problem resolution via mediated interaction, in and out of school settings. Cyberinfrastructure can provide the tools, applications, and media needed to instantiate transformative models of K-12 education.

Conclusion

This chapter sketches a vision, not a prediction, of how emerging ICT might shape the evolution of teaching, learning, and schooling (Dede, 1990). A prediction portrays the future as like a train track, leading us to a predestined outcome for which we must prepare. In contrast, a forecast depicts the future as like a tree: one trunk (the past and present), with many branches (alternative futures). In this model of the future, individuals and institutions are like ants crawling up the trunk toward the branches, moving through the present to the future. Decisions made in the present strengthen and weaken various branches (fortify and undermine possibilities) because the choices not made are constrained as alternatives; by the time our present becomes our future, only one branch is left (the new trunk).

How difficult in 2007 is developing forecasts about the effects on civilization of ICT in 2022 and beyond, at a period during which today's students are assuming roles of responsibility in society? The equivalent in recent history would be describing, in 1992, the impact of computers and telecommunications in 2007. In the early 1990s—before the World Wide Web, universal email, digital telephony, massively multiuser virtual worlds, and similar civilization-wide advances—scholars did accurately articulate many of the shifts in society we see today (Dede, 1992; Naisbitt & Aburdene, 1990 ; Schwartz, 1991). However, very few people predicted some important changes, such as sociosemantic networking, and many "futurist" forecasts (e.g., widespread, sophisticated artificial intelligence) were unrealized.

At this point in history, the primary barriers to altering curricular, pedagogical, and assessment practices toward the transformative vision of ICT in education this chapter advocates are not conceptual, technical, or economic, but instead *psychological, political,* and *cultural.* We now have all the means necessary to implement alternative models of education that truly prepare all students for a future very different from the immediate past. Whether we have the professional commitment and societal will to actualize such a vision remains to be seen.

NOTE

1. Education has many responsibilities other than aiding economic development, and this chapter does not attempt to portray the full range of educational missions or the instructional strategies needed for success across this spectrum of goals. However, all those other responsibilities are possible only if education succeeds in providing the foundation for a prosperous future. This does not mean that education for economic development is privileged more than other objectives. Nonetheless, those who want education to succeed in resolving major concerns (e.g., equity, moral citizenship, self-realization) need to incorporate perspectives about preparation for 21st-century work into their planning.

REFERENCES

Barab, S., Thomas, M., Dodge, T., Carteaux, R., & Tuzan, H. (2004). Making learning fun: Quest Atlantis, a game without guns. *Educational Technology Research & Development, 53*(1), 86–108.

Barab, S.A., & Plucker, J.A. (2002). Smart people or smart contexts? Cognition, ability, and talent development in an age of situated approaches to knowing and learning. *Educational Psychologist, 37*(3), 165–182.

Brown, J.S., Collins, A., & Duguid, P. (1989). Situated cognition and the culture of learning. *Educational Researcher, 18*(1), 32–42.

Business Roundtable. (2005). *Tapping America's potential: The education for innovation initiative.* Washington, DC: Author.

Business–Higher Education Forum. (2005). *A commitment to America's future: Responding to the crisis in mathematics & science education.* Washington, DC: Author.

Clarke, J., Dede, C., & Dieterle, E. (in press). Emerging technologies for collaborative, mediated, immersive learning. In J. Voogt & G. Knezek (Eds.), *The international handbook of technology in education.* New York: Springer-Verlag.

Clarke, J., Dede, C., Ketelhut, D., Nelson, B., & Bowman, C. (2006). A design-based research strategy to promote scalability for educational innovations. *Educational Technology, 46*(3), 27–36.

Computing Research Association (CRA). (2005). *Cyberinfrastructure for education and learning for the future: A vision and research agenda.* Washington, DC: Author.

Dabbagh, N. (2006). *Select instructional models/Theories to develop instructional prototypes.* Instructional Design Knowledge Base, Graduate School of Education, George Mason University. Retrieved August 6, 2006 from http://classweb.gmu.edu/ndabbagh/Resources/IDKB/models_theories.htm

Dede, C. (1990). Futures research and strategic planning in teacher education. In R. Houston (Ed.), *Handbook of research in teacher education* (pp. 83–100). New York: Macmillan.

Dede, C. (1992, July). Education in the 21st century. *Annals of the American Academy for Political and Social Science, 522,* 104–115.

Dede, C. (2005). Planning for "neomillennial" learning styles: Implications for investments in technology and faculty. In J. Oblinger & D. Oblinger (Eds.), *Educating the net generation* (pp. 226–247). Boulder, CO: EDUCAUSE Publishers.

Dede, C. (in press-a). Theoretical perspectives influencing the use of information technology in teaching and learning. In J. Voogt & G. Knezek (Eds.), *International handbook of information technology in education.* New York: Springer.

Dede, C. (in press-b). *The role of information and communications technologies in the evolution of graduate education.* Washington, DC: Council of Graduate Schools.

Dede, C. (in press-c). *Reconceptualizing 21st century skills.* Raleigh, NC: The Friday Institute, North Carolina State University.

Dede, C., Korte, S., Nelson, R., Valdez, G., & Ward, D. (2005). *Transforming education for the 21st century: An economic imperative.* Chicago, IL: Learning Point Associates.

Dieterle, E., Dede, C., & Schrier, K. (2007). "Neomillennial" learning styles propagated by wireless handheld devices. In M. Lytras & A. Naeve (Eds.), *Ubiquitous and pervasive knowledge and learning management: Semantics, social networking and new media to their full potential* (pp. 35–66). Hershey, PA: Idea Group, Inc.

Duffy, T.M., & Cunningham, D.J. (1996). Constructivism: New implications for instructional technology? *Educational Technology, 31,* 7–12.

Edelson, D.C., Pea, R.D., & Gomez, L. (1996). Constructivism in the collaboratory. In B. G. Wilson (Ed.), *Constructivist learning environments: Case studies in educational technology.* Englewood Cliffs, NJ: Educational Technology Publications.

Engeström, Y., & Middleton, D. (Eds.). (1996). *Cognition and communication at work.* Cambridge: Cambridge University Press.

Friedman, T.L. (2005). *The world is flat: A brief history of the twenty-first century.* New York: Farrar, Straus, and Giroux.

Greeno, J.G., & the Middle-school Mathematics Through Applications Project Group. (1997). Theories and practices of thinking and learning to think. *American Journal of Education, 106*(1), 85–126.

Griffin, M.M., & Griffin, B.W. (1996). Situated cognition and cognitive style: Effects on students' learning as measured by conventional tests and performance assessments. *Journal of Experimental Education, 64*(4), 293–308.

Hutchins, E. (1995). *Cognition in the wild*. Cambridge, MA: MIT Press.

Jonassen, D.H. (1996). *Computers in the classroom*. Englewood Cliffs, NJ: Merrill.

Kafai, Y.B., & Ching, C.C. (2001). Affordances of collaborative software design planning for elementary students' science talk. *The Journal of the Learning Sciences, 10*(3), 323–363.

Kirschner, P.A., Sweller, J., & Clark, R.E. (2006). Why minimal guidance during instruction does not work: An analysis of the failure of constructivist, discovery, problem-based, experiential, and inquiry based teaching. *Educational Psychologist, 41*, 75–86.

Klopfer, E., & Squire, K. (in press). Environmental detectives: The development of an augmented reality platform for environmental simulations. *Educational Technology Research and Development*.

Klopfer, E., Yoon, S., & Rivas, L. (2004). Comparative analysis of Palm and wearable computers for participatory simulations. *Journal of Computer Assisted Learning, 20*, 347–359.

Krajcik, J.S., & Blumenfeld, P.C. (2006). Project-based learning. In R.K. Sawyer (Ed.), *Cambridge handbook of the learning sciences*, (pp. 317–333). Cambridge: Cambridge University Press.

Lave, J., & Wenger, E. (1991). *Situated learning: Legitimate peripheral participation*. New York: Cambridge University Press.

Lenhart, A., Madden, M., & Hitlin, P. (2005). *Teens and technology: Youth are leading the transition to a fully wired and mobile nation*. Washington, DC: Pew Internet & American Life Project.

Levy, F., & Murnane, R.J. (2004). *The new division of labor: How computers are creating the next job market*. Princeton, NJ: Princeton University Press.

Mitchell, W.J. (2003). *Me ++: The cyborg self and the networked city*. Cambridge, MA: MIT Press.

Naisbitt, J., & Aburdene, P. (1990). *Megatrends 2000*. New York: William Morrow.

National Academy of Science. (2006). *Rising above the gathering storm: Energizing and employing America for a brighter economic future*. Washington, DC: National Academy Press.

National Research Council. (2000). Committee on Developments in the Science of Learning and Committee on Learning Research and Educational Practice. In J.D. Bransford, A. Brown, & R. Cocking (Eds.), *How people learn: Brain, mind, experience, and school* (pp. 6–8). Washington, DC: The National Academies Press.

National Research Council. (2005). Committee on How People Learn, a targeted report for teachers. In M.S. Donovan & J.D. Bransford (Eds.), *How students learn: History, mathematics, and science in the classroom* (pp. 231–235). Washington, DC: The National Academies Press.

National Science Foundation Cyberinfrastructure Council. (2006). *NSF's cyberinfrastructure vision for 21st century discovery* (draft 7.1). Washington, DC: National Science Foundation.

Pear, J.J., & Crone-Todd, D.E. (2001). A social constructivist approach to computer-mediated instruction. *Computers & Education, 38*(1), 221–231.

Pintrich, P.R., & Schunk, D. (2001). *Motivation in education: Theory, research and applications* (2nd ed.). New York: Pearson.

Rheingold, H. (2002). *Smart mobs: The next social revolution*. Cambridge, MA: Perseus Publishing.

Roberts, D.F., Foehr, U.G., & Rideout, V. (2005). *Generation M: Media in the lives of 8–18 year-olds*. Menlo Park, CA: Kaiser Family Foundation.

Salomon, G. (Ed.). (1993). *Distributed cognitions: Psychological and educational considerations*. New York: Cambridge University Press.

Schwartz, P. (1991). *The art of the long view*. New York: Doubleday Currancy.

Simpson, T.L. (2002). Dare I oppose constructivist theory? *The Educational Forum*, 66(4), 347–354.

VanLehn, K., Lynch, C., Schulze, K., Shapiro, J.A., Shelby, R., Taylor, L. et al. (2005). The Andes physics tutoring system: Lessons learned. *International Journal of Artificial Intelligence in Education*, 15(3), 147–204.

Wenger, E., McDermott, R., & Snyder, W. (2002). *Cultivating communities of practice*. Cambridge, MA: Harvard Business School Press.

Wiske, M.S., Franz, K.R., & Breit, L. (2004). *Teaching for understanding with technology*. New York: Jossey-Bass.

The Internet Landscape in College

STEVE JONES, CAMILLE JOHNSON-YALE, FRANCISCO SEOANE PÉREZ, AND JESSICA SCHULER

It goes without saying that in the United States college students are Internet users. A 2002 Pew Internet and American Life Project report titled "The Internet Goes to College" (Jones, 2002)[1] made it abundantly clear that college students were indeed regular users of the Internet (74% of those surveyed reportedly using the Internet 4 or more hours per week). This is not surprising in light of the development of Internet technologies themselves. Many applications (Napster and Facebook, for instance) were created by college students, on college campuses, and targeted college student users (who took them up in droves). The Internet itself was initially developed at research universities and some of the earliest Internet users were college students.

Since that 2002 report much has changed about the Internet and its users. In the United States Internet adoption has continued to grow, and minority users, previously less well-represented, have increasingly gone online. So-called "Web 2.0" technologies (social networking, video sharing, etc.) have become prominent. And a generation of college students has come and gone. Pew undertook a follow-up study of college students' Internet use in 2005 to get a better sense of today's college students' Internet use and to determine whether there were any differences in use since the 2002 survey. The goal of this chapter is to report key results from this research (which at this time has not yet been published) and to draw conclusions from the data that documents the differences between students' and professors' use of and attitudes toward Internet technologies, along with the potential impact of these differences.

Steve Jones is Professor of Communication and Associate Dean of Liberal Arts and Sciences at the University of Illinois at Chicago and Senior Research Fellow at the Pew Internet and American Life Project. Camille Johnson-Yale is a doctoral candidate in the Institute of Communications Research at the University of Illinois, Urbana-Champaign. Francisco Seoane Pérez is a Ph.D. student at the Institute of Communications Studies at the University of Leeds. Jessica Schuler is a Master's student in Communication at the University of Illinois at Chicago.

TABLE 1
GENDER

	2005 Survey (%)	NCES Survey (%)
Men	43.5	42.5
Women	56.5	57.5

NCES, National Center for Education Statistics.

TABLE 2
RACE

	2005 Survey (%)	NCES Survey (%)
Black	11.7	12.0
American Indian	1.0	1.0
Asian	6.1	5.9
Latino	9.7	11.0
White	64.9	59.5
Missing/Unknown	6.7	7.5

NCES, National Center for Education Statistics.

Our research is based on the findings from an online survey given to college students at 2-year and 4-year public and private colleges and universities in the continental United States during the spring 2005 academic term. Invitations to participate were sent via email to every student at 29 college campuses, and to a random sample of students stratified by class (freshman, sophomore, etc.) at 11 other campuses. In all, 7,421 surveys were completed. Participants and their colleges remain anonymous in this report, as the surveys asked questions regarding students' feelings and attitudes about certain aspects of Internet usage along with other information that might have been considered personal, sensitive, or critical of their college.

The campuses were chosen to represent a broad cross-section of higher education institutions in the United States (public/private, flagship/regional, urban/rural, research-oriented/teaching-oriented, etc.). The overall sample was also tested against demographic data for all U.S. college students as reported by the National Center for Education Statistics (NCES).[2] In both cases (individual campuses and overall) the samples were tested against known population parameters (gender, race, age; see Tables 1–3) and found to be reflective of the national population of college students as reported by *The Chronicle* and reflective of individual campus student populations. For results based on the total sample, we can say with 95% confidence that the error attrib-

TABLE 3
AGE

	2005 Survey (%)	NCES Survey (%)
14–17	—	1.5
18–19	25.1	28.7
20–21	34.2	28.2
22–24	21.2	19.2

NCES, National Center for Education Statistics.

utable to sampling and other random effects is plus or minus one percentage point. In addition to sampling error, question wording and practical difficulties in conducting surveys may introduce some error or bias into the findings.

In addition to the surveys, ethnographic data was collected during the fall 2005, spring 2006, and fall 2006 academic terms by a team of graduate and undergraduate student researchers from the University of Illinois at Chicago. The researchers were recruited to observe the behaviors of college students at several institutions of higher education in the upper Midwest. The researchers were trained in ethnographic methods of observation and data collecting, and rotated the times of the day and days of the week they spent in various public settings where college students could be found using the Internet.

Academic Uses of the Internet

General Activities and Attitudes

College students continue to have a positive opinion about the Internet's impact on their educational experience. The percentage of college students with a positive opinion has risen to 84%, compared to 79% in the 2002 survey. On the other hand, 7% of today's students disagree with a positive assessment of the Internet's impact on their academic experience, compared to 4% in the 2002 survey. Far fewer are now of the belief that its impact has been neutral, with 8% choosing that response today compared with the 16% who chose it in 2002. While these figures do not portend a very strong shift in students' assessment of the Internet in relation to their academic life, they may be evidence of a shift nevertheless, and will be worth tracking over time.

No matter their assessment, all college students (100%) use the Internet for information searching. Their preferred means of information searching are search engines such as Google or Yahoo! (95% of college students reported using those), followed by library websites (68%), news websites (64%), and online encyclopedias (48%).

Communications with Professors

The vast majority of college students surveyed (84%) are using the Internet to communicate with professors, a number similar to the 2002 figure (87%). Email is the most popular method for doing so, with 79% of college students using it to reach their instructors. Course websites and email lists were also popular means of communication with professors, with about one-quarter (23%) using email lists and close to half (45%) using course websites. Instant messaging (IM), wikis, and chat rooms represented only a small percentage of students' means of communication with faculty (4% combined). Although email continues to be most used by students to get in touch with professors, it is less used now than was reported in 2002, when 94% of college students reported using it. Email lists and course websites have risen in popularity since 2002, when 8% and 20% of students reported using those (respectively). In 2005 only 6% of college faculty reported using email lists, although 55% reported using course websites (Jones & Johnson-Yale, 2005).

Frequency. Students generally stated that the frequency of their communications with professors via the Internet is seldom or rare, with most having contact every 2 weeks or less (61%). Only about one in eight (12%) described themselves as being in frequent or very frequent contact with professors via the Internet (defined as several times a day or week). However, those who reported contacting their professors occasionally—about once a week—has more than doubled since 2002, from 11 to 26%. Fewer than half (43%) report that they are required by professors to use email to contact them, but nearly all students (92%) reported that they used email to contact professors.

Purpose. At least half the students cited the following as a primary reason for emailing professors: to report an absence (68%), for clarification of an assignment (68%), to set up an appointment (57%), and to discuss or find out a grade (56%). Over three quarters (78%) of students surveyed had emailed assignments to professors. These results are consistent with those collected in the 2002 college student survey. Additional reasons for contact with professors provided by today's college students included alerting their instructors to websites or information related to class and asking for recommendation letters. Conversely, the primary reasons, according to students, that professors contact them via the Internet are to share class announcements (74%), information about class assignments (68%), and additional course material and information (58%). Less than half (42%) reported that they received feedback via the Internet from professors on class assignments. Students felt that professors were less likely to use email to send grades (44%), discuss course-related problems or complaints (41%), or handle attendance matters (16%).

Relationships. Just over half (53%) of students felt that they had more face-to-face than email communication with professors, although one in five (18%) felt they had more communication with professors via email. These findings are consistent with student responses in the 2002 report. However, college students appear slightly less satisfied than they were in 2002 with email as a communication tool for expressing ideas to professors. Thirty-eight percent of students agreed or strongly agreed that email allowed them to express ideas to professors that they would not have expressed in class, down from 46% in 2002. Close to half (44%) of students did not believe they knew their professors any better because of email contact with them; the same number disagreed or strongly disagreed that their professors knew *them* better because of email. Those who felt email had enhanced their relationships made up about a quarter of respondents—24% agreed or strongly agreed that they knew their professors better, and 26% agreed or strongly agreed that their professors knew them better as a result of email correspondence. These findings are consistent with student responses from 2002, and point toward email serving a functional, rather than personal, purpose in regard to student–professor communication.

Interviews with college students revealed that they made very conscious decisions about which medium to use to communicate with professors. Several said they often felt uneasy talking to their professors in person, and even more awkward speaking to them on the phone. One student described feeling like it was an "intrusion into [a professor's] personal life" to call them on their cell phone, even if the professor gave the class his or her cell phone number. The students generally agreed that email seemed the least personal contact method, and that meeting with a professor after class was usually less time consuming and more relevant to the students' interests. But students also agreed that email led to less pressure on them, because, for instance, a professor could not ask them questions to which they would have to respond immediately, as would be the case in a face-to-face meeting. Some students also mentioned hesitation about using the telephone to call a professor based on a concern about calling at an awkward or inconvenient time and getting on his or her "bad side" as a result.

Nevertheless, half of college students surveyed (51%) felt that email in particular had improved their interactions with professors and only 2% felt that email had worsened their interactions with professors. When evaluating the impact of Internet communication on the overall quality of their relationships with professors, almost half (47%) agreed or strongly agreed that the Internet has had a positive impact.

Internet Communication with Classmates

More than three-quarters (78%) of college students use the Internet to communicate with one another about their classes. Email and IM are the most common means of communication (55% and 33%, respectively), but in response to open-ended questions, some students also reported using Facebook for academic purposes. While 40% of students reported that they were required to use the Internet to communicate with classmates, more of them (58%) reported that they were not required to do so. Unlike their communications with professors, students were more frequently in contact with classmates via the Internet, with 30% reporting communicating with classmates several times a week and 8% reporting daily contact. Over half (55%), though, described their contact with classmates online as seldom (every few weeks) to rare (once or twice per semester/term).

Collaboration on group projects was the primary reason cited by students for contacting other classmates using the Internet, with 55% of college students reporting it as their reason for such contact. Exchanging notes (47%) and studying for exams (43%) were also common reasons. Many students reported that they often contacted classmates for assignment clarifications and to find out what work they had missed after missing a class meeting. Students' feelings about the impact of the Internet on their relationships with fellow students were about the same as those found in our 2002 report. About two-thirds (63%) were in agreement that the Internet had had a positive impact on their relationships with classmates, while only about 5% disagreed with that assessment.

College Students and Online-Only Courses

Much has been written about online education, and much research has been undertaken to try to determine the value of the Internet for teaching and learning. There are likely very few courses at U.S. colleges that do not employ the Internet in some way or another, even if it is only to use courseware or to facilitate communication between professors and students. "Blended" or "hybrid" courses, courses that use the Internet in lieu of some (but not all) class meetings, lectures, discussions, etc. are increasingly common at many U.S. college campuses, according to a 2007 report from the Sloan Consortium, Eduventures, and the Babson Survey Research Group (Allen, Seaman, & Garrett, 2007).

Since the 2002 Pew report of college students' Internet use, there appears to have been a substantial increase in the number of students who have taken an online-only course, from around 6% in 2002 to over one-quarter (27%) of today's college students. The latter are also more satisfied with the quality of online-only courses than those surveyed in 2002. About two-thirds (67%) reported that taking an online-only course was a satisfying experience, and almost as many (61%) said an online-only course was worth their tuition dollars.

By comparison, however, only about one in four (27%) felt the online learning experience was comparable to a traditional, face-to-face course. Interestingly, around half (53%) felt they learned less in their online course than they might have learned in the same class meeting face to face. This finding is consistent with our 2002 report data. In terms of course difficulty, 20% of students actually felt the online course was *more* difficult than a traditional face-to-face equivalent would have been. Another 42% felt their online course was easier than a traditional course; one-third (36%) neither agreed nor disagreed when asked whether the online-only course was harder or easier than the traditional equivalent.

The majority of students (69%) who had taken online-only courses reported that the course they took was not offered by colleges other than the one from which they were going to earn their degree; in other words, the course was unique and not available elsewhere.

Academic Dishonesty and the Internet

Plagiarism has long bedeviled Internet use in education. Websites such as http://www.turnitin.com that purport to detect plagiarism have proliferated amid claims that the Internet has made it easier than ever to copy and paste others' work into one's papers or homework assignments. Some teachers use search engines to detect whether parts of a paper may be found online, indicating that a student may have copied and pasted it. There are many websites that sell term papers on numerous topics. Given recent trends in the use of collaborative online technologies (such as wikis), some students may believe that it is all right to copy and paste someone else's material, or to turn in material they may not have entirely authored themselves. As the waters are still as muddy as when the web first gained widespread use, it is important to know students' opinions and ideas about, as well as behaviors related to, this type of cheating.

Fewer than 2% of college students admitted submitting an assignment to a professor in which they had copied and pasted material from the Internet and claimed it as their own. Only 25 of the over 7,000 college students surveyed reported having purchased a paper online and turning it in as their own work. However, close to half (46%) of students reported knowing someone who had copied materials from the Internet to submit as their own work for an assignment. Of those who admitted copying material, only 15% said they were caught plagiarizing. Given the publicity surrounding plagiarism detection tools available to teachers, it is worth pondering why so few report being caught.

When students were asked whether they felt it was okay to copy and paste a paper posted on the Internet for use as their own work in a class, 88% disagreed or strongly disagreed that it was okay to do so. The others were mostly neutral on the issue (10%), with only a few (2%) agreeing that it was acceptable to copy and paste material they found online and claim it as their own work. When asked how they would feel about the practice of copying and pasting papers posted online for use as their own if they knew they would not be caught, students were slightly less disagreeable. About three-quarters (76%) still disagreed with the practice, while those who were neutral rose to 18%, and those who agreed that it would be acceptable rose to 4%.

Students also seemed aware of limited paraphrasing as being a type of plagiarism. When asked whether changing a few words in each paragraph of an Internet document was all right in comparison to copying and pasting whole papers, the major of students disagreed (84%). About one in seven (14%) agreed that limited paraphrasing of online material was acceptable. Most students (84%) also felt that they were very careful to cite others' material, and most (96%) believed that claiming others' work as one's own was one of the worst academic offenses. Nearly one-third (31%) of students surveyed said they knew someone who had used a cell phone, laptop computer, or personal digital assistant to cheat on an exam by storing answers in the device, contacting a friend for answers, or other similar activities. Connecting to the Internet during class for personal (i.e., not related to the course) reasons is a somewhat common practice, with just over one-quarter (26%) of college students reporting having done this.

Conclusions and Implications

In some ways little has changed since our first look at college students' Internet use in 2002. Internet use is thoroughly woven into a college student's life. Today's student has for all intents and purposes grown up with early knowledge of, if not significant access to, the Internet. Computers have been commonplace in school and at home. By the time these students entered high school, nearly all had Internet access. Indeed, computers and the Internet are so common at college that Rebekah Nathan's recently published book *My Freshman Year* (2005) barely mentions them beyond noting that students often multi-tasked and some took courses online. Reading her fascinating, under-cover anthropological account of passing as a college freshman, one gets the impression of an almost complete absence of computers and online activity. What her book reveals by omission is that this technological communication infrastructure is so much a part of the college landscape—so ubiquitous—as to be unnoticeable.

Whereas it was true in 2002 that college students took Internet access for granted, today they take almost everything *about* the Internet for granted. Today's college students are at the forefront of the use of social networking sites such as Facebook and MySpace. But there is little of the kind of "buzz" and hype about these technologies among the users that one finds in many blogs, newspapers, and magazines—they are simply part of daily life for many. Email is still the tool the majority of college students use most often. More of them are blogging now than before, and on a percentage basis there are more bloggers among college students than among the general population (Lenhart & Fox, 2006). But even though they are heavy users of Web 2.0 tools, most of them seem to consider those tools primarily as a part of college *life* and not as much a part of college *education*, using them mainly to communicate with new friends, old friends, and family. It is not clear that students see other purposes for these tools, and so one is left to wonder whether to believe the hype surrounding predictions about the use of such technologies for education, business, or politics in the future.

Will college students' attitudes toward Internet use mean that the innovation in Internet use and applications that have so regularly been spawned on campuses will dry up? That is not likely, if only because there are undoubtedly many individual students who do not fit the general pattern—students for whom the Internet is an obsession and for whom developing new tools (and hacks) is a passion. Nor does it mean that college students will not take up new applications when they arrive.

Quite the contrary; they remain eager early adopters—but they are more likely to use an application than they are to tout it or flout it.

Interestingly, from observation and interviews, it seems most college students (as opposed to educators) seem nonplussed about *Second Life*, an online virtual environment described on its website as "a 3-D virtual world entirely built and owned by its Residents. Since opening to the public in 2003, it has grown explosively and today is inhabited by a total of 9,703,110 Residents from around the globe"—residents who live, socialize, buy, sell, and trade (see http://secondlife.com/whatis for more details). They are unable to comprehend its attraction and do not show an interest in using it for distance learning. They find little point to *Second Life*, because there are no obvious rewards or "levels" as there are in video games, and the graphics seem far less impressive than they do in the games to which they have become accustomed. It is likely that as displays get larger, network connections become faster, and more media and classes move online into *Second Life*-like virtual environments that college students will for all intents and purposes be forced to spend time in those environments, but it would behoove educators (particularly ones for whom *Second Life* retains some "Wow!" factor) to consider that for students the environment may be unexciting, at best. In other words, although *Second Life* may have interesting uses for education, it is important to remember that the experience of it as a technology for college students appears to be simply boring.

Online Education

While today's college students are increasingly partaking of online courses as compared to those surveyed in 2002, they are not moving to online education in droves. Their choice to take an online course seems, more often than not, to be predicated on convenience both in regard to time and to place. If an online course can solve a scheduling problem (and one must keep in mind that a "scheduling problem" may mean simply avoiding having to go to a class on Fridays) or help a student avoid going to a class in a building far away from one's residence hall or apartment, the choice to take it is clear. Such decision making, coupled with a newfound interest on many campuses in accommodating more students without new building construction—freeing up classroom space with online and "hybrid" or "blended" courses—will likely continue to fuel growth in online education. Whether the majority of college students, however, are likely to make online education a significant part of their time in college is unknown, because there are many aspects of college life that are nonacademic and strongly tied to place.

As Nathan (2005) noted, "Most professors and administrators overestimate the role that academics plays in student culture, and as a result magnify the impact of teachers and classes on student life and decisions" (p. 140). Today's college students are, if nothing else, smart consumers. Whether one agrees or disagrees with their decisions, they rarely make uninformed choices, and usually carefully weigh the pros and cons of most everything related to their college life (of course, teachers, and adults generally, may not understand the metrics they use for those measurements). The extent to which they choose online courses will, for the majority of them, ultimately be driven by the quality and value of the courses on a number of different levels.

There is every reason to think that upon graduation college students will in general continue to be heavy Internet users. And as new demands such as jobs and families become a part of their lives they will likely incorporate Internet use into those areas as well. The same seamlessness with which the Internet coexists with their college life may elude them somewhat (particularly as they come to be responsible for their own connectivity at home, and move between jobs that may have better or worse access), but there is little question that the Internet is part of their communication, information, and entertainment "mix," and its absence would leave a notable gap not only in their social and leisure lives but also in their knowledge of everything from world affairs to movie showtimes.

Privacy and Social Circles

Concerning college students' understanding of the line between the personal and the public, our study shows that the majority of college students, nearly three-quarters, are at least somewhat concerned about the privacy of their personal data on the Internet (only 3% are not at all concerned); nonetheless, they continue to post personal information online. This is not a contradiction for them, but rather a matter of multiple definitions of the personal, of private and public. While they are concerned about the security of passwords, credit card numbers, and social security numbers, they are not very concerned about sharing what might seem like private behavior on social networking sites such as MySpace and Facebook. The reason for their lack of concern is partly a result of the degree to which these sites "feel" private; one "invites" friends to them, and the notion that they are easily viewed by anyone is often ignored, overlooked, or simply not understood. In some cases, one's home page and profile can be kept private, and the availability of the option may be enough to cause a user to believe it *is* private.

(Perhaps if the sites were to reverse the option, i.e., to require users to make sites public and by default make them private, then less personal information would be publicly shared.) However aware they may be of online predation, security concerns, and the like, many college students simply do not believe that they will face significant consequences from posting private information online.

Thanks at least in part to social networking sites, college students now have a broader social circle than ever before. As Facebook has made inroads in high schools and in the corporate sector, it is becoming possible for college students to maintain connections to high school friends, as well as connections with college friends once they graduate and move into the workforce. The rise in popularity of these sites is not a surprise when viewed through the lens of today's college students' lives. As Nathan (2005) pointed out in *My Freshman Year*, students' (offline) personal networks are very deliberately and consciously constructed in the context of what she calls an "over-optioned" system in which life is "an optional set of activities and a fluid set of people whose paths are ever-shifting" (p. 40). It is not likely that today's college students will have as many social options after they leave college, if only because they are unlikely to ever again find themselves in a situation that immediately and on a large scale puts them in close personal contact with so many new people. It may be that the social ties formed in college, both offline and online, will become increasingly important as the number of new social contacts diminishes. It would be particularly interesting to track today's college students and monitor their social circles over time, perhaps along the lines of Michael Apted's *7Up* film series (which has followed a set of friends and resulted in a new film every 7 years that captures their lives and relationships), to view the ebb and flow of offline and online social networks.

Perhaps the most surprising finding of the Pew study is of the absence of particularly innovative uses of the Internet either in academic or social activities. That is not to say that college students are not doing interesting things online, or that there are no academic programs that utilize the Internet in useful and interesting ways. However, generally speaking, our study did not uncover evidence of any disruptive technology (Christensen, 1997). By and large Internet technologies are supplanting or replacing traditional methods of instruction and communication, but they would appear to be doing so in a relatively steady manner. While much has changed about the technology a college student encounters today compared with the technology one encountered 20 years ago, it is likely that the vast majority of other aspects of college life have changed little. And, even in those technological areas in which change has been greatest, the change that has occurred has for the most part been in service of the existing interests (social, leisure, and academic) of college students, so that changes have largely been experienced in regard to quantity (the variety of music one encounters, the number of friends with whom one stays in touch, the amount of information to which one has access, the amount of communication one has with professors, etc.) and not very much in regard to quality.

The National Survey of Student Engagement (2006) listed numerous aspects of student success, including "persistence and graduation rates, student goal attainment, course retention, transfer rates and transfer success, success in subsequent coursework, degree/certificate completion, student satisfaction, [and] personal and professional development" (p. 33). Perhaps technology, with its advances and effective implementation (individually and institutionally), can contribute to maintaining or even increasing multiple facets of student success. It is critical that our deepening understanding of students' Internet use be framed by these understandings of success.

NOTES

1. All references in the text to the "2002 report" or "2002 survey" are to this report.

2. National Center for Education Statistics, College Student Population in the USA 2003–04, data accessible at http://nces.ed.gov/ipeds/. Data for the period 2004–05 were not available at the time of writing. However, a review of changes from year to year between 1994 and 2004 revealed very little difference from one year to the next, typically no more than 0.1% in any category of race.

REFERENCES

Allen, I.E., Seaman, J., & Garrett, R. (2007). *Blending in: The extent and promise of blended education in the United States*. Retrieved May 5, 2007, from http://www.blendedteaching.org/special_report_blending_in

Christensen, C. (1997). *The inventor's dilemma*. Boston: Harvard Business School Press.

Jones, S. (2002). *The Internet goes to college: How students are living in the future with today's technology*. Pew Internet and American Life Project. Retrieved May 18, 2007, from http://www.pewInternet.org

Jones, S., & Johnson-Yale, C. (2005). Professors online: The Internet's impact on college faculty. *First Monday*, 10(9). Retrieved May 20, 2007, from http://firstmonday.org/issues/issue10_9/jones/index.html

Lenhart, A., & Fox, S. (2006). *Bloggers: A portrait of the Internet's new storytellers*. Pew Internet and American Life Project. Retrieved June 24, 2007, from http://www.pewinternet.org/pdfs/PIP%20Bloggers%20Report%20July%2019%202006.pdf

Nathan, R. (2005). *My freshman year*. New York: Penguin Books.

National Survey of Student Engagement (NSSE) (2006). *Engaged learning: Fostering success for all students: Annual report 2006*. Retrieved July 8, 2007, from http://nsse.iub.edu/NSSE_2006_Annual_Report/index.cfm

Teacher Education and Technology: Initial Results from the "What Works and Why" Project

JAMES W. PELLEGRINO, SUSAN R. GOLDMAN, MERYL BERTENTHAL, AND KIMBERLY LAWLESS

The education policy and practice fields are rife with questions and controversies about the effectiveness of teacher education programs, but we lack an adequate base of research and/or theory to answer them (e.g., Levine, 2006). While there is documented evidence of wide variability in teacher candidates' experiences during their preservice preparation, the nature of the impact of this variation on teacher effectiveness in K-12 classrooms is unknown. Take for example the preparation of teachers to integrate the technologies of the 21st century into their subsequent K-12 teaching. Although there seems to be general agreement that such preparation is desirable, there is no systematic evidence regarding the kinds of preparation that are needed, nor the best ways to provide such preparation. All that is agreed upon is that teachers' lack of knowledge of how to integrate technology for a positive impact on student learning will constrain the potential of electronic and multimedia technologies in K-12 education. Indeed, over the past 25 years there have been a number of initiatives to provide teachers with opportunities to acquire such knowledge, and billions of dollars have been invested in technology by state and federal governments, private foundations, and the public. Programs such as *Preparing Tomorrow's Teachers to Use Technology* (PT³) expended millions of dollars in training teachers to use technology. Business leaders are demanding that students emerge from schooling armed with the technological literacy that is needed for

James W. Pellegrino is Distinguished Professor of Cognitive Psychology and Education and Co-director of the University of Illinois at Chicago's (UIC) Learning Sciences Research Institute. Susan R. Goldman is Distinguished Professor of Psychology and Education and Co-Director, Learning Sciences Research Institute, UIC. Meryl Bertenthal is Visiting Director of Research Programs, Learning Sciences Research Institute, UIC. Kimberly Lawless is Associate Professor of Curriculum and Instruction and Project Director of Teachers Infusing Technology in Urban Schools at UIC.

economic success and productivity in the 21st century. More than 40 states have implemented technology standards for students and/or teachers. Finally, there is a growing learning sciences research base that is identifying strategies for uses of technology that can support learning and instruction in principled ways. Support for these claims can be found in various sources, including the annual "EdWeek Technology Counts" special report (see e.g., *Education Week*, 2007).

Our goal in this chapter is to suggest a strategy for exploring the issues surrounding the preparation of teachers to integrate technology effectively in classrooms to support learning. We do so in the context of our *What Works and Why* (WWW) project, a multiyear research project that is attempting to examine the instructional and learning experiences of students in eight major teacher preparation programs.[1] Each of these institutions has a reputation for integrating technology into the fabric of its program. Central to our strategy for exploring these issues is the use of contemporary principles of how people learn and develop competence in academic content domains to guide our data collection and analysis. We examine technology with respect to the roles it can play in enacting these principles and thereby support-ing effective teaching and learning. The chapter is organized into three major sections. In the first we review what is currently known regarding technology integration in teacher education. These data provide a context for the WWW project. The second section examines the theoretical and empirical approach of the WWW project. We then present initial data on technology integration in the teacher prepara-tion programs of the eight focal institutions of our study. In the con-clusion we discuss the implications of the findings for practice and policy. Our discussion extends to contemporary issues involving the educational software industry as well as the instructional and assess-ment climate that now pervades K-12 education.

Technology Integration in Teacher Education: A Critical Appraisal of What is Known

The investment made in transforming teacher education with respect to technology integration is now substantial by several metrics, especially when considered in terms of typical federal, state, and local institutional dollar investments in the teacher education enterprise. A rough estimate based on dollars from the U.S. Department of Educa-tion's (USDOE) PT[3] program, including the required one-to-one dollar match in this program, plus other state and federal initiatives to support technology infusion in teacher education, yields a figure between $750 million and $1 billion. This does not include the considerable dollars that K-12 systems have simultaneously invested in technology using local, state, and federal funds.

While much has and will continue to be spent on information and communications technologies, very little of a systematic nature at the K-12 or higher education level is known about what people have been doing, why they followed the path they did, and what impact it is having on things that matter—what teachers do and the resultant student learning outcomes! This is true even in those institutions of higher education (IHE) programs that are typically thought of as "cutting edge."

Actions Lacking Strong Theory and Data

Much of the activity underway across multiple levels of the educational system appears driven by the strong perceived need for action, but it is not guided by any substantial knowledge base derived from research about what works and why with regard to technology, teaching, and learning. Support for this claim comes from the collective set of papers presented by experts at a conference on educational technology research held by SRI International for USDOE in 1999. The conclusion was that "multiple and complementary research strategies are needed to measure the implementation and impacts of learning technologies. No single study, genre of studies, or methodology is adequate to the task" (Haertel & Means, 2003, pp. 257–258). Based on their analysis and synthesis of the research strategies proposed by multiple experts, Haertel and Means argued that substantial funding is needed for a coordinated, large-scale program of research on educational technology and learning in K-12 schools. Such a program would, of necessity, require the use of multiple research and data-collection approaches to address the many questions still in need of answers.

The importance of technology in educational settings has also prompted various organizations, including those responsible for accrediting teacher training programs, to develop technology-based standards. This activity has ensued despite the lack of a compelling knowledge base for understanding technology's impact on student learning. The recently released National Educational Technology Standards (NETS) for Teachers and NETS for Students, both from the International Society for Technology in Education (ISTE), the National Council for Accreditation of Teacher Education 2000 Teacher Education Program

Standards, and individual state licensure standards are cases in point. The clear prediction is that further, and possibly quite substantial, changes will occur in these areas over the next decade, especially as attempts are made to give the standards meaning by designing assessments that purportedly reflect them. In turn, teacher training programs within IHEs have begun altering their practices. However, in the absence of empirically grounded knowledge about how to most effectively integrate technology, instruction, and learning into a coherent whole, the current model of innovation seems to be best characterized as "letting a thousand flowers bloom."

What We Know and Do Not Know

A review of existing evaluation reports on the state of technology implementation in teacher education programs shows a lack of attention to cross-institutional and/or longitudinal studies. We found no systematic, conceptually driven effort to study the effectiveness of technology integration across multiple IHEs. Many "evaluation reports" and case studies exist for individual programs (e.g., Barker, Helm, & Taylor, 1995; Curry School of Education, 1997; Duran, 2000; Glenn, Reed, & Rhodes, 2001; Vermillion, Young, & Hanafin, 2007), and there are quite a few "reports" that urge IHEs to work harder at integrating technology (e.g., Carnegie Forum of Education and the Economy, Task Force on Teaching as a Profession, 1986; National Commission on Teaching and America's Future, 1996; Office of Technology Assessment [OTA], 1995). However, only a few studies have attempted to look at technology integration across institutions (e.g., American Association of Colleges for Teacher Education [AACTE], 1998; Campus Computing Project, 2001; Fulton, Glenn, & Valdez, 2003; Mergendoller, Johnston, Rockman, & Willis, 1994; Moursund & Bielefeldt, 1999; Persichitte, Tharp, & Caffarella, 1997). None have studied the effects of that integration across institutions (see Baker & Herman, 2000) or the differential impact on teacher candidates' learning and subsequent teaching.

Those studies that have compared institutions have often relied on simple mailed surveys, with all of their inherent limitations (for a discussion of the problems see Moursund & Bielefeldt, 1999). Most cross-institutional comparisons have also suffered from a lack of attention to the context or intended outcomes of each institution (Baker & Herman, 2000). Further, although many advocates have argued that technology must be deeply embedded in practice teaching as well as coursework, most studies looked only at the use of technology in IHE courses.

Finally, with the exception of the Fulton and colleagues (2003) study cited earlier, no studies that we found looked at the use of technology by new teachers after they completed their teacher education program and moved into teaching assignments.

What is known can be summarized as follows from a large-scale survey of over 400 IHEs and their graduates (Moursund & Bielefeldt, 1999). First, while most institutions report that their technology infrastructure is adequate, about a third say that they are limited by facilities. Second, although faculty information technology skills are comparable to the students' information technology skills, most faculty members do not model the use of those information technology skills in teaching. Third, despite the fact that most institutions report that information technology is available in their field experience classrooms, most student teachers do not routinely use information technology during field experiences and do not work under master teachers and supervisors who can advise them on such use. Fourth, the best predictor of technology integration by program graduates is their basic technology proficiency, yet technology-specific coursework at the IHE does not seem to correlate with eventual integration of technology in teaching. In other words, technology-specific coursework at the IHE does not seem to improve graduates' basic technology proficiency or their eventual use of technology in teaching. The authors concluded, on the basis of these findings, that the best predictor of eventual use of technology may be what the teacher candidates bring with them from their prior experiences, rather than what happens within IHEs!

Moursund and Bielefeldt (1999) argued that in order to increase the technology proficiency of new teachers, teacher education programs needed to increase the level of technology integration in their own programs. This integration should not be in stand-alone courses and should be based on an institutional plan. Student teachers should be able to use technology during field experiences. Faculty should be encouraged to model use of technology in their courses. The authors suggested that more in-depth study of technology integration would be useful at this stage, and urged researchers to concentrate on "concrete evidence of effectiveness," including observations, interviews, and examination of work samples. They also urged attention to the organizational history of those institutions whose survey results show high levels of capacity for technology integration, and concluded, "Public agencies and foundations should develop and solicit research proposals that will address these issues" (p. 25).

The What Works and Why Project

Theoretical Framework

The theoretical framework of the WWW project takes as axiomatic that preparing teachers and assessing that preparation occurs in a complex, multifaceted landscape. There are multiple contextual variables that make simple causal connections between preparation and K-12 student performance problematic at best. Perhaps because of this, systematic research on connections among teacher education, teacher learning, teaching practices, and K-12 student outcomes is lacking (e.g., Cochran-Smith & Zeichner, 2005). However, the current policy environment is one in which teacher preparation programs are being challenged to demonstrate that they are producing high-quality teacher candidates for our nation's schools. Some policymakers are attempting to infer evidence of the quality of teaching from standardized achievement tests. There are two major problems with this approach. First, these tests were not designed to assess teaching effectiveness and may or may not be sensitive to variations in K-12 students' instructional experiences (e.g., Pellegrino, Chudowsky, & Glaser, 2001).

Second, and more critical from our perspective, is that this form of accountability ignores the multiple influences on what and how teachers teach that may mediate the impact of teacher preparation programs on the achievement of students taught by their graduates. That is, teachers and students exist in classrooms within schools within districts within communities within states. Each level in this multiple embedded system sets conditions on the teaching–learning process through its policies and procedures regarding all aspects of the educational environment.[2] For example, in some districts teachers are required to use prescribed curricula and follow the "script" provided by the publisher. In others, they may choose their own programs. With respect to technology some districts and schools encourage and support its extensive use, while in others technology use is dependent on individual teachers' interests and skills. Funding policies at state and community levels affect class size, as do federal policies associated with entitlements. Thus, while a teacher candidate might emerge from a preparation program prepared to provide high-quality instruction, many variables and conditions codetermine what teachers can and do realize in their practice once they are located in classrooms of their own. Unfortunately, there is virtually no empirical data on the degree to which teachers actually do implement what they have learned in their teacher preparation programs, nor the conditions that

FIGURE 1

A REPRESENTATION OF THE LANDSCAPE IN WHICH NEW TEACHERS LEARN HOW
TO TEACH
HPL: How people learn

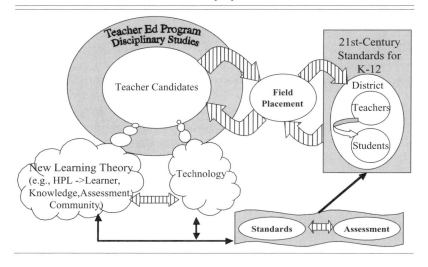

facilitate as compared to inhibit their ability to do so. In the absence
of such data, it is indeed problematic to hold schools of education
solely responsible for how their graduates teach.

Teacher preparation programs are also embedded in multiple contexts, including state and federal, political and professional. In the
design of the WWW project, we wanted to take into account these
multiple contexts of both IHE-based teacher preparation programs and
K-12 teaching settings. The schematic in Figure 1 is our representation
of the "space" of IHE and K-12 settings. Although within the context of
the WWW project we could not investigate all levels and all influences
in depth, we identified a sample of institutions that reflected variation in
the IHE and the K-12 contexts and considered each a case study, as
described subsequently. In the remainder of this section, we elaborate
on the representation in Figure 1.

The IHE context. Teacher preparation programs differ along a
variety of structural and philosophical dimensions that might be
expected to impact how they prepare teachers:

- Program size—ranging from small boutique programs (often at private universities and colleges) as compared to large programs run by state and state-related universities and colleges;
- Program mission—ranging from preparing small, select cohorts of innovators as compared to being the major supplier of a state's teaching force;
- Identity of the teaching faculty—ranging from a majority of tenure-track faculty to a largely clinical and adjunct faculty;
- Qualifications of the teacher candidates admitted to the program—ranging from highly selective to minimum entrance requirements; and
- Involvement of the disciplines in teacher preparation—ranging from highly collaborative interactions around content and content pedagogy among faculty from departments such as English, Chemistry, and Mathematics and teacher educators, to largely separated subject-matter courses that make little contact with teacher-preparation needs and/or faculty.

Although such differences exist across institutions, the ways in which these differences influence the knowledge and practices of their graduates has not been investigated (Cochran-Smith & Zeichner, 2005; Levine, 2006). Moreover, Kennedy (1999) pointed out that within different kinds of teacher preparation courses there are multiple kinds of practice, but we know little about if or how such differences affect teacher-candidate learning, let alone their practices in their own classrooms.

Beyond structural and philosophical differences there are also differences in the content that is taught. In Figure 1 we indicate that what is taught is, in part, determined by state and federal standards for teacher certification and technology competencies. Many state and national standards for assessing the qualifications of teacher candidates and awarding teaching credentials include technology literacy requirements (for an overview of state requirements, see the Digital Decade, *Education Week*, 2007, pp. 44–47). Such standards also impact the teacher preparation curriculum in other ways. For example, there are state specifications that indicate the number of hours in different course areas; the courses that may be taken as pre- versus post-undergraduate degrees; whether teacher candidates are required to have a substantive undergraduate major instead of, or in addition to, teacher preparation; whether teacher preparation occurs at the undergraduate level or subsequent to it; and the documentation of performance that IHEs are required to provide in connection with the credentialing of teacher candidates. Thus, the state in which an IHE resides can have a powerful influence on the structure and content of the teacher preparation experience.

The WWW project is particularly interested in differences in the IHEs' approach to learning and technology, especially along dimensions that reflect traditional as compared to contemporary approaches to learning, instruction, and assessment and enabling roles for technology. Many of the most important ideas about learning, instruction, and assessment have been explicated in the past few years in syntheses produced by the National Academy of Sciences, as well as other sources. As argued in reports such as *How People Learn* (Bransford, Brown, Cocking, Donovan, & Pellegrino, 2000) and *Knowing What Students Know* (Pellegrino et al., 2001), this knowledge base needs to be systematically incorporated into the preparation of future teachers and school leaders. In addition, one implication of contemporary approaches to learning is that teacher candidates need to experience, and not just listen to lectures about, different ways of teaching. Thus, one goal of the WWW project was to characterize the content of the teacher preparation courses with respect to evidence of contemporary approaches to learning, instruction, and assessment as reflected in the National Research Council (NRC) synthesis reports. As Grossman (2005) wisely noted, research on how prospective teachers are taught is of critical importance, because most research on teacher education focuses on the structure of programs rather than on issues of instruction. In teacher education, she argues, "*how* one is taught is part and parcel of *what* one teaches" (p. 425).

Furthermore, a major element of the knowledge base of contemporary theory concerns ways in which technology can and should be integrated into the teaching and assessment of school subject matter learning. This literature is largely based on work in K-12 classrooms, but there is some on uses of technology in undergraduate and teacher preparation programs (Goldman, Lawless, Pellegrino, & Plants, 2005/06 for overview; Pellegrino & Altman, 1997). In other words, we were interested in whether the content of the IHE courses included information on the integration of technology into K-12 teaching. Our current understanding of technology's role in teaching and learning goes well beyond the benefits of using general technology tools; it now incorporates specific materials and instructional programs that have been shown to dramatically change what is learned and how well student mastery of the content can be monitored and supported through intelligent, content-based assessment practices (see Goldman et al.). For example, technology tools can provide access to simulations, visualizations, video-based problem-solving environments, concept mapping, graphing applications, and computational aids such as calculators and spreadsheets. These kinds of tools can help students learn important content with understanding rather than merely memorizing it (see Bransford et al., 2000, chapter 9; Cognition and Technology Group at Vanderbilt [CTGV], 1996 for examples). These same technology tools can also support the learner by providing dynamic visual images and simulations, by making students' thinking visible, and by providing chances for self-assessment (Goldman et al.).

Other forms of technology can support formative assessment. The Diagnoser software for physics and mathematics (Hunt & Minstrell, 1994) provides information on students' preconceptions. Latent Semantic Analysis (e.g., Landauer, Foltz, & Laham, 1998) can be used to score essays, summaries, and answers to questions. It can also provide students with information regarding sections of the material that they have failed to demonstrate an understanding of. The Interactive Multi Media Exercises (IMMEX) system provides feedback on solution processes in complex problems (Hurst, Casillas, & Stevens, 1997). Other software gives students, teachers, and parents a picture of the child's progress over time on specific skills, for example, curriculum-based measurement (Fuchs, Fuchs, Hamlett, & Stecker, 1991). Electronic portfolio software can also help students (as well as teachers, parents, and others) see records of progress over time (see http://www.CILT.org). Other software applications use small portable devices such as personal digital assistants (PDA) to help teachers implement performance assessments of presentations and other kinds of activities.

Multimedia technologies can help classes create group products that can be shared with outside audiences. Networked and web-based communications technologies such as email, listservs, and more sophisticated knowledge-building software such as Speak Easy (Linn & Hsi, 2000) or Knowledge Forum (Scardamalia, Bereiter, & Lamon, 1994) can also help students form a community around important ideas. Such technology helps capture ideas that otherwise can be ephemeral and it supports communication that is asynchronous as well as synchronous.

Consistent with Grossman's (2005) point about teachers teaching the way they were taught, we were interested not only in whether the content of IHE courses dealt with learning-based uses of technology, but also in the degree to which IHEs integrated technology across the teacher preparation program. We hypothesized that if teacher candidates were not experiencing new roles for technology in their own education, there would be little chance that they would use technology in innovative ways in their own classrooms (subject of course to potential school-site influences on their practices).

The K-12 context. The right side of the schematic in Figure 1 depicts the K-12 context, its connection to the IHE through field placements, and the embedded contexts that we discussed earlier. The field placement basically bridges the IHE and K-12 worlds. Field placements, including student teaching, place constraints on what teacher candidates actually have an opportunity to observe or enact when they are in K-12 classrooms. There may be bidirectional opportunities for influence, in that student teachers can potentially introduce practicing teachers to different ways of teaching and using technology in the K-12 classroom. In the other direction, the K-12 context impacts the issues that are highlighted for student teachers in their day-to-day lives during their field placements. The degree to which they feel prepared to deal with these issues often comes back to the IHE in the context of student-teaching seminars that occur in coordination with the field placement. This may act as a feedback loop to the IHE regarding ways in which they need to better prepare their teacher candidates for operating in real classrooms. One question of interest for the WWW project was the nature of these potential feedback and feed-forward loops.

Figure 1 also shows the influence of state and national contexts that we exemplified earlier. The districts and states in which graduates of teacher preparation programs teach vary in terms of their demographics, economics, and standards. Differences in teaching quality related to these variables have been well documented (Darling-Hammond, 2000). This analysis of the ecology of teaching and learning suggests that to understand the impact of teacher preparation programs, one must also understand the impact of the placements where student teachers and new teachers begin to enact their practice, at least insofar as the nature of the constraints these may place on teachers with respect to what and how they teach. Can student teachers and new teacher graduates enact the knowledge and skills they have acquired in their methods classes? Is technology part of the school infrastructure? Is there a collegial atmosphere of collaboration among the teacher community or are newcomers regarded as plebes who have to learn the ropes? The design of the WWW project enabled us to follow student teachers from their coursework through their field placements and into their initial year or two of teaching. Thus, we have the potential for tracing, at least in terms of case study methodology, the potential roles of the various constraints operating at multiple levels in the overall educational system.

Design of the WWW Project

The overall design of the WWW project is an embedded longitudinal case study that follows cohorts of teacher candidates at specific institutions through their coursework and into their field placements and initial years of teaching. This design enables us to trace relationships among teacher candidates' experiences in their preparation programs, their field placements, and their own K-12 classrooms. The goal is to trace, over time, the links between what prospective teachers learn and experience concerning effective instruction and assessment (of which technology is a part) and the effects of this training on their practices when they enter teaching. We are using multiple sources of evidence and multilevel data collection and analyses to associate the knowledge, skills, and classroom practices of beginning teachers with the organizational contexts and characteristics of their teacher preparation programs.

The project was designed to examine variation in faculty practices with technology and the effects on the practices of teacher candidates across, as well as within, institutions. We are interested in identifying and tracing (1) the experiences with technology that are part of specific teacher preparation programs, and (2) the influences that these experiences have in shaping the subsequent instructional uses that teacher graduates implement in their own classrooms to support learning. The project's longitudinal, multilevel data-collection model traces the resiliency of two important strands of knowledge and skills—the establishment of learning environments that reflect contemporary understandings of how people learn and the integration of technology into instruction. In this chapter we emphasize only the technology strand. The project is a series of case studies of the participating institutions. Within each institutional case, there are three embedded cases corresponding to different groups of participants (administrators, faculty, and teacher candidates) (Yin, 1994).

Selection of the IHE

The IHEs that are the focus of the WWW study were selected through a multistep process. The initial step involved identification of a candidate set of teacher education programs that have been nationally recognized as being especially effective. To identify the candidate program pool, we examined published review materials and national recognition programs from selected organizations focused on issues of educational reform, especially the integration of educational technology into teacher education. The organizations and recognition programs whose materials were examined included

- Carnegie Corporation—Teachers for a New Era Project;
- AACTE—Best Practice Awards for the Innovative Use of Technology;
- ISTE—NETS Distinguished Achievement Award;
- George Lucas Educational Foundation;
- North Central Regional Educational Laboratory—Preparing Technology-Competent Teachers for Urban and Rural Classrooms: A Teacher Education Challenge; and
- USDOE—PT³ Program.

IHEs that were highlighted as of 2002 by more than one of the organizations listed were identified. In some cases, the organizations identified teacher education institutions based on their overall success in teacher education. In other cases, they specifically identified teacher education programs that were considered exemplary in the integration of technology in teacher education. However, even when the selection was based on overall teacher education program performance, there was still a specific emphasis on the diffusion of technology throughout the program. The result was a pool of 16 institutions clearly recognized as leaders in technology and teacher education. Each of these was recruited for participation in this project and eleven institutions agreed to participate in initial on-site interviews that generally occurred over one and one-half days. Each institutional visit contained between five and nine separate interviews with deans, other administrators, and key teacher education program staff. Based on the interview process and other factors such as institutional type, geographic location, and willingness to participate in a long-term, multifaceted data-collection process, the pool was ultimately narrowed to a set of eight institutions.

The eight case-study institutions. The final set of institutions includes over 4,000 teacher education students distributed across the Mid-Atlantic, South, Midwest, Southwest, and Western regions of the United States. The institutions are representative of teacher education programs at highly selective Research 1 institutions as well as programs at state and regional institutions that produce large numbers of teachers. The set includes both public (six) and private (two) IHEs. Five of the institutions participate in the Carnegie Foundation

FIGURE 2

QUESTIONS AND ISSUES ADDRESSED AT EACH ANALYSIS LEVEL OF THE WHAT
WORKS AND WHY PROJECT

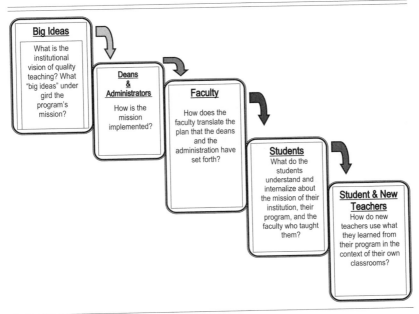

Teachers for a New Era project and the other three are highly respected
programs that have made notable attempts to integrate technology
into the teacher education curriculum. Additionally, seven of the eight
have been recipients of USDOE PT[3] grants. Each institution constitutes an individual case study, reflecting its unique characteristics. At
each institution, deans and program coordinators of the elementary
education teacher preparation program, faculty who teach the foundational courses in the elementary education teacher preparation
program, and teacher candidates volunteered to participate in the
WWW project.

Questions of Interest, Design, and Data Collection

The multilevel design of the WWW project has allowed us to
examine the orientation of each IHE, including its emphasis on contemporary learning theory and technology. Figure 2 depicts these
multiple levels of data collection and analysis as well as the types of

FIGURE 3

SOURCES OF DATA AT EACH ANALYSIS LEVEL OF THE WHAT WORKS AND WHY
PROJECT

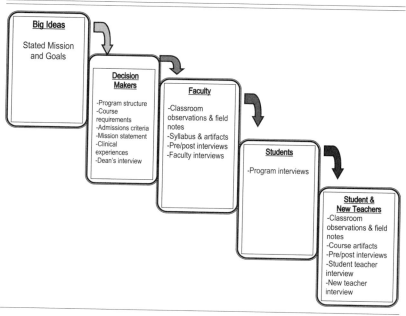

issues and questions addressed at each level. Specifically, we collected
data from administrators (e.g., deans and associate deans), program
coordinators, and faculty responsible for teaching the specific courses
that comprise the elementary teacher education program. Impact on
teacher candidates' knowledge is accessed through self-reports about
their coursework and overall program experience, plus observations of
their practices during student teaching and of their first years of teaching in their own classrooms. These observations were accompanied by
interviews that provided an additional window into the knowledge and
skills of teaching that could (or could not) be traced back to their
experiences at the IHEs.

Figure 3 provides additional detail on the specifics of the questions
we attempted to address for each strata of participants. Data collection
at the institutional level is focused on questions about (1) the organization of the program and its articulated philosophy regarding contemporary theory and research on teaching, learning, and technology,

and (2) the core courses and experiences that comprise the foundation of the institution's typical program for prospective elementary school teachers. In particular, we are interested in how technology is viewed by the institutional leadership with regard to its philosophical and structural role in the overall teacher education program and in their vision regarding the knowledge and skills of the programs' graduates. Sources of data at this level include interviews with the deans of the colleges of education and with heads or program coordinators of the teacher preparation programs about the program's history and mission, goals for graduates, and efforts to incorporate technology into teacher preparation.

At the level of the teacher preparation program, we targeted those courses identified as foundational by the deans and program administrators and which were offered in some form or another at each of the institutions in the sample. These courses include language arts/reading and mathematics methods courses and courses that cover research and theory on human development, learning, curriculum, and instruction. We interviewed the faculty teaching these courses regarding their course objectives, philosophy of teaching, and intended outcomes for students; observed course sessions using a time-sampling observation instrument for capturing specific features of the learning environment (e.g., grouping, content emphasis, materials used) and accompanying narrative field notes; and collected artifacts (syllabi, student work) associated with the course. In these courses, we are interested in seeing how often technology is used and the ways in which it is used. In other words, we are interested in what pedagogical practices faculty are modeling for their students.

At the student level, data collection is focused on three sets of outcomes: (1) student perceptions of what they have learned in their program, (2) the student teaching experiences and practices of selected student teachers, and (3) the pedagogical practices and instructional philosophies of program graduates during their first and second years of actual teaching. We focus on how frequently they use technology as a key component of their pedagogy, and in what ways they use it to support their own practice and their students' learning. Sources of data at the student teacher/new teacher level include:

- interviews with teacher candidates about their philosophy of teaching, influences on their practice, their experiences in their teacher preparation programs, and their student teaching experiences; and

- observation of their classrooms during their student teaching and first and second years of teaching. These observations use the same instrument and data collection procedure as the observations conducted in their teacher preparation courses.

Status of the Data Collection

We are currently 2 years into a 3-year data-collection effort and have completed collection of the interviews with deans and program coordinators. We are approximately three-fourths of the way toward completing the targeted course observations and interviews with the faculty who teach them, and have conducted a limited number of observations of teacher candidates during their student teaching. We have just begun the observation of these teacher candidates in their initial years of teaching.

In the present context, we present some preliminary descriptive results focused on the integration of technology in the teacher education programs of the eight IHEs. The data reflect analyses to date of three of the levels of data collection and analysis shown in Figures 2 and 3: deans and administrator interviews, observations of IHE courses, and observations of teacher candidates during their student teaching. Because we are still in process of analyzing the interviews with faculty and teacher candidates, those data do not contribute to what we present. We wish to emphasize that, given the ongoing nature of the data collection and analysis process, the picture we provide here is, of necessity, incomplete. Furthermore, we are not attempting to provide an evaluation of the quality of the instructional and learning experiences of students enrolled in any individual IHE program or the collective set of programs. What we do present is a snapshot of the current state of affairs regarding technology integration into the instructional milieu *across* teacher preparation programs as we understand it and have been able to map it thus far.

Dean and Program Administrator Interview Results

The dean and program coordinator interviews were focused on the "institutional" mission and overall vision for their teacher graduates and how technology was positioned with respect to these goals. Semi-structured interviews were conducted at each IHE; the number of respondents at each institution ranged between six and 13. The protocol is provided in Table 1, and all interviews were conducted by a member of the project staff. Respondents were encouraged to provide as much

TABLE 1
DEAN AND ADMINISTRATOR INTERVIEW QUESTIONS

1. What are the big ideas that influence your teacher education program?
   a. Is there a guiding vision of the graduating teacher candidate? If there is, how widely shared is it among faculty?
   b. Are there mechanisms in place to determine whether that vision is being achieved? If so, what are they?
   c. How have you promoted faculty involvement in your efforts?
2. As you know, we wanted to talk with you because your institution is recognized as a leader with respect to integrating technology into teacher education.
   a. Can you tell us how this came about and what supports its maintenance and further development?
   b. What are program areas where there is more versus less integration of technology?
   c. Are there instances where the availability of certain technologies has stimulated thinking about program change?
3. What are the plans for enhancing current programs with respect to content, technology, or their integration?
4. What have been the obstacles, stumbling blocks, and hurdles in the technology integration process? How have they been dealt with?
5. What have been the pleasant surprises in the technology-integration process?

detail as possible regarding the specifics of each answer. The interviewer was free to pursue specific topics that arose in the course of the interview through additional probes. All interviews were tape-recorded and later transcribed for coding and analysis purposes.

Three researchers triangulated on the themes present in the interviews with respect to the big ideas influencing the program; how technology was integrated into the program and the expectations for graduates with respect to technology skills; the genesis of technology in the teacher education program; ways in which they perceived technology to have changed teaching at the IHE; pleasant surprises and obstacles to technology integration; and plans for moving ahead with technology. Highlights of these analyses are reported here.

There was consistent mention across institutions of technology as a key feature of the program. We note however that at least one dean reported that technology integration was much stronger in the secondary program than in the elementary program. This may account for some of our findings about elementary-level courses and the practices of student teachers, as we focused our observations at the K-8 level. At each IHE, at least one key administrator mentioned technology integration in instruction as a "big idea" influencing the structure and functioning of the teacher education program. Also apparent is the image of the program graduate as someone who has mastered technology and is using it to support learning. That being the case, within most of the institutions there was no single, coherent vision about the connections among technology, teaching, and learning that was articulated by all administrators associated with the teacher education enterprise. Rather, there was a general sense that technology was an important part of both the preparation of new teachers and the transformation of how faculty were to go about the business of educating the students. The clearest visions came from the technology directors or coordinators, those who were typically charged with overseeing the integration of technology into the program, teaching instructional technology courses, and/or providing professional development support for faculty and staff.

In terms of the locus of a transformative process, the mathematics and language arts/reading methods courses emerged as critical. However, the transformation was discussed more in terms of generic technology tools or software, rather than in terms of software or courseware that is focused on the learning of critical content or in terms of how to teach this content, in either methods area. The lack of a clear focus on specific content-based applications and the emphasis on more generic software tools for presentation and access to information is generally consistent with the results described below for uses of technology observed in the methods courses.

Another common theme emerging in these interviews was the role of external resources to facilitate the technology-infusion process, in addition to the cadre of dedicated faculty who were willing to play a leading role in the process. These were the people who typically pursued the PT^3 grants and then were responsible for the development of training programs for faculty, staff, and students. The obstacles were common—the technology itself was often a problem and a source of frustration to all, because it was far less than an infallible instructional and learning resource. Nevertheless, people persisted, and there was a general sense of personal and institutional commitment to making it part of the fabric of the instructional program.

In summary, the interviews accord well with the reputations and histories of the IHEs in the area of technology integration into teacher education. Technology was not a mystery nor was it a driving force. Rather, it was perceived to be an important and inevitable component of the training of educational professionals. If there was an obstacle it was getting the faculty to use it in important and meaningful ways. What is also important to note is that across the set of IHEs, no single, powerful view of technology for teaching and learning emerged. Rather, each program had followed its own path in adopting technologies and in incorporating them into the lives of the faculty and students in the program. This has implications regarding the nature of technology use in higher education and in the K-12 arena.

IHE Course Observation Results

Direct observations were made of over 2,000 10-minute "teaching episodes"—data that were collected across all eight IHEs. The observations were derived from courses at each IHE that covered mathematics and reading methods, as well as other foundational content areas. With each instructor we conducted a course interview prior to the first observation and pre- and post-observation interviews that corresponded to the actual observation. Specific courses were observed three times over the course of the semester or quarter. The duration of each observation was equivalent to the number of hours the class met in a week. In the case of classes that met for 3 hours once per week, observers were present for the entire 3 hours; if classes met multiple times during the week, the observer attended all sessions in that week. Observations were distributed over the duration of the course (beginning, middle, end).

All observations were conducted by research assistants trained by WWW project staff to use an instrument specifically developed for this purpose (Carney, Oney, Goldman, & Pellegrino, 2004). The observation tool is a specialized *Filemaker®* application that utilizes two methods of data capture. An observation episode consists of two phases: a descriptive field note phase followed by a checklist phase. During a 10-minute episode, the first 5 minutes consist of entering "running" descriptive field notes of what is being observed during that 5 minutes into a text field that appears side by side with the checklist. After 5 minutes, observers read over their notes and characterize the 5 minutes of activity by checking off the relevant descriptors on the checklist. They are encouraged to refer to their field notes as they complete the checklist. This completes an episode. They then begin a new 10-minute episode by resuming the observing and field-note writing for 5 minutes, then completing the checklist. This cycle repeats for the duration of the observation period. Users are free to define the length of the episode and there is a clock on each checklist to facilitate time keeping. The software automatically time codes the field notes and checklist completion for each episode. The data are exported to an Excel file that can be manipulated. Information about the Classroom Observation Tool (© Center for the Study of Learning, Instruction, and Teacher Development, 2004) is available at http://litd.psch.uic.edu/

FIGURE 4

RECORDING SCREEN FOR AN EVENT = EPISODE FROM THE CLASSROOM
OBSERVATION TOOL
CENTER FOR THE STUDY OF LEARNING, INSTRUCTION, AND TEACHER
DEVELOPMENT, 2004

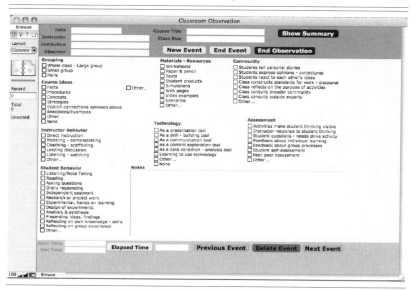

research/projects/ww/tools.asp. Figure 4 provides a screen shot of the episode template (called Event in the template) and checklist.

The Classroom Observation Tool allows for the coding of multiple aspects of the instructional context and activity, including the use of technology. Descriptors of observations are grouped into the following conceptual and functional groupings: student grouping or configuration; course ideas; focus; instructor behavior; student behavior; materials; technology; community; and assessment. Under each category are two to 13 checklist items, and also a checklist item for "none" and "other." Checklist descriptors are at an intermediate "grain size" or level of abstraction from what can be observed. They are specific about characterizing activity in such a way that we can make useful distinctions regarding features that tend to characterize powerful learning environments within the framework described in the *How People Learn* (Bransford et al., 2000) report, but they are broad enough to be applicable across a variety of instructional contexts. Each observer can choose as many of these descriptors as make sense based on the content

TABLE 2
DESCRIPTIONS OF CODING CATEGORIES REGARDING HOW ELECTRONIC
TECHNOLOGY WAS USED DURING THE OBSERVATION BLOCK

Presentation Tool	This was to be selected if the technology was used primarily to help the instructor or students present or convey course ideas.
Skill-Building Tool	This was to be selected when technology was being used to help students build or become automatic with certain skills. Examples might be typing or mathematics, or spelling drill and practice programs.
Communication Tool	This was to be chosen when the class used technology for in-class communication or for communicating with others outside the classroom. This descriptor could also be used when the instructor used a technology that makes student ideas public (such as Inspiration).
Content-Exploration Tool	This was to be used when students and/or the instructor used technology for using prepared materials about classroom content. This could be done through accessing information, running simulations, or otherwise.
Data Collection-Analysis Tool	This was to be selected when students used technology for data collection or analysis. The use of Palm technology for data collection or the use of statistical packages for data analysis would fall under this description, as would any creation of graphs or charts with technology.
Learning to Use Technology	This was to be selected when students were simply learning how to use a certain kind of technology rather than using it to build knowledge.
Personal Tool	Students were using laptops or other computers on their own initiative rather than as directed by the teacher. These tasks could include note taking, making calculations, or checking email.
None	No technology was used during the time block.
Other	Technology was used to serve another purpose during the time block. Clicking on *other* produced a dialogue box that allowed entry of a description.

of the field notes. The checklist is designed so that the data can be examined separately for each item on the checklist or by considering co-occurrences of checklist items. As shown in Table 2, the coding categories for technology allow for the capture of multiple different uses of technology. The coding categories in Table 3 were not meant to be mutually exclusive and multiple codes could be used for a single observation episode.

In order to fully understand how technology was integrated into instruction during the episodes observed, we first identified those episodes that were coded as having some type of technology present. For

TABLE 3

DESCRIPTION OF CODING CATEGORIES FOR FUNCTIONAL USES OF TECHNOLOGY

Delivery	Technology solely used to convey/present information to students. In most cases, this was a PowerPoint presentation in which the main ideas of a lesson/topic were simply displayed.
Productivity	Technology used for word processing/note taking, emailing, conducting web searches.
Pedagogical Affordance	Technology used to actively engage students in processing and exploring content material, usually in a group rather than individual configurations; providing opportunities for students to exchange ideas and share related experiences. Frequently, this was accomplished by using video of K-8 classrooms to bring actual classroom situations into the IHE course. Often such videos featured both the thinking out loud of an elementary student and a teacher guiding the learning. Teacher candidates typically discussed what they observed, including their thoughts about what students in videos were thinking and the strategies utilized by the teacher to assist and support learning. Sometimes the IHE instructor asked teacher candidates to hypothesize about other possible strategies that could be employed.
Assessment	Technology used for the purposes of informal, formative assessment, where student thinking, understanding, and/or products were visible and allowed for meaningful instructor and/or peer feedback. These interactions often stimulated deeper discussion, and sometimes were used by the instructor to determine the next steps for instruction. A typical example of this category is students posting their ideas, reflections, or responses related to a particular topic or assignment to a blog that was then displayed in class, affording deeper level engagement by both the instructor and students.
Learning to Use Technology:	These are cases where the students are learning how to use a certain type of technology. An example of this could be students learning how to use content specific software or being instructed in webpage development. Although this category has the same label as one in Table 2, the application of this category in the context of functional analysis is far more restricted than it was for the technology use coding.

these episodes, we tabulated the frequency of use of technology in each activity category shown in Table 2; this was done on a course-by-course basis. These data thus provide information about the general types of technology-based activities that were engaged in by instructors and/or students. Evidence was in fact obtained for activities encompassing each of the coding categories shown in Table 2, although the absolute and relative frequencies of occurrence vary substantially, as we shall illustrate. We also pursued an analysis of the instructional function associated with each technology-based activity. To do so we combined information from the actual-use codes checked off on the observation tool and the descriptive field notes recorded by the observer. An examination of both the type of activity that involved technology and its functional use in instruction provides a richer and more complete understanding of the nature and quality of technology integration in the instructional environment within a given course and across episodes. We were able to narrow the functional uses of technology to five distinct categories, as described in Table 3. Each episode involving technology-based activities was then coded based on this functional use scheme. If an episode happened to include multiple functional uses of technology, this was captured during the coding process.

Table 4 provides the results of the analyses of technology use in terms of (1) the total number of episodes observed and (2) separately, by type of course. As shown in the top rows of Table 4, the use of technology was observed in approximately 47% of the episodes. Actual variation across IHEs in technology usage ranged from a low overall value of 34% to a high value of 54% of episodes. The summary provided in Table 4 also indicates that there was variation in the overall frequency of technology use across the different courses. Not surprisingly, the highest percentage use of technology was in the educational technology courses where it was ubiquitous, whereas the lowest frequency of occurrence was in the student teaching seminar/discussion courses. The language arts/reading methods courses, as well as the educational psychology and the curriculum and instruction courses, did not vary greatly in overall occurrence, with values between 47% and 54%. The lowest frequency of occurrence was in the mathematics methods courses, with a value of 35%. Thus, it seems logical to conclude that technology was a reasonably frequent feature of the learning/instructional environments in each of the IHEs and that it was generally present in a range of courses and instructional contexts.

Of particular interest are the types of activities that technology supported and the instructional functions that were fulfilled. The middle rows of Table 4 provide a summary of the data on the types of activities based on the coding categories from Table 3. When technology was present, 66% of the time it was used as a lecture/presentation tool. This predominant use of technology was remarkably consistent across course contexts, ranging from 59% to 73% of all episodes where technology use was coded. The second most frequent activity (30%) was use as a personal tool, and this was also very stable across course contexts with the exception of the teaching seminar courses (58%). None of the other activities that involved technology use exceeded 11% overall, and there was general consistency in the patterns across all the

TABLE 4
DESCRIPTIVE DATA ON ACTUAL AND FUNCTIONAL TECHNOLOGY USE IN IHE INSTRUCTIONAL EPISODE

	Total # of Episodes	Math Methods	Lang Arts/Reading Methods	Ed Psych	Ed Tech	Teaching Seminar	Curriculum and Instruction
Total IHE Episodes	2141	491	612	385	151	161	341
Total IHE Tech Episodes	995	171	288	209	134	33	160
Tech Episodes as % of Total	46.50	34.8	47.10	54.30	88.70	21	46.90
Activities Using Technology			Frequency (% of tech episodes)				
Presentation Tool	658 (66.1)	125 (73.1)	171 (59.4)	139 (66.5)	85 (63.4)	21 (63.6)	117 (73.1)
Skill-Building Tool	53 (5.3)	9 (5.3)	30 (10.4)	0 (0)	13 (9.7)	0 (0)	1 (.6)
Communication Tool	76 (7.6)	17 (9.9)	22 (7.6)	5 (2.4)	10 (7.5)	0 (0)	22 (13.8)
Content-Exploration Tool	110 (11.1)	34 (19.9)	26 (9.0)	13 (6.2)	24 (17.9)	0 (0)	13 (8.1)
Data-Collection/Analysis Tool	14 (1.4)	2 (1.3)	0 (0)	2 (1.0)	5 (3.7)	0 (0)	5 (3.1)
Learning to Use Technology	85 (8.5)	7 (4.1)	31 (10.8)	1 (.5)	43 (32.1)	0 (0)	3 (1.9)
Personal Tool	294 (29.5)	33 (19.3)	83 (28.8)	75 (35.9)	45 (33.6)	19 (57.6)	39 (24.4)
Instructional Function			Frequency (% of tech episodes)				
Delivery	582 (58.5)	87 (50.9)	145 (50.3)	136 (65.1)	81 (60.4)	21 (63.6)	112 (70.0)
Productivity	354 (35.6)	52 (30.4)	123 (42.7)	64 (30.6)	46 (34.3)	17 (51.5)	52 (32.5)
Pedagogical Affordance	141 (14.2)	57 (33.3)	37 (12.8)	21 (10.0)	15 (11.2)	0 (0)	11 (6.9)
Learning to Use Technology	45 (4.5)	4 (2.3)	12 (4.2)	0 (0)	27 (20.1)	0 (0)	2 (1.3)
Assessment	17 (1.7)	2 (1.2)	1 (.3)	5 (2.4)	9 (6.7)	0 (0)	0 (0)

courses. The one exception was in the educational technology courses where 32% of the episodes involving technology included activities associated with learning to use some form of technology, a result that is not surprising given the course context.

The lower rows of Table 4 present the results regarding the instructional functions that the technology served based on the coding categories in Table 4. These data provide a very clear and consistent pattern overall and across courses. The primary instructional function of technology was to deliver content; this was true 59% of the time when technology was used, and it varied between 50% and 70% across course contexts. The second most frequent instructional use of technology was as a productivity tool (36%) and the variation across course contexts was not large (30% to 52%). It is also clear that the instructional functions least often served were assessment (2%) and learning to use technology (5%).

The results in Table 4 for instructional function also make it clear that the more powerful pedagogical affordances of technology, that is, those that would support student engagement with critical concepts and procedures, were not abundant, occurring 14% of the time when technology was used. Interestingly, the only course context wherein the percentage use in this instructional function category was greater than 13% was in mathematics methods (33%). Examples of the use of technology to fulfill this instructional function are useful, because they help illustrate some of the ways in which the use of technology to present material can be coupled with a deep engagement with the content to support future pedagogy. In one such episode, IHE students watched a video of elementary school students sharing solutions to geometry problems, reacting to each other's ideas and presenting alternate ways of solving the problems. Then the IHE faculty instructor asked students what they saw as well as what they would do differently. In another example, a video showed students working out problems with Unifix cubes, and IHE students were asked to follow along while using their own cubes and to think about the strategies the elementary students were using. The instructor stopped the video throughout to probe for students' ideas about the children's misunderstandings.

As might be expected, there was variation across individual courses in the use of technology—both in frequency and in type of use—as a function of the individual instructor. We have yet to probe all the other sources of information, such as faculty interviews, to obtain a more complete picture of how faculty view technology in their own pedagogy and what they are attempting to model, if anything, for prospective teachers. It may well be the case that technology had a more prominent role in the learning of IHE students but that this occurred outside normal classroom instructional time. Evidence to that effect will come from further analyses of the faculty interviews and the course syllabi and assignments. At present, however, all we can tentatively conclude is that the IHEs' efforts to infuse technology into the teacher education instructional milieu were effective only to the extent that PowerPoint has become the preferred means to present information and may well have replaced the ubiquitous overhead transparency as the medium of delivery.

Student Teaching Observation Results

A version of the classroom observation tool similar to that described earlier for use in the IHE classroom was used to collect data on the characteristics of student teachers' instruction. For each student teacher who agreed to participate, observations were collected of instruction in two separate content areas—reading/language arts and mathematics. These data were collected at different times for each student teacher using the same sampling and recording method described previously. At present, we have fewer total cases of these instructional observations than those of faculty and not all of the IHEs are represented in the data to be discussed.

Given the data summarized earlier for the uses of technology by faculty in IHE courses and learning contexts, perhaps it is not surprising that observations of teacher candidates during their student teaching of mathematics and reading lessons revealed a very low baseline level of technology use, especially in the context of mathematics instruction (5% of all math instruction episodes). The data are shown in Table 5. Of 710 total episodes of student teaching that were observed and coded for technology use, only 11% showed any evidence of the use of technology as part of the student teachers' pedagogy. Contributing to this low percentage of technology use is the fact that only 20 of the 69 student teachers who were observed used any technology whatsoever during their student teaching. When technology was used by these 20 student teachers, 26% of the time it was as a presentation tool and 44% of the time it was for skill building. When the episodes are examined in terms of the instructional functions served by use of technology, the data reveal very few deep pedagogical uses of technology. The primary functional use of technology was for personal productivity, and this was consistent across mathematics and reading instructional contexts.

TABLE 5
DESCRIPTIVE DATA ON ACTUAL AND FUNCTIONAL TECHNOLOGY USE IN STUDENT TEACHER INSTRUCTIONAL EPISODES

	Total # of Episodes	Math Instruction	Language Arts/Reading Instructions
Total Student-Teacher Episodes	710	335	375
Total Student-Teacher-Technology Episodes	78	17	61
Technology Episodes as % of Total	11	5	16.3
Activities Using Technology	Frequency (% of tech episodes)	Frequency (% of tech episodes)	Frequency (% of tech episodes)
Presentation Tool	20 (25.6)	11 (64.7)	9 (14.8)
Skill-Building Tool	34 (43.6)	7 (41.2)	27 (44.3)
Communication Tool	6 (7.7)	5 (29.4)	1 (1.6)
Content exploration Tool	19 (24.4)	0 (0)	19 (31.1)
Data Collection/Analysis Tool	12 (15.4)	4 (23.5)	8 (13.1)
Learning to Use Technology	15 (19.2)	3 (17.6)	12 (19.7)
Personal Tool	23 (29.5)	0 (0)	23 (37.7)
Instructional Function	Frequency (% of tech episodes)	Frequency (% of tech episodes)	Frequency (% of tech episodes)
Delivery	18 (23.0)	7 (41.2)	11 (18.0)
Productivity	46 (59.0)	11 (64.7)	35 (57.4)
Pedagogical Affordance	13 (16.7)	1 (5.9)	12 (19.7)
Learning to Use Technology	6 (7.7)	0 (0)	6 (9.8)
Assessment	3 (3.8)	1 (5.9)	2 (3.3)

The data in Table 5 are consistent with other studies that have looked at technology use by teachers. For example, Russell, Bebell, O'Dwyer, and O'Connor (2003) found evidence that teachers use technology more for preparation and presentation than for delivering instruction or assigning work that utilizes technology to students. Further, they found that teachers who were new to the field, such as the students we observed, were less likely to use technology than their experienced peers despite being more comfortable with technology as a personal tool.

As was true for the IHE faculty, these results beg the question of why technology was such a missing part of the instructional equation. Perhaps it is a function of the limited availability of technology in the K-8 classrooms where these instructional episodes transpired. But this may not be the only reason. Interview data with the student teachers surrounding these instructional events will help fill in some of the explanatory gaps. For example, several teacher candidates who had had experience with technology as a learning/instructional tool at their IHE mentioned that despite this exposure, they had had no specific instruction on how to use that technology with their own students, and consequently did not feel comfortable doing so. Others mentioned the lack of technology use by cooperating teachers as a factor; while others highlighted the lack of time, lack of resources, and/or lack of confidence. We must be guarded in drawing conclusions about the capabilities and predispositions of the student teachers and beginning teachers to use technology in their own instruction until we have a larger data set and can probe other aspects of the interview data.

Discussion and Implications

Information technology has become an ubiquitous aspect of our daily lives, from the iPods and cell phones we carry around to the computers we use to access the web, write papers, and present material. The generation of students now in schools and those entering teacher education programs are considered "digital natives," a term that captures the idea that anyone born after 1980 embraces technology as a natural fact of life (Prensky, 2001). The lives of K-12 students, as well as current teacher education students, are dominated by information and communication technologies. Those of us who predate that time are considered "digital immigrants."

But despite the presence of technology all around us, we still seem to know so little about how technology is or should be affecting the educational process. Nowhere has this been more obvious than in the context of teacher preparation. In the early 1990s much was written about the need to prepare teachers, both through inservice and preservice programs, to make use of information technology as a key feature of their pedagogy. And in the last 15+ years, considerable time, effort, and dollars have been expended on the integration of technology into the instructional environments and preparation of new teachers. In this chapter we have reported some of the initial results of our attempt to probe more deeply into exactly what is happening in teacher preparation as regards technology and pedagogy. Our look at teacher education and technology is not intended as a random or representative sample of the over 1,000+ institutions across the country that prepare teachers. On the contrary, we deliberately attempted to look in places where an investment and institutional commitment has been made, over time, to prepare the next generation of digitally literate teachers.

Perhaps it is useful then to take a step back and consider what we expected or perhaps hoped to see as a context for evaluating and discussing what we have been able to ascertain from our data thus far. One reasonable expectation is that technology would be omnipresent in the lives of the students learning to become teachers and that a major aspect of its presence would be in the environments for learning where they were interacting with higher education faculty. A second expectation is that these prospective teachers would be comfortable with using these technologies to accomplish tasks associated with their own learning. A third expectation is that there would be a clear and consistent vision about how technology was to be used by teachers to support their students' learning and an accompanying execution of this vision in the courses and experiences of the prospective teachers. One way to express the latter expectation is that it would be clear to everyone—administrators, faculty, prospective teachers—what was new, different, and important about the use of technology in the teaching and learning process as related to important curricular content, and that prospective teachers would get opportunities to develop understanding and facility in the uses of technology for pedagogy.

The results we have obtained to date certainly accord well with the first two expectations. Technology was indeed omnipresent in the lives of the teacher education students. It was used in their courses by most of their faculty instructors and it was used by the students to accomplish various tasks and objectives. In fact, one would be hard-pressed these days to find a higher education context where technology was *not* a critical part of the teaching and learning context. So one might justifiably conclude that the digital natives who are learning to be teachers and the digital immigrants who are responsible for their training and preparation are at least in the same ballpark when it comes to some of the many uses of technology for educational purposes. Compared to studies and data obtained in the 1990s, we would have to conclude that teacher education has changed substantially with regard to the presence and use of technology. It is no longer the case that only a few selected instructors are using technology in the design and delivery of some aspects of their instruction. Clearly, we observed the use of technology across a range of critical course contexts.

In contrast, however, our initial results are somewhat troubling relative to the third expectation described earlier. No clear vision about the role of technology in transforming the teaching and learning process was apparent in the rhetoric or execution of the IHE programs. Furthermore, the data on instructional episodes reveal remarkably limited evidence of deep and powerful integration of technology into the learning environments experienced by prospective teachers. Most of that integration was restricted to the use of technology as an information-presentation and content-delivery tool. There was relatively little evidence of technology serving as a vehicle for restructuring the content and/or format of instruction for prospective teachers. This occurred despite the fact that the eight IHEs were originally selected for their investment in technology and its integration into the fabric of their teacher education program. Even more troubling is the fact that a very small percentage of the instructional episodes observed for the student teachers showed any evidence of the use of technology as an innovative part of their pedagogy. Thus, whatever they did learn about the uses of technology to facilitate pedagogy and learning was not easily or readily applied in their initial teaching experiences, whether in mathematics or reading instruction. Instead, they used technology in their teaching in ways that mimicked the higher education context—as a content-delivery and personal-productivity tool—adding further support for the general proposition that a person "teaches the way they were taught."

There are multiple valences that can be applied to the results we have reported. On the one hand there is reason to look positively on the situation, because it is clear that technology for teaching and learning is part of the daily fabric of the instructional lives of these prospective teachers. The fact that it is present to a fairly high degree in their courses and program experiences means that they have expectations regarding its use in their personal and professional lives. Unfortunately, the negative perspective on these very same data is that they are coming to view technology as a means to reinforce traditional modes of teaching and learning—ways of doing the same things, only more quickly or efficiently. This is not an uncommon way in which technology affects multiple aspects of our daily lives. What is happening is that prospective teachers are not learning about transformative ways to use technology to support deep engagement with content and to support the design and delivery of learning environments that are more consistent with what we know about how people learn. This suggests that the teacher education enterprise now needs to move to a new stage of technology integration in teacher preparation—we are beyond the phase of needing to make it available and accessible to faculty and students. Rather, we need to engage faculty and students with examples and experiences that capitalize on the power of new media and tools to support learning with understanding. The worst thing that could happen is that teacher education becomes complacent and assumes that the problem is solved. Perhaps another way to say this is that the digital immigrants who have learned to use technology need to move beyond the ways in which they learned and were taught. Making this shift will require a concerted effort and a new investment of resources focused on the transformation of pedagogy in the IHE. Simply making one's lectures available via Podcasts is not the answer . . . although it may be part of the solution, because doing so opens up time for fundamentally different, content-based interactions between teachers and students when they do meet.

Although the primary focus of this report has been higher education, it is but one aspect of the complex landscape of factors influencing how teachers teach and how their students learn, as discussed earlier and depicted in Figure 1. The other major aspect is the K-12 context. As yet, we have not obtained data on what happens to the graduates of the eight teacher preparation programs when they enter school districts and have their own classrooms. Perhaps things will look different, but one must wonder if that is possible, given that the experiences that precede taking control of one's own classroom establish a necessary if not sufficient condition for predicting how technology will be used for instruction in the K-12 classroom. What worries us even more is that the trends in K-8 instruction, especially with regard to uses of technology (see e.g., *Education Week*, 2007), are moving toward the use of applications that emphasize assessment and accountability, and that can lead to the narrowing of curriculum and instruction. If new teachers do not have a powerful vision of the types of learning and teaching they wish to support with technology, they will have a difficult time making intelligent choices about technology use in their professional lives as teachers.

NOTES

1. This work is supported by a grant to James Pellegrino and Susan Goldman from the Atlantic Philanthropies. The results reported in this paper are the product of the data collection and analysis efforts of many individuals who have contributed to the project since 2002. Special acknowledgement goes to Kamila Brodowinska, Cynthia Mayfield, and Blythe Miller who supervise and coordinate the data collection and data analysis efforts at UIC.

2. Talbert and McLaughlin (1993) refer to this as multiple embedded contexts.

REFERENCES

American Association of Colleges for Teacher Education (AACTE). (1998). *Best practice: Innovative use of technology award* (Press release). Washington, DC: Author.

Baker, E., & Herman, J.L. (2000). *Technology and evaluation*. Los Angeles: Center for Research on Evaluation, Standards, and Student Testing, University of California, Los Angeles.

Barker, B.O., Helm, V., & Taylor, D.R. (1995). *Reforming teacher education through the integration of advanced technologies: Case study report of a college model*. Paper presented at the annual meeting of the American Association of Colleges for Teacher Education. Washington, DC (ERIC document reproduction Service No. ED 379 274).

Bransford, J.D., Brown, A.L., Cocking, R.R., Donovan, S., & Pellegrino, J.W. (Eds.). (2000). *How people learn: Brain, mind, experience, and school* (expanded edition). Washington, DC: National Academy Press.

Campus Computing Project (2001). *eCommerce comes slowly to the campus*. Claremont, CA: Campus Computing Project. Retrieved April 12, 2007, from http://www.campuscomputing.net/pdf/2001-CCP.pdf ().

Carnegie Forum on Education and the Economy, Task Force on Teaching as a Profession (1986). *A nation prepared: Teachers for the 21st century*. Washington, DC: Carnegie Forum on Education and the Economy.

Carney, K.E., Oney, B., Goldman, S.R., & Pellegrino, J.W. (2004, November). *Interpreting the How People Learn framework: What lies in the overlaps?* Working paper. Chicago, IL: University of Illinois at Chicago.

Cochran-Smith, M., & Zeichner, K. (Eds.). (2005). *Studying teacher education: The report of the AERA panel on research and teacher education*. Mahwah, NJ: Lawrence Erlbaum Associates.

Cognition and Technology Group At Vanderbilt (CTGV). (1996). Looking at technology in context: A framework for understanding technology and education research. In D.C. Berliner & R.C. Calfee (Eds.), *The handbook of educational psychology* (pp. 807–840). New York: Simon & Schuster Macmillan.

Curry School of Education (1997). *The Curry School technology strand*. Unpublished manuscript, University of Virginia, Charlottesville.

Darling-Hammond, L. (2000). Teacher quality and student achievement: A review of state policy evidence. *Educational Policy Analysis Archives, 8*(1). Retrieved May 5, 2007, from http://epaa.asu.edu/epaa/v8n1

Duran, M. (2000). *Examination of technology integration into an elementary teacher education program: One university's experience*. Unpublished dissertation, Ohio University. Athens, OH.

Education Week (2007, March 29). *Technology Counts 2007: A digital decade* [Special report].

Fuchs, L.S., Fuchs, D., Hamlett, C.L., & Stecker, P.M. (1991). Effects of curriculum-based measurement on teacher planning and student achievement in mathematics operations. *American Educational Research Journal, 28*, 617–641.

Fulton, K., Glenn, A., & Valdez, G. (2003). *Three preservice programs preparing teachers to use technology: A study in partnerships.* Naperville, IL: Learning Point Associates.

Glenn, A., Reed, R., & Rhodes, E. (2001). *Purdue University P3T3 Grant, Year 1: Report of the external evaluation team.* West Lafayette, IN: Purdue University. Retrieved May 13, 2007, from http://p3t3.soe.purdue.edu/ExternalYear1.pdf

Goldman, S.R., Lawless, K., Pellegrino, J.W., & Plants, R. (2005/06). Technology for teaching and learning with understanding. In J.M. Cooper (Ed.), *Classroom teaching skills* (8th ed., pp. 185–234). Boston, MA: Houghton Mifflin.

Grossman, P.L. (2005). Research on pedagogical approaches in teacher education. In M. Cochran-Smith & K. Zeichner (Eds.), *Review of research in teacher education* (pp. 425–476). Washington, DC: American Educational Research Association.

Haertel, G.D., & Means, B. (2003). *Evaluating educational technology: Effective research designs for improving learning.* New York: Teachers College Press.

Hunt, E., & Minstrell, J. (1994). A cognitive approach to the teaching of physics. In K. McGilly (Ed.), *Classroom lessons: Integrating cognitive theory and classroom practice* (pp. 51–74). Cambridge, MA: MIT Press.

Hurst, K.C., Casillas, A.M., & Stevens, R.H. (1997). *Exploring the dynamics of complex problem-solving with artificial neural network-based assessment systems.* (CSE Tech. Rep. No. 387). Los Angeles: University of California Los Angeles, Center for Research on Evaluation, Standards, and Student Testing.

Kennedy, M. (1999). The problem of evidence in teacher education. In R. Roth (Ed.), *The role of the university in the preparation of teachers* (pp. 87–107). Philadelphia: Falmer.

Landauer, T.K., Foltz, P.W., & Laham, D. (1998). Introduction to latent semantic analysis. *Discourse Processes, 25*, 259–284.

Levine, A. (2006). *Educating school teachers.* Princeton, NJ: Education Schools Project.

Linn, M.C., & Hsi, S. (2000). *Computers, teachers, peers: Science learning partners.* Mahwah, NJ: Lawrence Erlbaum Associates.

Mergendoller, J.R., Johnston, J., Rockman, S., & Willis, J. (1994). *Exemplary approaches to training teachers to use technology, vol. 1: Case studies.* Washington, DC; Novato, CA: Office of Technology Assessment; Beryl Buck Institute for Education.

Moursund, D.G., & Bielefeldt, T. (1999). *Will new teachers be prepared to teach in a digital age? A national survey on information technology in teacher education.* Eugene, OR: International Society for Technology in Education.

National Commission on Teaching and America's Future (1996). *What matters most: Teaching for America's future.* New York: Author.

Pellegrino, J.W., & Altman, E.A. (1997). Information technology and teacher preparation: Some critical issues and illustrative solutions. *Peabody Journal of Education, 72*(1), 92–93.

Pellegrino, J.W., Chudowsky, N., & Glaser, R. (Eds.). (2001). *Knowing what students know: The science and design of educational assessment.* Washington, DC: National Academy Press.

Persichitte, K.A., Tharp, D.D., & Caffarella, E.P. (1997). *The use of technology by schools, colleges, and departments of education 1996.* Washington, DC: American Association of Colleges for Teacher Education.

Prensky, M. (2001). Digital natives, digital immigrants. *On the Horizon, 9*(5), 1–6.

Russell, M., Bebell, D., O'Dwyer, L., & O'Connor, K. (2003). Examining teacher technology use: Implications for pre-service and in-service teacher preparation. *Journal of Teacher Education, 54*(4), 297–310.

Scardamalia, M., Bereiter, C., & Lamon, M. (1994). The CSILE project: Trying to bring the classroom into world 3. In K. McGilly (Ed.), *Classroom lessons: Integrating cognitive theory and classroom practice* (pp. 201–228). Cambridge, MA: MIT Press.

Talbert, J.E., & McLaughlin, M.W. (1993). Understanding teaching in context. In D.K. Cohen, M.W. McLaughlin, & J.E. Talbert (Eds.), *Teaching for understanding: Challenges for policy and practice* (pp. 167–206). San Francisco, CA: Jossey-Bass.

U.S. Congress, Office of Technology Assessment (1995, April). *Teachers and technology: Making the connection.* OTA-EHR-616. Washington, DC: U.S. Government Printing Office.

Vermillion, J., Young, M., & Hanafin, R. (2007). An academic technology initiative for teacher preparation candidates: Implications for preservice teacher programs. *Journal of Computing in Teacher Education, 23*(3), 99–104.

Yin, R.K. (1994). *Case study research: Design and methods* (2nd ed.). London, UK: Sage Publications.

Teacher Professional Development and ICT: Strategies and Models

CHARALAMBOS VRASIDAS AND GENE V GLASS

The continuous striving for better teachers and better schools has taken many different paths. One such path involves the use of Information and Communication Technologies (ICT) in teaching and learning. It is clear that ICT is increasing access to information, inspiring new developments in teaching, and allowing individuals and communities to interact at any time. Debates between technology supporters and skeptics about the use of ICT in classroom teaching have been growing. Although disputes over the value of using ICT in education are one factor, the lack of availability of ICT in schools is another reason its use is limited. Other dynamics include the realities and culture of the typical classroom and teachers' knowledge, skills, beliefs, and expertise (CEO Forum on Educational Technology, 2000; Cuban, 2001; Moursund & Bielefeldt, 1999; Vrasidas & Glass, 2005), and particularly the lack of teacher professional development.

Attempts to integrate ICT into the classroom are influenced by such things as the availability of the necessary technology infrastructure, support for teachers, accessible change models, teachers' practices, curriculum constraints, assessment practices, education policies, and professional development. Education reform efforts have emphasized the importance of integrating ICT in the classroom, citing these factors, and the need for quality teacher professional development to do so (Donnelly, Dove, Tiffany-Morales, Adelman, & Zucker, 2002; McIntyre & Byrd, 1998). Preservice teacher education programs are by no means sufficient to prepare teachers to be effective users of ICT in

Charalambos Vrasidas is Executive Director of the Centre for the Advancement of Research and Development in Educational Technology (CARDET) and Associate Professor of Learning Technologies at the University of Nicosia, Cyprus. Gene V Glass is Regents' Professor of Education at Arizona State University and Director of Research & Policy, Centre for the Advancement of Research & Development in Educational Technology, Nicosia, Cyprus.

the classroom. As technology evolves rapidly, lessons learned even a few years earlier no longer suffice. Several scholars have argued that existing professional development programs are inadequate for preparing teachers for the 21st century (Ball & Cohen, 2000; Borko, 2004). Ongoing professional development is essential for school improvement, and it can empower teachers to address the challenges they face in their everyday teaching and to meet demands for teacher quality and school accountability.

Before discussing strategies and models for professional development, it is important to emphasize that successful technology integration in schools requires ICT as an integral part of teacher preparation programs (Duffield, 2005; Vrasidas & Glass, 2005). Teachers tend to teach as they were taught. If teachers are expected to teach using ICT, they should be taught by teacher educators who use ICT and who structure their courses so as to model expert ICT approaches in teaching. Teacher preparation programs should not simply offer one isolated course in educational technology; rather, they should demonstrate sound use of ICT in teaching teachers content and pedagogy. For faculty to be able to act as experts in integrating technology, they need to have the knowledge, skills, and expertise to teach with technology. Partnerships between teacher education faculty and technology experts help faculty develop the expertise needed to act as role models for preservice teachers.

The purposes of this chapter are to describe successful approaches that have been taken to prepare teachers to teach with technology and to explicate a set of design suggestions culled from promising technology integration approaches. We discuss strategies and models of teacher professional development with an emphasis on programs designed to prepare in-service teachers to integrate ICT into their classrooms. We will use examples and findings from our work and from work conducted by our colleagues. For teacher professional development to succeed, educators must take a fresh look at curriculum, pedagogy, assessment, education policy, research, and evaluation. We argue that teachers, administrators, policymakers, and other stakeholders should collaborate and participate in the decision-making process, as well as in the design, implementation, and evaluation of professional development programs. In the first section, we discuss themes and issues that relate to professional development aimed specifically at preparing teachers to integrate ICT in their teaching. We then discuss models and strategies and share lessons we have learned from our involvement in teacher professional development programs.

ICT-Related Professional Development: Themes and Issues

Effective professional development for teachers has several characteristics that are common across various subject matters (e.g., science education, math education), such as a focus on content and engaging teachers in active learning opportunities related to their classroom practice; however, there are some issues that are unique to ICT-related professional development. We first discuss the ways in which technology encourages new professional development delivery vehicles (interactive self-paced tutorials, online education) and how it changes the nature of interactions (sustained online communities, global community, and sharing of ideas). In this section we also explore how learning to integrate technology differs from some of the other components of teacher development (e.g., curriculum, subject area development, instructional strategies). We then explore the challenges that stem from ICT being a "moving target," constantly changing and requiring that we all become lifelong learners.

Technology Affordances for Professional Development

The use of ICT and the evolution of online learning environments provide an opportunity to innovate and reform teacher professional development. ICT allows access to knowledge and expertise that were previously unavailable, enabling new relationships and new models of professional development. The demands of work and family life for teachers, many of whom are women, underline the need for professional development activities that can be delivered anytime, anywhere. Several studies have shown that the blended approach of a combination of face-to-face workshops and online interaction can provide a sustainable model for ongoing teacher development (Clark, 2000; Vrasidas & Glass, 2004).

Although online professional development is widely used, there are many barriers to effective participation in such initiatives. One of these is teachers' limited access to the Internet, which results in certain groups of teachers being disadvantaged and a greater gap between the "haves" and "have-nots" (Clark, 2000). Because of this, some skeptics question the use of online education (Fabos & Young, 1999; Zembylas, Vrasidas, & McIsaac, 2002). Some of this skepticism disappears when one takes a broader, more international view of online education and considers the opportunities that it can offer. In many parts of the world, there can be no professional development without asynchronous online delivery because of the remoteness of the locations in which teachers practice, the cost of transportation, and the shortage of persons trained to conduct professional development. It is easy to be skeptical, but it is also easy to forget that in many places there is no practical alternative to online delivery of instruction (Vrasidas, Zembylas, & Glass, in press).

One of the main themes guiding the development of online professional development is that of *communities of practice* (Vrasidas & Glass, 2004; Wenger, 1999). The concept of community is fundamental to an understanding of how people learn and how professional development can take place online. Communities of practice are groups of individuals bound by what they do together—anything from engaging in informal discussions to solving problems—and by what they have learned through their mutual engagement in these activities. Thus, communities of practice are sites of mutual learning and important contributors to the success of knowledge-dependent organizations (Vrasidas & Zembylas, 2004). Such online communities provide both formal and informal professional development opportunities for teachers.

In the last decade or so, there has been increasing interest in constructing e-learning spaces to support communities of practice (Schlanger & Fusco, 2003; Schwen & Hara, 2003). Listservs®, bulletin boards, and course management systems can offer alternative methods of constructing and supporting communities of teachers to serve professional development needs. Dede, Whitehouse, and Brown L'Bahy (2002), for example, describe how ICT are facilitating the development of virtual communities for creating, sharing, and mastering knowledge. An introductory course they designed to offer teachers a better understanding of ICT capabilities clearly illustrates the complexities of learning and teaching across distance and time. Teachers gain skills in using various media (e.g., discussion forums and videoconferencing) by participating in activities that encourage their use and through the development of learning activities integrating ICT to achieve specific instructional objectives.

Another example of a model for ICT-related professional development is illustrated in the program Supporting Teachers with Anywhere/ Anytime Resources (STAR)-Online (http://www.star-online.org). STAR-Online is a model for continuing education and professional development for teachers that draws on the notion of communities of practice. More than 20,000 teachers have benefited from this project. Teachers can access mentors, colleagues, and resources via a web-based Virtual Teaching and Learning Community (VTLC) system, which provides interactive, self-paced, and collaborative development. The

VTLC is an online model that allows teachers to develop knowledge and gain ICT skills in the application of educational technology. They develop lesson plans, share them with experts and peers, receive feedback, and comment on others' work. Through the VTLC, teachers can participate in quality online training modules, access resources, build an online portfolio, and collaborate with other teachers throughout the United States.

As noted, research has shown that teachers tend to teach as they were taught (Ball, 1990; Lortie, 1975). Teachers themselves have spent upward of 20 years as students in elementary, secondary, and college classes. Consequently, their experiences as learners are often indelibly etched in their minds and shape their daily teaching. One of the advantages of ICT-related professional development is that it can support reflection in ways that help teachers unlearn the old ways of thinking about teaching and learning. ICT afford multiple kinds of interaction and the design of learning environments that support the development of communities of inquiry, collaboration, negotiation, and problem solving within authentic contexts. In order for teachers to unlearn old ways and relearn how to teach using ICT, they need to be provided with enough time and support (Adelman et al., 2002; Vrasidas & Glass, 2005). Removed from familiar surroundings and circumstances, teachers may be more willing to entertain alternative approaches to teaching.

ICT Professional Development Challenges

Teachers need time to use ICT and gain the needed skills and competencies to integrate them successfully into their classroom. According to Donnelly and colleagues (2002), studies have shown that teachers need 3–6 years of sustained practice to integrate ICT fully into the classroom. Adelman and colleagues (2002) found that teachers identified time as the most significant barrier to integrating ICT in the classroom—time to learn how to use ICT, how to develop educational activities, and how to implement them in the classroom.

One of the most vigorous discussions in teacher professional development focuses on the importance of the successful integration of ICT into current curricula (Mumbi & Mesut, 2004). Access to quality digital content is crucial, and trying to develop one's own digital curricula is a task that very few teachers can be expected to undertake. However, it is not simply a matter of aligning the curriculum to new technologies. Technology has changed dramatically during the last few decades, but school curricula have not. Imposing innovative technologies on old curricula is a serious challenge. The affordances of ICT require that we revisit fundamental assumptions about teaching and learning. Computers were initially designed to serve the needs of businesses, not education. Yet what we know about pedagogy requires that technology-integration efforts be driven by the needs of education rather than the business sector from which technological advancements typically arise. Trying to force the use of technology in the classroom, for which it was not designed, often presents insuperable difficulties. ICT is always used within a context (e.g., to teach math, social studies, and the like); integrating the technology seamlessly within the content area is not always successfully achieved. Current uses of ICT in the classroom are not always transparent; rather, ICT use is often "added on" to the curriculum.

Another difficulty stems from the reality that teachers are often asked to learn to use technological tools that become out-of-date with new development; as a result, the need for ongoing professional development never ends. Education software and applications can become obsolete quickly. Today, social networking software (e.g., Wikis, blogs, YouTube, and the like), mobile technologies (Blackberrys, cell phones, iPods), and games are popular among students, but the technologies and skills of ten years from now cannot be imagined. Cyprus's Project HANDLEARN,[1] which focuses on preparing teachers to use mobile technologies for environmental education, has struggled with choosing the most cost-effective mobile learning tools that will not be out-of-date before the end of the 2-year project.

Finally, another unique characteristic of ICT-related professional development is the importance of infrastructure and technical support for implementing what is learned and for using new skills with students. In our experience from working in more than 20 countries, there are large discrepancies in the availability of ICT for this purpose. We have encountered instances in the United States and Europe where every student in a classroom has a computer, whereas in certain countries in Africa and Asia, a school with more than 2,000 students has only a few dozen computers at their disposal (Vrasidas et al., in press).

While a great deal of funding and sweat equity have been invested to improve teacher preparation programs and increase professional development opportunities so as to meet the new demands of technology for teaching and learning, few visible uses of technology to meet educational goals are observed in either higher education or K-12 classrooms (see Pellegrino et al., this volume). This observation stems, at least in part, from the fact that we know relatively little about what constitutes *effective practice* for teaching teachers how to use technology. What follows are common themes and strategies that have emerged from a comprehensive review of the literature on technology professional development. For each of these themes, we provide an illustration.

Strategies for Effective ICT-Related Professional Development

Based on our experiences and on a review of the literature, we summarize in Table 1 the key issues and strategies for effective professional development. These strategies are well documented and are demonstrated in several of the models and cases discussed in earlier sections. Education programs depend heavily on context, learners, and goals; therefore, program designers should carefully choose those strategies that best serve their needs.

Learning Designs

Much has been discovered in the last 5 decades about how humans learn. Students learn best when they are actively engaged in meaningful activities; when they collaborate with peers, exchange ideas, and provide and receive peer feedback; when they reflect critically on what they are doing; when they work on real-world, challenging, authentic activities; when their work is constantly evaluated; and when they are intrinsically motivated (Bransford, Brown, & Cocking, 1999). But it is easily forgotten that teachers/adults learn best in the same ways (Putnam & Borko,

TABLE 1
KEY ISSUES AND STRATEGIES FOR ICT-RELATED PROFESSIONAL DEVELOPMENT

Key Issue	Strategy
Learning designs	Design programs based on what we know about how ICT can support learning
Authentic engagement within teacher's contexts	Situate programs in teachers' context so that activities are authentic
Opportunities for reflection	Design activities that encourage participants to use ICT and reflect on their practice
Collaborative efforts	Encourage the use of ICT for collaboration among all stakeholders in the design, implementation, and evaluation of programs
Ongoing support	Use ICT and online technologies to provide ongoing support
Informal learning	Provide opportunities for informal learning and support
Systemic effort	Coordinate professional development with broader ICT and school improvement efforts
Leadership	Foster leadership that nurtures innovation, change, and the creation of schools as learning organizations

2000). Good professional development for teachers will resemble the best teaching for *all* learners, as we are beginning to understand it (Gross, Truesdale, & Bielec, 2001; Vrasidas & Glass, 2005).

Authentic Engagement

Effective professional development is situated in teachers' everyday practice, and distributed across communities, tools, and contexts. As such, it provides authentic opportunities for teachers to think like experts in making instructional decisions, structuring learning activities, and employing sound pedagogical strategies. One such example is project ENVETI (Environmental Education and Technology Integration),[2] a teacher professional development program developed by the Center for the Advancement of Research and Development in Educational Technology (CARDET) and implemented in Cyprus. Professional development experiences take place in a coherent framework that provides participants with a clear view of the connections between what they learn during professional development and their classroom practice. Project ENVETI emphasizes two critical areas: environmental education and technology integration. The use of ICT creates new opportunities for Cypriot teachers to enrich their pedagogical knowledge of how to deal with health and environmental issues that affect Cyprus and the Mediterranean basin (Vrasidas, Zembylas, Evagorou, Avraamidou, & Aravi, 2007). Experts from local universities and research centers establish partnerships with local teachers and schools and develop curricula that integrate technology in environmental education and at the same time promote multiculturalism and peace. Teachers work in teams to identify specific thematic units aligned with local curricula. These units serve as the focus of the professional development program. Following the identification of the content, training is offered (face-to-face and online) to a core group of teachers who in turn serve as trainers to teachers at their local schools. Teachers collaborate with experts and they share and discuss their findings online and face-to-face. They then develop lesson plans on environmental education that will be implemented in their classrooms.

In programs we developed for teachers in Europe, the United States, and Asia-Pacific, we worked with local stakeholders, evaluated the ICT infrastructure, conducted a needs assessment, and developed material with the help of local teachers and experts, ensuring the alignment of professional development with local curricula, cultures, and contexts. In projects TECHNOSKEPSI,[3] HANDLEARN, and ENVETI teachers are taught how to integrate online technologies and web-based tools in their teaching by participating in workshops that are offered face-to-face and supported within an online learning environment. Thus, they actually participate and moderate online discussions similar to those they are asked to facilitate for their students. Teachers are provided with opportunities to interact with experts and peers as they develop and implement lesson plans integrating ICT into their classrooms.

Reflection

Teachers need time to develop, master, and reflect on technology-based learning approaches. They need to be given ample opportunities to engage in meaningful activities, collaborate with peers, exchange ideas, provide feedback to peers and receive feedback from them, reflect critically on their work, and engage in real-world, challenging, and authentic activities (Chitpin & Evers, 2005). It is essential that professional development policies be established that promote technology integration and provide incentives to encourage teachers to engage in lifelong learning. Using web-based portfolios can be a valuable tool that will allow teachers to document their knowledge and reflect on their practice. In projects we developed and implemented, teachers were required to create lesson plans, implement them, and then reflect on them using an online portal (e.g., see http://www.enveti.org).

Another program that supports reflection was designed by Riel, DeWindt, Chase, and Askegreen (2005), who employed multiple strategies for fostering teacher learning with technology and presented several approaches to professional development for promoting attitudes, aptitudes, and practices supporting an ongoing process of inquiry and learning. Each approach depicts teacher learning as a process that is directed by the learner, socially constructed, and continuous. One such approach focuses on the use of a mentor who works with student teachers in planning and implementing action research projects prepared to help teachers integrate ICT into their classroom. Reflection on practice and revision of plans are fundamental characteristics of such models.

Collaborative Efforts

One of the key characteristics of successful professional development programs is collaboration among all stakeholders (Gross et al., 2001; Manke, Ward, Lundeberg, & Tikoo, 2005; Vrasidas & Glass, 2005). Collaborative efforts among in-service and preservice teachers, university faculty, technology experts, and policymakers will ensure the commitment needed for the success of professional development programs. The participatory nature of collaborative projects provides for a shared ownership and understanding of the project among all participants. Innovative professional development involves opportunities for teachers to share their expertise, learn from peers, and collaborate on real-life projects. Teachers' needs are better served when they are able to make connections between their daily work and professional development (Darling-Hammond & McLaughlin, 1995). Radinsky, Smolin, and Lawless (2005) reported a case study of the construction of a professional development program in which teacher education faculty, technology experts, and teachers collaborated to design modules integrating ICT into the curriculum. This collaborative curriculum design anchored the process of learning to use ICT in an exploration of what it meant to teach and learn the subject; for example, students learn to create web-based hypertext documents in order to support historical arguments that are built upon primary source documents.

In Teaching and Learning Online (TLO), a teacher professional development initiative designed to prepare Illinois teachers to use technology and teach online classes, administrators from school districts, teachers, and experts from academia collaborated on the design, implementation, and evaluation of the program (Vrasidas & Chamberlain, 2005). Collaboration on this project took place at several levels. First, a needs assessment was conducted. Then schools and school districts in the state of Illinois collaborated with each other in the development of curricula designed to meet some of the needs and to facilitate coordination of the project. All stakeholders in the project wanted to empower teachers to use ICT successfully to create and teach online classes. Once the project entered its development stages, schoolteachers and school administrators collaborated with the design team in developing the classes. Expert teachers served as trainers for colleagues in their schools and received ongoing support throughout the stages of the project. Educational technologists and experts worked with teachers and schools to establish the program policies. Findings from project evaluations revealed that one of the core strengths of the program was the close collaboration among all stakeholders. This is another example of a professional development program where multiple "models" have been applied: train the trainer, school-to-school partnership, curriculum development, and the university–schools partnership.

Another approach illustrating the importance of collaboration comes from a project by Thompson, Schmidt, and Davis (2003), which used Goodlad's (1994) model for simultaneous renewal as its foundation. Goodlad argued that for a successful school renewal, both schools and teacher preparation programs should collaborate in simultaneous reform efforts. Thompson and colleagues developed a project that brought together K-6 in-service teachers, preservice teachers, and university faculty to share resources and expertise with the goal of integrating ICT in the classroom and improving teaching and learning. Preliminary evaluation showed that the project was successful in demonstrating effective simultaneous renewal, and that it changed attitudes and practices among teachers and university faculty.

Collaboration can take place at many levels. At one level, collaboration takes place between schools and universities. Through such partnerships, expert teacher educators collaborate with teachers in developing and implementing programs that serve the teachers' needs (Smolin, Lawless, & Radinsky, 2005). Good partnerships between universities and schools are essential for the success of education initiatives such as ENVETI, TLO, and STAR-Online. All partners worked closely to develop the material, train the teachers, and implement the programs, and to bring solid theoretical and research grounding that helped shape the planning, implementation, and evaluation of these programs. Schools and teachers contributed the real-world, pragmatic view of teacher needs. Furthermore, collaboration within the same school or among schools allowed teachers to learn from their peers and exchange ideas. Collaborative projects allowed teachers to have access to each other's expertise and increased the sense of interdependence among participants. This collaboration often took place online via the project portals.

Ongoing Support

One of the major criticisms of professional development programs is that they often take the form of a one-shot 3-hour workshop with no follow-up activities. Teacher support should not be based on such models; it must be ongoing and embedded. Projects like STAR-Online and ENVETI provide teachers the ongoing support and resources they need to integrate ICT in their classroom. Follow-up activities are structured to ensure that professional development makes a difference. Teachers participate in face-to-face and online workshops and at the same time receive ongoing support via an online portal. This portal provides teachers with resources, support, and opportunities to share and discuss lessons and activities with peers and exchange resources with other teachers. Such blended models of professional development can better serve the needs of today's teachers.

Informal Learning

A significant amount of professional development takes place informally. Researchers are only just beginning to explore the ways in which informal learning affects teacher technology use in the classroom. Teachers often engage in informal learning activities during which they explore their own research interests, learn with family and friends, chat with colleagues online or in person, and post questions on discussion forums (Adelman et al., 2002). These opportunities are at least as important as formal ones and develop knowledge and ICT skills. Adelman and his/her colleagues found that 78% of teachers reported that they participated in informal ICT-related activities and that the effects of both formal and informal learning were similar in nature and strength. Given the fact that a large number of teachers indicate that this "informal professional development" has contributed to their use of technology in the classroom, it seems useful to support opportunities that allow for informal professional development to take place. One simple way of doing so would be to provide, within online portals, areas where unstructured interactions can take place among teachers. Another way would be to encourage teachers to maintain their own blogs, sharing their experiences using ICT, which can be read and commented on.

Systemic Effort

Teacher professional development to integrate ICT into the classroom needs to be systemic, which will necessitate addressing some obstacles, as already noted. These include the school culture's traditional resistance to change; the lack of ICT infrastructure, teacher technology skills, appropriate and accessible technologies, and teacher support; curriculum constraints; education policy that mandates technology use but provides little in the way of guidelines and funding; and assessment problems. ICT-related professional development programs are rarely coordinated or integrated with systemic education reform efforts.

Meaningful systemic efforts at school improvement place an emphasis on lifelong learning, and presumably, schools aim to develop autonomous learners by developing lifelong learning skills and competencies in their students. For this to occur consistently, schools have to change from institutions that "transfer" knowledge into true learning organizations (Coppieters, 2005). A learning organization is one that has the capacity to learn, change, and adapt to rapidly changing contexts (Argyris, 1999). When schools become learning organizations, they embrace change and innovation and nurture lifelong learning for both teachers and students. ICT is a tool that allows both teachers and students to become and remain lifelong learners. One of the most important skills that a person must now have is the ability to learn online—skills like searching for information, critically evaluating such information, and using it to solve specific problems will be essential for both teachers and students. ICT can be instrumental, indeed it might be the key instrument, in turning schools into learning organizations.

Leadership

Strong leadership commitments from schools and colleges of education around the integration of ICT and professional development can help establish the conditions and the support teachers need to succeed. Leadership must emphasize lifelong learning and the transformation of schools into learning organizations within which all members are engaged in learning and leading. Leading, like learning, is shared and distributed among all members of the community (Spillane, 2006). In terms of professional development, distributed leadership supports and values teachers' agency in driving educational change. In projects we developed and implemented in Asia, for example, special workshops were offered to administrators to help them better understand the value of ICT, the complexities in integrating ICT in the classroom, and the support teachers need to flourish—critical understandings in fostering distributed leadership for technology use in their schools.

Conclusion

In this chapter, we have shared strategies and models of teacher professional development aimed at integrating ICT into classroom teaching. Several of these strategies can be applied to a variety of professional development contexts other than ICT. We have presented a number of ideas, strategies, and models that cover design issues, the importance of shared ownership and vision, a systemic approach to teacher development, and the collaborative nature of successful professional development projects. While we have identified a number of influences affecting successful professional development programs, more research is required to understand the complexities of teachers' practices and how professional development can help teachers better serve their students' needs.

There are several lines of research related to preparing teachers to teach with technology that teacher educators can pursue. These include:

- What technologies can be used to undertake the kinds of tasks that teachers cannot easily perform, making room for teachers to focus on the tasks they do best?
- How has technology made some professional development content obsolete and other content more important than ever?
- What professional development content should be relegated to machines instead of taught to humans?
- What combination of technologies, content, context, and instructional methods are appropriate for what kinds of instructional goals, teachers, and learners?
- What changes need to be made in our current teacher education programs to better facilitate technology use in schools?
- How can in-service teachers be retrained so that they integrate technology for teaching, learning, and assessment?
- What is the role of informal learning and how can we foster informal learning to facilitate teacher professional development?

NOTES

1. Project HANDLEARN is run by CARDET and supported by the Cyprus Research Promotion Foundation.

2. ENVETI is supported by the United Nations Development Program (UNDP), Action for Co-operation and Trust, which receives support from the American people through a grant from the United States Agency for International Development (USAID). The views expressed in this publication are those of the authors and do not necessarily represent those of the United Nations or its Member States, UNDP, or USAID.

3. Project TECHNOSKEPSI is run by CARDET and supported by the Cyprus Research Promotion Foundation.

REFERENCES

Adelman, N., Donnelly, M.B., Dove, T., Tiffany-Morales, J., Wayne, A., & Zucker, A. (2002). *The integrated studies of educational technology: Professional development and teachers' use of technology*. Arlington, VA: SRI International.

Argyris, C. (1999). *On organizational learning*. London: Blackwell.

Ball, D.L. (1990). The mathematical understandings that prospective teachers bring to teacher education. *The Elementary School Journal, 90*(4), 449–466.

Ball, D.L., & Cohen, D.K. (2000). Developing practice, developing practitioners: Toward a practice-based theory of professional education. In L. Darling-Hammond & G. Sykes (Eds.), *Teaching as the learning profession* (pp. 3–31). San Francisco: Jossey-Bass.

Borko, H. (2004). Professional development and teacher learning: Mapping the terrain. *Educational Researcher, 33*(8), 3–15.

Bransford, J.D., Brown, A.L., & Cocking, R.R. (1999). *How people learn: Brain, mind, experience, and school*. Washington, DC: National Academy Press.

CEO Forum on Educational Technology (2000). *School technology and readiness: A focus on digital learning*. Washington, DC: Author. Retrieved January 5, 2007, from http://www.ceoforum.org/downloads/report3.pdf.

Chitpin, S., & Evers, C.W. (2005). Teacher professional development as knowledge building: A Popperian analysis. *Teachers and Teaching Theory and Practice*, *11*(4), 419–433.

Clark, T. (2000). *Online professional development: Trends and issues*. Macomb, IL: Center for the Application of Information Technologies.

Coppieters, P. (2005). Turning schools into learning organizations. *European Journal of Teacher Education*, *28*(2), 129–139.

Cuban, L. (2001). *Oversold and underused: Computers in the classroom*. Cambridge, MA: Harvard University Press.

Darling-Hammond, L., & McLaughlin, M.W. (1995). *Policies that support professional development in an era of reform*. Retrieved January 26, 2004, from http://www. middleweb.com/PDPolicy.html

Dede, C., Whitehouse, P., & Brown L'Bahy, T. (2002). Designing and studying learning experiences that use multiple interactive media to bridge distance and time. In C. Vrasidas & G.V. Glass (Eds.), *Distance education and distributed learning* (pp. 1–29). Charlotte, NC: Information Age Publishing, Inc.

Donnelly, M.B., Dove, T., Tiffany-Morales, J., Adelman, N., & Zucker, A. (2002). *Technology-related professional development in the context of educational reform: A literature review*. Arlington, VA: SRI International.

Duffield, J. (2005). Mentoring a teacher preparation faculty toward technology integration. In C. Vrasidas & G.V. Glass (Eds.), *Preparing teachers to teach with technology* (pp. 325–342). Charlotte, NC: Information Age Publishing, Inc.

Fabos, B., & Young, M.D. (1999). Telecommunications in the classroom: Rhetoric versus reality. *Review of Educational Research*, *69*(3), 217–259.

Goodlad, J. (1994). *Educational renewal*. San Francisco: Jossey-Bass Publishers.

Gross, D., Truesdale, C., & Bielec, S. (2001). Backs to the wall: Supporting teacher professional development with technology. *Educational Research and Evaluation*, *7*(2–3), 161–183.

Lortie, D.C. (1975). *Schoolteacher: A sociological study*. Chicago: University of Chicago Press.

Manke, M P., Ward, G., Lundeberg, M.A., & Tikoo, S. (2005). An effective model of professional development in technology for multiple constituencies: The Technology Leadership Cadre. In C. Vrasidas & G.V. Glass (Eds.), *Preparing teachers to teach with technology* (pp. 343–358). Charlotte, NC: Information Age Publishing, Inc.

McIntyre, D.J., & Byrd, D.M. (Eds.). (1998). *Strategies for career-long teacher education*. *Teacher Education Yearbook VI*. Thousand Oaks, CA: Corwin Press.

Moursund, D., & Bielefeldt, T. (1999). *Will new teachers be prepared to teach in a digital age? A national survey on information technology in teacher education*. (ERIC document reproduction Service No. ED428072.) Santa Monica, CA: Milken Exchange on Education Technology.

Mumbi, K., & Mesut, D. (2004). Using anchored instruction to teach preservice teachers to integrate technology in the curriculum. *Journal of Technology and Teacher Education*, *12*(3), 431–445.

Pellegrino, J.W., Goldman, S.R., Bertenthal, M. & Lawless, K. (2007). Teacher education and technology: Initial results from the "What Works and Why" project. In L. Smolin, K. Lawless, & Burbules, N.C. (Eds.), *Information and communication technologies: Considerations of current practice for teachers and teacher educators. The 106th yearbook of the National Society for the Study of Education*, Part II (pp. 52–86). Malden, MA: Blackwell Publishing.

Putnam, R., & Borko, H. (2000). What do new views of knowledge and thinking have to say about research on teacher learning? *Educational Researcher*, *29*(1), 4–15.

Radinsky, J., Smolin, L., & Lawless, K.A. (2005). Collaborative curriculum design as a vehicle for professional development. In C. Vrasidas & G.V. Glass (Eds.), *Preparing teachers to teach with technology* (pp. 369–380). Charlotte, NC: Information Age Publishing, Inc.

Riel, M., DeWindt, M., Chase, S., & Askegreen, J. (2005). Multiple strategies for fostering teacher learning with technology. In C. Vrasidas & G.V. Glass (Eds.), *Preparing teachers to teach with technology* (pp. 81–98). Charlotte, NC: Information Age Publishing, Inc.

Schlanger, M.S., & Fusco, J. (2003). Teacher professional development, technology, and communities of practice: Are we putting the cart before the horse? *Information Society, 19*(3), 203–220.

Schwen, T.M., & Hara, N. (2003). Community of practice: A metaphor for online design? *The Information Society, 19*(3), 257–270.

Smolin, L., Lawless, K.A., & Radinsky, J. (2005). The technology mentor model: Infusing technology into student teaching placements. In C. Vrasidas & G.V. Glass (Eds.), *Preparing teachers to teach with technology* (pp. 257–270). Charlotte, NC: Information Age Publishing, Inc.

Spillane, J.P. (2006). *Distributed leadership*. San Francisco: Jossey-Bass.

Thompson, A.D., Schmidt, D.A., & Davis, N.E. (2003). Technology collaboratives for simultaneous renewal in teacher education. *Educational Technology Research and Development, 51*(1), 73–89.

Vrasidas, C., & Chamberlain, R. (2005). The LUDA-VHS model: The role of the university in virtual schools. In B. Zane & T. Clark (Eds.), *Virtual schools and K-12 learning: Planning for success* (pp. 172–182). New York: Teachers College Press.

Vrasidas, C., & Glass, G.V. (Eds.). (2004). *Online professional development for teachers*. Charlotte, NC: Information Age Publishing, Inc.

Vrasidas, C., & Glass, G.V. (Eds.). (2005). *Preparing teachers to teach with technology*. Charlotte, NC: Information Age Publishing, Inc.

Vrasidas, C., & Zembylas, M. (2004). Online professional development: Lessons from the field. *Education and Training, 46*(6/7), 326–334.

Vrasidas, C., Zembylas, M., & Glass, G.V. (Eds.). (in press). *ICT for education, development, and social justice*. Charlotte, NC: Information Age Publishing, Inc.

Vrasidas, C., Zembylas, M., Evagorou, M., Avraamidou, L., & Aravi, C. (2007). ICT as a tool for environmental education, peace, and reconciliation. *Educational Media International, 44*(2), 129–140.

Wenger, E. (1999). *Communities of practice: Learning, meaning and identity*. Cambridge: Cambridge University Press.

Zembylas, M., Vrasidas, C., & McIsaac, M.S. (2002). Of nomads, polyglots, and global villagers: Globalization, information technologies, and critical education online. In C. Vrasidas & G.V. Glass (Eds.), *Distance education and distributed learning* (pp. 201–223). Charlotte, NC: Information Age Publishing, Inc.

Technology Tools for Collecting, Managing, and Using Assessment Data to Inform Instruction and Improve Achievement

GENEVA D. HAERTEL, BARBARA MEANS, AND WILLIAM PENUEL

The purpose of this chapter is to examine the ways in which technology is transforming practices of assessment and educational decision making. We will make the argument that the use of information and computer technology for these purposes is becoming increasingly common, but that the various technology applications are still fragmented and education has yet to realize the full potential of using technology to integrate instructional activities, assessment, and data-informed decision making. The specific categories of technology-supported tools reviewed here are (1) student data management systems; (2) technology-supported assessments for accountability; (3) technology-supported formative assessments; and (4) classroom communication systems. We will first provide a brief sketch of the national policy context for educational technology, and then describe each of these categories of technology applications and highlight findings from available research on their effects on student achievement, concluding with a framework for their integration.

The Broader Educational Technology Policy Context

Since the early 1980s, educational settings have been irrevocably changed by the implementation of technologies in classrooms. We have witnessed the introduction of both the technical infrastructure of computers, wiring, software applications, laser discs, and digital cameras in classrooms nationwide and the implementation of the organizational infrastructure of technical support for all this equipment, including the

Geneva D. Haertel is Director of Assessment Design and Research at the Center for Technology in Learning at SRI. Barbara Means is Director of the Center for Technology in Learning at SRI. William Penuel is Director of Evaluation Research at the Center for Technology in Learning at SRI.

professional development of teachers and school administrators. Supporting the infusion of these technologies into our schools is a loosely knit coalition of policymakers, corporate executives, technology vendors, public officials, educators, and parents.

Early federally funded educational technology programs promoted access to instructional content for underserved students through telecommunications (Star Schools) and schools' involvement in developing innovative educational programs supported by technology (Technology Innovation Challenge Grants). Both of these programs were competitive, requiring Local Education Agencies and their partners to develop ideas for technology use that would compete against other grant proposals. Hence, federal support for K-12 technology integration was selective—more suited to catalyzing the development of model programs than to ensuring universal access.

In 1996, Congress created the Technology Literacy Challenge Fund (TLCF), the first program of block grants for the purpose of supporting the integration of technology into the K-12 curriculum. Over a period of 4 years, this legislation made nearly $2 billion available to states to build the technology infrastructure necessary for schools to move into the digital age. States received block grants under TLCF in amounts proportional to the number of low-income students served in their schools. Within states, districts competed for TLCF funds, writing proposals for how they would use the money. The national educational technology plan issued in conjunction with TLCF described four "pillars" or goals that the funds would support. The first two of these—making computers accessible to every student and connecting classrooms to each other and to the world outside of schools—were access goals. The other two goals were integrating "engaging" educational software into the curriculum and preparing teachers to use and teach with technology.

Technology access was also the focus of the "E-rate," a universal discount phone service subsidy providing assistance in the form of subsidized Internet connection rates and payment for the cost of wiring classrooms in schools. The program was intended to help improve access to educational technology, especially in rural areas and in low-income districts. At the same time, private ventures such as Net Day enlisted massive numbers of volunteers to help wire schools for Internet access.

Statistics collected by the National Center for Education Statistics (NCES) documented remarkable progress in providing access to computers and the Internet within K-12 schools during the 1990s. The number of public school classrooms with Internet access rose from 3% to 87% between 1994 and 2001 (NCES, 2005). This progress, coupled with the achievement and accountability focus of No Child Left Behind (NCLB), heralded a new emphasis in national educational technology policy. John Bailey, then director of the U.S. Department of Education's Office of Educational Technology, announced "We have reached an important technology goal by connecting our schools to the Internet. ... Now we must use these connections for a far more important goal of improving student achievement" (U.S. Department of Education, 2002).

Federal support for integrating technology into schools was authorized under Title II of the NCLB Act and reflected that legislation's emphasis on raising achievement and using scientific evidence as the basis for selecting educational practices. According to this legislation (Public Law 107–110; Part D, Section 2402), a key purpose of the program was to provide assistance to states and localities for the implementation and support of a comprehensive system that effectively uses technology in elementary and secondary schools to improve student academic achievement.

Federal grants to states to support K-12 educational technology were continued in the form of the Enhancing Education Through Technology (EETT) program. EETT called on states to distribute EETT funds to districts serving low-income students, with half the funds distributed on a competitive basis (as was done under TLCF) and half distributed by a formula based on the number of low-income students that the district served. During the first year of EETT (fiscal year 2002), the funding level of $700 million was a high point for educational technology grants to states, but subsequently funding levels were cut, and by FY 2006 were down to about $250 million a year. This funding reduction for educational technology no doubt reflected general pressures on the federal budget, but also was prompted by the assumption that the challenge of access had been largely overcome and by uncertainties about the value of many of the ways that technology was being used in schools.

A new national educational technology plan was issued in 2004, and that plan included a goal that had not appeared in earlier national plans—to use integrated and interoperable data systems to allow teachers and administrators to access student, subgroup, classroom, and school-level data for the purpose of raising student achievement. This use of technology is the first category of applications to be reviewed in this chapter.

Student Data Management Systems

The 2004 national educational technology plan (U.S. Department of Education, Office of Educational Technology, 2004) emphasized the use of interoperable data systems to improve education. The plan articulated the expectation that such data systems would provide multiple benefits to classrooms, schools, and districts, including increased efficiency in the operation of districts and schools, better alignment of resources meant to be allocated to those students with the greatest achievement needs, streamlined purchasing, and more frequent and appropriate use of assessment results to inform and differentiate instruction for every child.

As the plan notes, most school districts were far from the idealized goal of integrated, interoperable systems. The average school district worked with multiple "silos" of data concerning different functions, from food service to buses to instructional programming and planning to student achievement to purchasing and resource allocation. Lack of integration and interoperability of data systems prevented all parties from seeing the "big picture" to efficiently coordinate data to drive policy and decision making. The plan touted the ability of an interconnected and interoperable network from which data could be mined to highlight relationships between different system components, resulting in greater efficiency, better allocation of resources, and better alignment between instructional practice, professional development, and assessment. Most importantly, the use of data from such systems to improve instruction for students was expected to enhance achievement. The plan cited Poway Unified School District, a suburban district near San Diego, California, as an example of a district using data to enhance student performance. Poway Unified had built a data warehouse that integrated data from the district's student information, human resources, special education, and assessment systems and made it available to teachers. Teachers were expected to use the database to develop queries about their students' performance and then use the data to differentiate instruction based on those results.

Over the past 4 years, the assessment and data reporting requirements of NCLB have motivated states and districts to adapt or acquire database systems capable of generating the required student data reports. A national Data Quality Campaign has articulated 10 essential features for student data systems, notably the use of a unique student identifier that enables longitudinal tracking of a student's progress from year to year (see http://www.dataqualitycampaign.org/ for details). In addition to serving accountability reporting requirements, these student data systems are promoted as the foundation for data-driven decision making. The use of data to inform decision making has long been central to business concepts of "total quality management" (Deming, 1986), and the idea that education would benefit from a similar focus on collecting and reflecting upon data has been promoted for several decades (Popham, 1995; Schmoker & Wilson, 1995). But the increase in the amount of annual testing conducted by states and the requirements for analysis of student subgroup performance and performance changes over time, coupled with the consequences of the failure to make progress that are part of NCLB, gave a huge impetus to the data-driven decision-making movement. As one journalist summarized, "There is no denying that an integral part of the business of K-12 education today is to collect, manage, analyze, and learn from a wide array of data" (Salpeter, 2004). The hierarchical nature of school systems and the fact that student data are generated at the classroom, school, and district levels and used both at these three levels and by state and federal decision makers call for technology tools and interoperable data systems. Since the passage of NCLB we have seen an explosion of student data systems, system use guidelines, and professional development offerings coming out of both the public and the commercial sectors (see Wayman, Stringfield, and Yakimowski, 2004 for a review of many of these commercial software products).

Many of these commercial products involve multiple modules so that districts have the option of purchasing one or all of them. Typically systems include student assessment data, student demographic data and educational history (e.g., English language learners [ELL] status, attendance), teacher professional and personnel data, perceptions data about school climate from relevant stakeholders, and school program data (e.g., effectiveness of curricular programs). Wayman (2005) loosely categorizes data systems into three types: (1) student information systems that provide real-time accounting of student daily school functions (e.g., attendance, disciplinary actions), but are not available beyond the current school year; (2) student data from standardized, large-scale assessments that readily organize and analyze frequent benchmark assessments but do not provide such data over time; and (3) data warehousing systems that provide historical data of all kinds but are not available for immediate turnaround of analyses of new data.

Although many of these systems can accommodate any type of student data that schools and districts choose to incorporate, in practice, the databases typically contain little in the way of student learning outcomes other than scores on mandated tests. Significantly, there are few data on instructional practices or program participation that would allow district officials, local school leaders, or teachers to link learning outcomes to specific instructional strategies. In a similar vein, many of the systems support flexible data queries on the part of users, but most usage involves the generation of standardized reports.

Empirical Findings

Research on the use of student data systems has burgeoned during the past 5 years. Several researchers have provided positive reports of successful implementations (Cromey, 2000; Feldman & Tung, 2001; Light, Wexler, & Heinze, 2004). The implementation of the Grow Network reporting system in New York City was studied by Light and colleagues using data from 15 city schools. Surveyed and interviewed teachers reported using assessment data for their students in both broad and specific planning to help set whole-class priorities, make weekly and yearly lesson plans, construct specific daily lesson plans and mini-lessons, individualize instruction, group students, and pair high- and low-achieving students for peer tutoring. Student achievement was not measured using assessment data; thus, it is unclear how much of the information obtained from the Grow Network system simply confirmed what teachers already knew about their students' achievement levels.

Wayman and Stringfield (2006) examined the efforts of three schools to involve entire faculties in a review of student data that was supported by efficient data systems. The researchers reported results that indicated that administrative supports were key in fostering the use of such data systems and that improved teaching practices were often associated with the use of data. However, they were circumspect in their conclusions about the impact of such systems on student achievement, saying

Finally, our study was not designed to address the causal relationships among data use, educational practice, and student learning. The teachers in our study felt the improvement in their practice benefited students and led to improved student learning, and administrators cited increased test scores. Still, without a longitudinal experiment, it is impossible to extend beyond these anecdotal associations, nor is it possible to attribute test score increases to this or any other initiative. Future research should be conducted experimentally that demonstrates the effects of data initiatives, such as those undertaken in these districts, on student performances and learning. (p. 569)

Herman and Gribbons (2001) studied a high school where overall student performance looked good when compared with national norms, but that had a subgroup of economically disadvantaged ELLs from outside the local area who had poor test scores. Looking at the data more closely, the staff discovered that poor attendance and lower enrollment in more demanding mathematics courses were associated not so much with where students lived as with where they had attended middle school. A misalignment between the mathematics sequences at the high school and some of the middle schools outside the local area made the transition into higher-level math courses in ninth grade difficult for these students. This discovery led staff to the understanding that ELLs' math deficiencies were based more on prior learning opportunities than on socioeconomic status and helped the faculty identify the kinds of learning opportunities that students from these particular middle schools would need to successfully transition into the higher-level mathematics courses.

One conclusion that can be drawn from several of these case studies is that schools that implement data-driven decision making successfully have a preexisting common vision for the district as well as a supportive leader who promoted the data management tool and set aside time for teachers to engage in data review and reflection (Cromey, 2000; Herman & Gribbons, 2001). However, this optimistic picture is balanced in the literature by a number of concerns. Many teachers and administrators express distrust of the standardized test scores that these systems typically employ (Cromey; Herman & Gribbons). While standardized-test data can be viewed as useful in framing annual analyses of student progress, such scores are inadequate for formative and diagnostic assessment (Thorn, 2002). Teachers express a preference for "real-time" data relevant to their professional circumstance (Mason, 2002).

Even promoters of data-driven decision making acknowledge that training of teachers and administrators in the use of data to make decisions is an area of need (Herman & Gribbons, 2001). Standard reports generated by assessment systems are often confusing to teachers and it is not clear that they appreciate such basics of assessment as "measurement error" and "sampling bias." Research has also shown that teachers and administrators using assessment data tend to focus on "bubble kids" just below the criterion for proficiency (Confrey & Makar, 2005; Light et al., 2004), the rationale being that these students, with a little work and a minimum investment of resources, can be brought over the proficiency threshold, thereby improving the school's progress metric in the accountability system. School staff fail to appreciate that given measurement error, many of these students would be expected to score above that cut point on a second testing without any intervention, and students who had scores just above the cut point have a similar likelihood of scoring *below* the cut on the next testing if there is no growth in their underlying proficiency (Confrey & Makar, 2005). More important, the focus on the "bubble kids" results in those farthest behind being neglected.

Research conducted thus far has tended to focus on identifying supporting conditions and implementation challenges for data-driven decision making (Marsh, Pane, & Hamilton, 2006). There is a pronounced lack of data on the prevalence of the use of these data systems and the ways in which system use is influencing the instruction received by students. Comparisons among school districts have found that those districts making more progress in terms of improving student achievement are also investing more effort in using data to inform decisions (Snipes, Doolittle, & Herlihy, 2002), but rigorous evidence with respect to the causal relationship, if any, between system-level data-driven decision making and student achievement is lacking.

Technology Supports for Assessments for Accountability

The movement toward standards-based reform that has gained increasing purchase within American education since the mid-1980s has emphasized the importance of articulating standards for the content that students should learn and the level of proficiency they should demonstrate. States and districts not only articulate these standards but also hold students, teachers, schools, and districts accountable for meeting them, a process that necessarily involves student assessment.

The NCLB legislation has given strong impetus to the increased use of assessments tied to standards. The requirement for annual student testing tied to state standards and the demonstration of annual yearly progress for students overall and for student subgroups has created a demand for efficient assessment tools that teachers and administrators can use to gauge student progress and identify potential trouble spots. If teachers regularly and efficiently test students on state standards, the reasoning goes, they will be able to use those test results in their lesson planning to focus instruction for both the whole class and for individual students. Many educators and policymakers see a role for technology in supporting assessments for accountability. By facilitating teacher assessment of student performance on standards, technology-based systems can strengthen each teacher's instructional focus and standardize the content addressed across classrooms, schools, and districts within a state (Means, 2006).

Advantages of Technology-Based Assessment Systems

Technology-based assessment systems offer a number of advantages. Standards-based assessments can be easily customized. Commercial vendors have large banks of test items mapped to specific skills and tests can be developed that fit a specific state's or district's standards for a particular grade level. Some systems allow teachers to modify items or add their own. If students take the assessments online, another advantage is rapid scoring. Rather than having to ship test answer sheets to a vendor for scoring and waiting for months to get reports of individual student performance, the teacher can get individual student and whole-class profiles nearly instantaneously. Administrators at the school and district level can get a similarly rapid and detailed look at how students are performing against standards. Some technology-based assessments are promoted as "benchmark tests," even providing predictions of the likelihood that a student or student group will attain proficiency on the end-of-year state assessment.

This increased emphasis on assessment for accountability purposes has stimulated the market for commercial, computer-based assessment systems. Accountability-related testing systems have been part of what *Education Week* called "the greatest pre-collegiate testing boom in history." By 2004, education technology directors in 16 states reported that their states were offering Internet- or computer-based assessments of student achievement (Bakia, Mitchell, & Yang, 2007). In 2005–06, the number of states offering computer-based assessments had increased to 22 (*Education Week*, 2006). Of these 22 states, 13 make current state assessment results available through a centralized portal, 11 make current state assessment subscale or item results available, 13 provide performance data over time, and 17 link individual identifiers to assessment results. Table 1 identifies a number of computer-based testing systems, briefly describes each system, and notes the system's stated purpose.

In addition to the technology-based assessments being used at the district and state levels, technology is being used increasingly in national and international assessment systems. For example, the science framework for the 2009 National Assessment of Educational Progress and the 2006 and 2009 cycles of the Program for International Student Assessment are piloting computer-based items or entire test forms.

TABLE 1

LIST OF TECHNOLOGY-SUPPORTED ASSESSMENTS FOR ACCOUNTABILITY PURPOSES

Assessment Product	Developer	Description	Purpose
Texas Math and Science Diagnostic System	State of Texas	Web based. Math component for grades 3–12, science grades 4–12. Benchmark assessment given at beginning of semester and at regular intervals thereafter. Content areas: geometry, spatial reasoning, measurement, probability and statistics, patterns, relationships, algebraic thinking (math), elementary and middle school science, high school physics, chemistry, and biology.	Test practice in mathematics and science for use in student remediation and acceleration.
FCAT Explorer	State of Florida	Web based. Test and skills practice keyed to FCAT. Grades 3 through 11. Content areas: math, science, reading, writing. Accessible by educators, parents, and students.	Test and skills practice, performance feedback, learning guidance, skill reinforcement, remediation, enrichment.
Progress Assessment Series	Pearson Education	Web based. Formative assessment series. Grades 3–8. Content areas: reading and math. Lexile scale used for reading, quantile scale for math. Reading component has pretest followed by three progress-monitoring tests, math component has pretest and six progress-monitoring tests designed for completion in one class period.	To measure student progress, tie assessment to classroom instruction, and forecast student performance on state-specific proficiency standards.

Product	Company	Description	Purpose
Pinnacle Plus	Excelsior Software	Web based. Integrated data system that provides educators, parents, and students with information on academic progress, attendance, grade reporting.	To assess student performance with multiple grading and weighting schemes and link performance to standards and benchmarks. To track and analyze student performance at the individual, class, and school level.
LearnerLink	HOSTS Learning	Web based. Provides resources to assist teachers in resource management, alignment of instruction to standards and benchmarks, diagnosis of student deficiencies or needs, prescriptive lesson planning and instruction, and access to data for decision making. Provides access to an assortment of assessment instruments and enrichment activities.	To provide teachers with formative assessment and lesson-planning assistance to align instruction with state/local standards and large-scale standardized tests. Provides access to instructional resources and assessment instruments. Provides data to identify student needs. Provides tools for resource and time management.
EduTest	PLATO	Web based. Grades K–8. Standards-based formative and benchmark assessment system. Assessment instruments may be customized to suit school and district needs. Data provided to educators to disaggregate and make decisions.	Classroom formative assessment and district benchmark assessments that provide midyear information on student progress with respect to NCLB requirements for annual improvement. Data provided for tracking student progress and needs and for decision making.

FCAT, Florida Comprehensive Assessment Test.
HOSTS, Helping One Student To Succeed.
NCLB, No Child Left Behind.

Empirical Findings

So far, the results of such investments show mixed returns. On the one hand, states have documented efficiencies in scoring, task presentation, and delivery linked to the use of online assessments. At the same time, few of the operational accountability systems, if any, are using the types of technology-based items that would leverage the capabilities of the technology to present complex problem-solving tasks such as animations and simulations. There also remain unanswered questions about whether the format of delivery (technology versus pencil–paper) affects students' academic performance in ways that disadvantage students who have limited access to technology for practice.

There have been laboratory-based studies of the comparability of paper–pencil and technology-based test forms that suggest why it is important to examine the effects of format on test performance. Since the 1990s, researchers have conducted rigorous and systematic studies of the features of assessments and their administration that might affect student performance when assessments transition from one presentation modality to another (Paek, 2005). Typically, researchers have examined the relationship of three variables to students' performances: (1) students' freedom to review and revise responses during the assessment; (2) features of the graphics and text on computer screens; and (3) students' familiarity with computers (Russell, Goldberg, & O'Connor, 2003). Such studies are conducted to reveal whether the psychometric qualities of the items and tests are affected when the mode of delivery changes from paper–pencil to technology-based. This type of research examines the differences in test-score and individual-item means and standard deviations, with little concern about underlying construct validity issues. Nor does this line of research examine comparisons of student achievement in schools or districts before and after implementing technology-based assessment systems.

At first, as technology entered the assessment world, the transition of a large-scale or standardized test from a paper–pencil administration to a technology-supported delivery was marked by few, if any, differences in the nature and types of items and tasks presented. In fact, the technology-supported version of the assessment was often exactly the same as the paper–pencil version except that the items and responses were presented on a computer screen. However, in the past 5–7 years, the science and art of technology-based assessment design and development has evolved to include new forms of assessment tasks such as simulations and animations that present visually rich stimuli, dynamic representations, inventive response formats, and the opportunity to assess different and more complex knowledge and skills (Quellmalz & Haertel, 2005). Technology has freed assessment designers from the constraints of only being able to present items on paper in a static format. With technology, assessment tasks and items can be presented dynamically, which greatly increases the kinds of knowledge and skills that can be assessed (Means & Haertel, 2003).

Opportunities to draw on new technologies to construct scenarios, interact with examinees, capture and evaluate their performances, and model the information they provide has opened a new era of assessment design and development. Computers and other media offer potential solutions to the practical challenges of assessing complex constructs such as model-based reasoning and science inquiry in the context of challenging content. Technology confers advantages in

- measuring phenomena that cannot easily be observed in real time, such as seeing things in slow motion (e.g., a wave) or speeded up (e.g., erosion). It is possible to freeze action or replay it.
- modeling phenomena that are invisible to the naked eye (e.g., movement of molecules in a gas).
- working safely in the simulation of a lab that would otherwise be hazardous (e.g., using dangerous chemicals) or messy and time-consuming in an assessment.
- conducting several repetitions of an experiment in limited assessment time while varying the parameters (e.g., rolling a ball down a slope while varying the mass, angle of inclination, or coefficient of friction of the surface).
- manipulating objects to solve problems or express solutions, such as moving concept terms and relationship labels in a concept map.

Interactive assessment tasks have been developed that demonstrate the advantages of technology-based assessments for assessing higher order knowledge and skills. Bennett and his colleagues at Educational Testing Service (Bennett, Jenkins, Persky, & Weiss, 2003), for example, developed a simulation of the physics of a hot air balloon that employed an interactive response format. Students are able to design and conduct experiments and interpret results. Researchers at SRI (Quellmalz et al., 2005) developed two computer-based simulations that assess science content and inquiry skills in the domains of force and motion and ecosystems. These tasks employ interactive response formats, including log files that can be analyzed by computer for evidence of solution paths. Robert Mislevy and his colleagues on the Principled Assessment Designs in Inquiry Project have adapted a well known paper–pencil assessment task, historically referred to as "Mystery Powders," to a technology-based assessment. This assessment, which was designed to assess scientific reasoning in the area of chemistry (Seibert, Hamel, Haynie, Mislevy, & Bao, 2006), employs a simulation and a selected response format in the context of a computerized adaptive test. While all the assessment tasks described earlier were developed with standardized, large-scale assessments in mind, the technologies that support them are also applicable for use in formative assessments (see the discussion of formative assessment that follows).

Technology-Supported Formative Assessments

Although vendors of the kinds of accountability-oriented assessment systems discussed earlier often describe their systems as "formative" in nature, most of the systems actually provide limited information that is usable for guiding instruction. Accountability-related assessments are designed to cover a broad collection of instructional objectives, with only a few items or even just a single item per objective. The performance reports received by teachers reveal which students are doing better and which more poorly on collections of objectives, but typically lack the kind of detailed information that could actually be used to shape future instruction for those who are not doing well. The teacher thus is put in the position of knowing who is struggling but not knowing the basis of their difficulties.

Furthermore, there is concern about the adequacy of the content covered by standardized tests. Measurement experts have pointed out the mismatch between current standardized tests and the needs of classroom teachers (Pellegrino, Chudowsky, & Glaser, 2001; Popham, 1995). Influential reform documents support curricular activities that foster deep understanding in subject areas. This understanding often is associated not only with fluency in the facts, concepts, and principles used in the domain, but also with the capability to think and reason like an expert. Commercial achievement tests that primarily provide evidence of reading comprehension and fact-based recall are insufficient to measure the learning associated with complex forms of reasoning, metacognitive strategies, and multi-step problem solving.

Lee Shulman (2007) distinguished the characteristics of classroom formative assessments from those of assessments for accountability in a recent opinion piece. He wrote:

Assessment should not only serve as an external evaluation and public con-
science . . . at the very least, it should do no harm to instruction, and at best, it
should guide, support, and enrich it. . . . Embedded measures will necessarily be
designed with a different "grain size" from those designed exclusively for external, high-stakes assessments. They will be more particular than general; more
dedicated to measuring individual student progress than institutional success;
repeatedly administered rather than being single, end-of-course events; and
highly transparent to students and teachers. They will have quick turn-around
times rather than providing highly secure, secretive, and delayed feedback of
current high-stakes environments. This is assessment as a regular physical exam
rather than a public autopsy.

In an influential review of research studies on formative assessment,
Black and Wiliam (1998) defined this practice as "all those activities
undertaken by teachers, and/or by their students, which provide information to be used as feedback to modify the teaching and learning
activities in which they are engaged" (p. 2). Thus, formative assessments
are designed specifically to inform future instruction (Black & Wiliam).
They argue that the "formativeness" of an assessment is found in the
test's intersection with the instruction that occurs in classrooms. State-
of-the-art thinking about assessment is built on a premise that insights
about students' learning will materialize from assessment items and
tasks that test deep conceptual understandings in content domains,
including the relationships among the concepts (Pellegrino et al., 2001).
As a result, formative assessments must go beyond providing information about whether a student has achieved mastery of particular standards or learning objectives. They must provide information about
student understandings in ways that teachers can use to improve students' deep understanding of the content. Formative assessments
emphasize depth of information about a narrow range of concepts and
skills in contrast to end-of-year state assessments, which prioritize
breadth of coverage. Black and Wiliam, in their review of the effects of
formative assessment on student learning, reported an average effect
size of .40. This is a substantial effect and demonstrates the potency of
assessments as a lever of positive change in student learning. They
concluded: "We know of no other way of raising standards for which
such a strong *prima facie* case can be made on the basis of evidence of
such large learning gains" (p. 19).

Advantages of Technology Supports for Formative Assessment

The prior section describes attributes and effects of paper–pencil
and hands-on performance assessments that have been designed to

gather formative information on students' performance. Such approaches, while fruitful, are limited to assessing content and processes that teachers can conduct in their classrooms or that use static pencil–paper formats. The use of technology-based assessments unleashes new possibilities for the content and processes that can be assessed. Technology can provide a means to assess high-level conceptual understanding, reasoning, and skills in formative, classroom-based assessment (Bennett, 2001; Linn, Lee, Tinker, Husic, & Chiu, 2006; Mislevy et al., 2003; Quellmalz & Haertel, 2005).

Technology can play a critical role in helping test developers address both domain and strategic knowledge through the use of assessment tasks that employ rich task environments, innovative response formats, immediate feedback, and reliable and informative scoring. For the purposes of this chapter, technology-supported formative assessments are those assessments delivered by computer to a student or group of students with the intent of providing information that describes the conceptual understandings and strategies that students possess within and across learning domains. The formative information the test provides must be linked to future instruction and the provision of particular learning opportunities. We envision the formative assessment of the future to be (1) inspired by the constructs that have emerged from the learning sciences; (2) designed so that teachers can readily identify gaps in students' learning; (3) delivered via technology; and (4) intimately associated with instruction.

"Facets." An example of technology-supported formative assessment can be offered from the work of Jim Minstrell and his associates. Minstrell has spent years compiling a set of student conceptions about force and motion based upon both the research literature and the observations of teachers. Some of these ideas, or "facets" in Minstrell's terminology, are considered scientifically correct (or at least correct to the degree one would expect at the stage of introductory physics). Others are partially incorrect, and still others are seriously flawed. The goal of Minstrell's "facets assessments" is to elicit student responses that reveal their underlying thinking. Having developed an inventory of knowledge facets, Minstrell and his colleagues proceeded to develop assessment items that would elicit different responses depending upon which facets a student held (Minstrell, 2001). For example, when asked to reason about the weight of objects totally or partially submerged in a liquid, one set of facets concerns separating the effect of a fluid or other medium from the effect of gravity. A student might think that surround-

ing forces do not exert any pressure on objects; alternatively, he might think that a fluid medium produces an upward pressure only or that the weight of an object is directly proportional to the medium's pressure on it. Some students may have memorized the mathematical formula for net buoyant pressure and may be able to apply it to some problems in order to obtain a correct answer, but might nonetheless lack the facet for a qualitative conceptual understanding (net upward push is because of differences in pressure gradients).

Minstrell and his colleagues (2001, 2003) have developed a computer-based assessment system to get at students' facets. The student is presented with a problem situation and a set of multiple-choice answers, each of which is associated with a specific facet. One example might be

A solid cylinder is hung by a long string from a spring scale above a container of water. The reading on the scale shows that the cylinder weighs 1.0 lb. About how much will the scale read if the cylinder which weighs 1.0 lb. is submerged just below the surface of the water?

After choosing an answer to the original question, the student is asked to provide the reasoning behind the original answer. The system compares the facet associated with the student's explanation to that associated with the original answer choice. Over multiple problems, the system diagnoses the student's probable facets and the consistency between student predictions and explanations and presents the teacher with reports of this diagnosis and with an instructional prescription appropriate for the diagnosed facets.

The FACETS web site (see http://www.facetinnovations.com/daisy-public-website/daisy/fihome/6.html) demonstrates the interplay between assessments and instruction. In addition to providing teachers with access to the diagnostic assessments, the site provides sample lessons geared to specific misconceptions. The purpose is to encourage students to apply their beliefs to new situations, examine their own reasoning, and see where their expectations are confirmed and where there are discrepancies between their beliefs and what they observe actually happening. By keying these experiences to students' specific misconceptions, teachers can increase the likelihood of conceptual growth.

Simulations. As noted in the prior section on assessments for accountability purposes, several assessment experts have developed interactive assessment tasks that use simulations to assess complex, multistep reasoning in various science domains (see Bennett et al., 2003;

Quellmalz & Kozma, 2003; Quellmalz et al., 2005; Seibert et al., 2006). Such interactive assessments can be used for both accountability and formative purposes. They can be used formatively if they are well aligned to the content being covered in a classroom, if they identify gaps in a student's understanding and skills, and if they can be used to prescribe participation in instructional activities, the review of content taught, or exposure to additional resources. The feasibility of using such interactive assessment tasks to assess students' higher order reasoning for formative purposes is being documented. Assessment data collected using the SRI science inquiry simulations and Bennett's hot air balloon simulation were tested in classrooms and indicate that computer-based simulation tasks can be successfully used to gather information on higher order, problem-solving science skills. In addition, teachers reported that the assessment data collected as part of the SRI science inquiry tasks was useful in informing their instructional decision making.

E-learning. In a final example of how interactive technology-based tasks are being used for formative purposes, we describe the use of such assessment tasks in a global e-learning program that was developed by the Cisco Networking Academies Program. The articles cited in suc-ceeding discussions provide detailed descriptions of how such interac-tive tasks can be designed using evidence-centered design and how they are presented and delivered online (Williamson, Bauer, Steinberg, Mislevy, & Behrens, 2004); the flexibility and power of the scoring and evaluation rules that can be used to provide useful information on student performances (DeMark & Behrens, 2004; Levy & Mislevy, 2004); and the types of psychometric analyses that can be conducted and reported within a formative assessment system (Levy & Mislevy).

The Networking Performance Skill System project, which supports the work of the Cisco Networking Academies, had as its goal the building of an online performance-based assessment prototype (Behrens, Mislevy, Bauer, Williamson, & Levy, 2004). This interactive prototype, when fully developed, was to be incorporated into the assess-ment system that served the Networking Academies. The assessment system included the use of online selected response items for formative as well as summative feedback to students and instructors. The selected response items were used in chapter, mid-term, and final examinations. The performance assessment tasks address four broad constructs: troubleshooting processes, implementation of those processes, design of solutions, and declarative knowledge about troubleshooting. The hope was that the use of online performance assessments that made use of open-ended response formats, rich and authentic presentations of situations that occur in the networking environment, and the use of multi-step problems would provide diagnostic feedback as well as situative information that would go well beyond the kinds of information provided by the selected response items. The online assessments that were developed illustrate the kinds of higher order, problem-solving tasks that can be presented using technology (Williamson et al., 2004), the use of natural language processing for understanding complex responses to free-response tasks (DeMark & Behrens, 2004), and the sophisticated measurement models and approaches to evidence accumulation (e.g., trace of interactions) that can be implemented for use with such tasks (Levy & Mislevy, 2004). The current formative system, as implemented by Cisco, does not use all of these features (e.g., natural language processing) but applies some of them. Evidence on the effectiveness of the formative interactive tasks as a means of improving student performances is not yet available, but there are plans to collect such data and share results.

Classroom Communication Systems

The vision of formative assessment painted earlier is one where assessment and instruction are intricately interwoven. Formative assessments probe students' understanding of the concepts being taught and provide the basis for designing further instruction for those concepts. This vision is consonant with the recommendations of learning scientists (Bransford, Brown, & Cocking, 2000; Pellegrino et al., 2001) and would be a major advancement in classroom instruction if consistently enacted. However, some learning technology researchers want to go a step farther—to harness the power of technology to greatly compress the timeframe of instruction–assessment–instruction cycles into minutes rather than days. They propose to do this by "instrumenting" the classroom with a communication system that can embed mini, just-in-time assessments into instruction (Crawford, Schlager, Penuel, & Toyama, in press).

Classroom communications systems consist of networked sets of computers, personal data assistants, or small wireless input devices. A teacher uses a laptop computer to project a question on a screen, along with answer choices for the question. Every student in the class can answer the question simultaneously, and either through a radio-frequency signal or a wireless network, student answers are aggregated and presented, usually in the form of a histogram. Typically, the correct answers are not displayed, so teachers may reteach, encourage peer discussion about the concept being taught, or ask for explanations before displaying and explaining the correct answer. Student responses are collected efficiently, facilitating a rapid cycle of question-and-answer and immediate feedback (Roschelle, Penuel, & Abrahamson, 2004). More advanced classroom network technologies also allow student input of text and graphical responses to teacher questions. The student input devices for such advanced applications could be either student laptops or graphing calculators.

Empirical Findings

Some of the best empirical evidence of the effectiveness of this technology on improving learning comes from the university-level physics instruction conducted by Eric Mazur and his colleagues (see Crouch & Mazur, 2001; Mazur, 1997). To support the development of conceptual understanding of physics content in his college students, Mazur uses a combination of a student response system and a technique he calls "peer instruction." After lecturing for a short time and posing a conceptual question, Mazur poses a question to his class and has each student use the classroom communication system to register a response. He then has his students work with one or two other students to discuss their answers and provide explanations to each other. After engaging in the peer activity, the same conceptual question is delivered to the class again using the communication system. Typically, the number of correct answers increases dramatically and Mazur proceeds to the next topic. However, if student responses indicate a widespread misconception, Mazur can immediately adjust his instruction to address it. Mazur and his colleagues report a positive association between students' understanding of introductory physics concepts and the use of a student response system supplemented with peer instruction (Fagan, Crouch, & Mazur, 2002; Mazur). Students in classrooms using interactive technologies and engagement methods similar to those used in peer instruction also make higher gains on measures of understanding than students in comparison classrooms (Hake, 1998; Sokoloff & Thornton, 1997). But the study designs do not support untangling the contributions of the communications technology as opposed to the nature of the questions posed and the peer instruction (Roselli & Brophy, 2002).

There exists a new class of technologies that rely on classroom networks and that extend the capabilities of classroom communication systems (Penuel & Riel, in press). These new technologies enable students to input a variety of responses, including open text and graphical images. Classroom network technologies are not content independent, as is the case when using student response systems; rather, the technology helps structure student interaction with content in ways that help make difficult concepts visible and more concrete. For example, in one application in mathematics (Hegedus & Kaput, 2004), students are given handheld computers connected to a classroom network, and a teacher's computer assigns them randomly to groups of three students each. The teacher can then assign a problem the students must collaborate to solve, such as matching a fraction to a decimal value. Each student has one fraction and decimal, and then uses her or his handheld device to "give" one of the two to a peer to create a match.

As a result of simulations and other forms of classroom activities that can be implemented using these devices, distinctive student roles emerge that teachers must be prepared to support. In particular, students become active agents in classroom activities; they are not manipulating the system or process from the outside but from within it (Colella, 2000). For example, in a simulation designed to teach students about how an infectious disease can spread within a population, students may act as individual organisms in the population, using their computers to interact with other organisms (other students). They unwittingly "infect" others with the disease, and like real agents know only whether they themselves are infected and have to infer underlying causes from the pattern of interaction they can recall or see. Specific subject matter plays a critical role in enabling and constraining the kinds of classroom activities that can occur when using network technologies such as these.

To date, there is little research on the effects of classroom networks on student achievement. However, there is some preliminary evidence that participatory simulations that rely on network technology can be effective in promoting learning (Hegedus, 2003; Lonsdale, Baber, & Sharples, 2004; Wilensky & Stroup, 2000). For example, Wilensky and Stroup present evidence that when students construct parameters that enable them to test different conjectures and hypotheses, there is an opportunity for them to come to a deeper conceptual understanding. In a simulation in which students are asked to model traffic flows in an urban area, students can test different hypotheses about the pattern of traffic lights that will produce the least traffic. They may arrive, through their experimentation, at a model that even approximates "timed" lights that have been developed in urban areas to increase flow on certain highly trafficked arteries. One advantage of using classroom communication systems for real-time diagnosis of student understanding is that a record of the performance of each student as well as the class as a whole can be maintained. Thus, detailed data on student learning are available for later analysis and reflection.

The Vision of an Integrated System

We have reviewed four categories of technology use to support assessment and student learning. Two of these categories are supports for different types of assessments—those we termed "accountability related" and "formative" assessments. We have noted that accountability-related assessments are a central tool of standards-based educational improvement and tend to cover broad areas of content and proficiency. While technology can provide advantages in terms of customizing and rapid scoring of large-scale assessments, the nature of these tests themselves limits their utility in guiding instruction. Formative assessments, on the other hand, have the potential to inform teacher choices of what and how to teach. Technology-supported formative assessments provide much more detailed information about student understanding and can do so at a point in time when further instruction can benefit from this information.

The other two categories of technology use discussed in this chapter involve systems for storing, aggregating, and displaying assessment data. In both cases, the purpose is to enable educators to use assessment results as part of their decision making. In the case of student data management decision systems, the data typically are scores on accountability-related assessments and the decision makers may be at the state, district, or school level. The express purpose for using the system is to distribute resources and refine curriculum and instruction in ways that increase student scores on accountability assessments. The assessment data in the student data system are likely to be "refreshed" only once or twice a year, and hence the data are more useful for "macro" education decisions and for planning major curriculum and professional development efforts rather than for day-to-day instructional decision making. The latter type of decision making is the target for classroom communication systems. These systems are designed for classroom-level decision making and are intended to support moment-by-moment adjustments in instructional approach and support.

But these differences in how the systems are typically used today in practice are not inevitable. In an ideal world, the instructionally diagnostic formative assessments and classroom communication system practices described here could be integrated with accountability systems to provide more complete data on students. As noted earlier, most of the student data management systems can incorporate multiple measures of student learning, and there is no *a priori* reason why they could not include results of multiple classroom diagnostic assessments. The stumbling block has been the labor required to put assessment results into this kind of system. The automated collection of formative assessment data that is supported by classroom communication systems has the potential to address this need for data input. Student responses made as part of classroom activities orchestrated through a classroom communication system could be uploaded to a student data management system to provide a detailed record of students' performances over time. Such an integrated system would enable administrators, teachers, parents, and students to review not just scores on accountability assessments but a detailed set of performances in specific content areas. The vignette that follows provides a glimpse of the potential such an integrated system could provide.

Integrating different types of systems is no small task from a technical standpoint, and creating the social and organizational climate that would support this kind of record of instruction and performance is perhaps an even greater challenge. But the commitment to improving all students' learning is exerting pressure in this direction, and technology will be an essential component of any integrated system.

The Integrated System in Practice: A Vignette

Our fictional eighth-grade science teacher begins her day by meeting with the middle school principal. In this meeting, the teacher discusses the performance of last year's students on the statewide science assessment, a discussion that is informed by data from the district's data management system. She then continues her day with several class periods during which she presents new science content and guides her instructional decision making using a classroom communication system. Later in the day she engages a small group of students in a simulation-based assessment on electric circuitry. Her day ends with a technology-based presentation to the parents of her students at the annual "Parents Night" activity. In this presentation, she uses the simulation-based assessment to illustrate the depth of knowledge that children will have to master to meet the standards set by the state. During the presentation, she relies on the district's data management system to provide charts and tables that compare their children with their counterparts in other schools within the district and the state.

*Using the District's Data Management System to View
Student Performance*

Before the beginning of the school day, our teacher meets with the school principal to discuss the performance of last year's eighth-grade students on the statewide science assessment. These students did not perform at what the district considers a satisfactory level on the science exam and, in particular, they were below the district and state averages on items measuring students' understanding of forces and motion as well as on items associated with the application of science inquiry skills. Students had difficulty with items that required the understanding that a variety of forces govern the structure and motion of objects in the universe. To make her points, the middle school principal goes online and accesses the district's data management system, which dynamically produces graphs and charts that compare the total score on the science exam of eighth graders in this school to their counterparts in other schools within the district and the state, and to eighth graders in other schools with similarly large proportions of low-income students.

The principal drills down into the assessment results to compare student performance on particular standards and items. She and the teacher find that while the performance of their students on items that measure knowledge of force and motion was only slightly lower than the district and state averages, there was a significant gap reflected in the performance of this school's eighth graders on the more complex, open-ended science inquiry items. Student performance was slightly below the district average on the items about electric currents and magnets exerting a force on certain objects and each other. However, in science inquiry, most students performed well below the district average on the items that required that they express a testable hypothesis, provide explanations, and make predictions. Using the data management system, the teacher and principal look at the specific items used to measure these science inquiry skills in last year's state test and can see examples of the responses of students from their school as well as some responses that the state has posted to illustrate proficiency on these open-ended items. The teacher realizes that students last year had difficulty distinguishing hypotheses from data and assures the principal that she will give more emphasis to that skill this year. After printing out copies of the assessment items and illustrative "Below Basic" and "Proficient" responses, the teacher starts thinking about her lesson plan for the day and how she can incorporate the insight she has gained in her discussion with the principal into her instruction.

Guiding Instruction Using a Classroom Communication System

In our teacher's first-period class, she presents basic information on force and motion, including definitions and examples of concepts such as acceleration, rate, and velocity. As part of the lesson, she demonstrates each concept using a physical apparatus (e.g., ball and ramp). After the demonstration, the students form small groups and each group conducts two simple experiments with the same materials the teacher used. The teacher uses the technology-based classroom communication system to project questions to which each group must respond. The questions call for predictions about what will happen in each experimental trial. The teacher takes care to use the term "hypothesis," which seemed to confuse some of last year's students when they took the state test. Each group transmits its answer to her question (i.e., their prediction) via the communication system, which posts the answers for the entire class to view. The groups then discuss the rationales they had for their conflicting hypotheses before following the protocol for using the balls and ramp, recording the results on their handheld computers and transmitting them to the teacher's laptop.

The teacher engages the class in a discussion about how their data compare to their hypotheses and why some of them were surprised by what happened. She notes with relief that these students seem to have a pretty good understanding of the difference between hypotheses and data and how examining data can lead to new hypotheses. But the predictions her students made and her discussion of their observations and what they would do next suggest that many of them are missing some key understandings in the physics of motion. Surprisingly, many of these students do not recognize that unbalanced forces acting on an object change both the object's speed and direction. She accesses an online item bank to pull up questions on this relationship, knowing that the questions in the online bank have been classroom-tested and are designed to reveal different physics misconceptions that research has shown students often have. She poses these questions to her students and has them respond individually using their response systems. A first quick look at the aggregated student responses tells her that only 40% of the class has mastered this key concept about motion. Looking at the student-by-question matrix of responses, the teacher can also see several clusters of students sharing the same misunderstanding. She puts an appropriate flag next to the online learning plan for each of these students and concludes that additional class time will need to be spent on the physics of motion, making a mental note to look up learning activities recommended for the misconceptions that she discovered at home tonight.

Assessing Inquiry Skills With Simulation-Based Assessment

In the late afternoon, the teacher meets with a small group of students who have been working on an independent science project focused on electrical circuitry. She believes that these students will be motivated by using a piece of software that simulates electrical circuits and responds dynamically when the student introduces a change in current, circuitry, or components (e.g., adds a resistor). Each student gets on a computer to work with the simulation. The students use the simulation to construct a model that accounts for how electric current moves in open and closed circuits in response to changing parameters. The software prompts them to predict the results of each change they choose to introduce, to analyze what happens when changes are introduced, and to verify quantitatively the scientific laws illustrated. The students explore circuit behavior enthusiastically, frequently calling on their friends to see what they have done and arguing good-naturedly about what will happen when the next change is introduced.

Students do not think of the activity as an assessment, but in fact the system is capturing a detailed trace of each student's work. Based on the assessment, both the teacher and the student can see how well the student understands the role of each parameter that influences electrical circuits and different ways of optimizing their values. The teacher moves around the room, looking over each student's shoulder and using what she has learned from the system's teacher feedback view to help frame questions tailored to the present knowledge state of the individual student, suggesting things they can try with the simulation.

Communicating With Parents Using Technology-Based Tools

At the end of her long day, our fictional teacher has one more professional responsibility—making a presentation to the parents of her students that describes the physical science curriculum in which their children will engage and the status of their children's knowledge of physical science. Our teacher begins by presenting a scope and sequence chart of the physical science curriculum that she is expected to teach this year. In addition to the range of topics that will be covered and the sequence in which they will be introduced, the teacher indicates the percent of time that she will devote to each topic. Having presented this overview, she wants to impress parents about the depth of knowledge and skills in physical sciences that students in her classes will be expected to attain. To make her point, she displays the simulation-based assessment on electrical circuitry that she used with the small group of students earlier in the day and poses some of the assessment questions to the parents. Her students' parents laugh nervously as they realize that they do not understand some of the concepts their eighth graders will be assessed on during state science testing.

After showing parents the simulation-based assessment items, the teacher accesses the district's data management system. She presents several histograms that show the performance of her eighth-grade classes from last year on the statewide exam. In response to a parent question, she shows how their performance compared with eighth graders from other schools in the district and with eighth graders from schools with similar populations. She illustrates in detail the science inquiry skill areas where last year's students did not perform as well as would be expected. She then switches back to the online assessment system to show where this year's eighth graders were with these skills at the first of the year as compared with today, when they engaged in the force and motion lesson. She is proud to be able to show that this year's students are already ahead of where last year's eighth graders were at spring testing.

REFERENCES

Bakia, M., Mitchell, K., & Yang, E. (2007). *State strategies and practices for educational technology*. Washington, DC: U.S. Department of Education, Office of Planning, Evaluation, and Policy Development.

Behrens, J.T., Mislevy, R.J., Bauer, M., Williamson, D.M., & Levy, R. (2004). Introduction to evidence centered design in a global e-learning program. *International Journal of Testing, 4*(4), 295–301.

Bennett, R.E. (2001, February). How the Internet will help large-scale assessment reinvent itself. *Education Policy Analysis Archives, 9*(5). Retrieved July 12, 2007, from http://epaa.asu.edu/epaa/v9n5.html

Bennett, R.E., Jenkins, F., Persky, H., & Weiss, A. (2003). Assessing complex problem-solving performances. *Assessment in Education, 10*, 347–359.

Black, P., & Wiliam, D. (1998). Assessment and classroom learning. *Assessment and Education, 5*(1), 7–74.

Bransford, J.D., Brown, A.L., & Cocking, R.B. (2000). *How people learn: Brain, mind, and experience*. Washington, DC: National Academies Press.

Colella, V. (2000). Participatory simulations: Building collaborative understanding through immersive dynamic modeling. *The Journal of the Learning Sciences, 9*(4), 471–500.

Confrey, J., & Makar, K.M. (2005). Critiquing and improving the use of data from high-stakes tests with the aid of dynamic statistics software. In C. Dede, J.P. Honan, & L.C. Peters (Eds.), *Scaling up success: Lessons learned from technology-based, educational improvement* (pp. 198–226). San Francisco: Jossey-Bass.

Crawford, V.M., Schlager, M., Penuel, W.R., & Toyama, Y. (in press). Supporting the art of teaching in a data-rich, high performance learning environment. In E.B. Mandinach & M. Honey (Eds.), *Linking data and learning*. New York: Teachers College Press.

Cromey, A. (2000, November). *Using student assessment data: What can we learn from schools?* (Policy Issues No. 6). Oak Brook, IL: North Central Regional Educational Laboratory.

Crouch, C.H., & Mazur, E. (2001). Peer instruction: Ten years of experience and results. *The Physics Teacher, 69*, 970–977.

DeMark, S., & Behrens, J.T. (2004). Using statistical natural language processing for understanding complex responses to free-response tasks. *International Journal of Testing, 4*(4), 371–390.

Deming, W.E. (1986). *Out of crisis*. Cambridge, MA: MIT Center for Advanced Engineering Study.

Education Week (2006). *Technology Counts 2006: A special state-focused supplement to Education Week*. Bethesda, MD: Editorial Projects in Education.

Fagan, A.P., Crouch, C.H., & Mazur, E. (2002). Peer instruction: Results from a range of classrooms. *The Physics Teacher, 40*(4), 206–207.

Feldman, J., & Tung, R. (2001). Using data based inquiry and decision-making to improve instruction. *ERS Spectrum, 19*(3), 10–19.

Hake, R.R. (1998). Interactive-engagement versus traditional methods. *American Journal of Physics, 66*, 64–74.

Hegedus, S. (2003, July). *Improving algebraic thinking through a connected SimCalc Mathworlds classroom*. Paper presented at the 27th Conference of the International Group for the Psychology of Mathematics Education held jointly with the 25th Conference of the PME-NA, Honolulu, HI.

Hegedus, S., & Kaput, J. (2004, September). *An introduction to the profound potential of connected algebra activities: Issues of representation, engagement and pedagogy*. Paper presented at the 28th Conference of the International Group for the Psychology of Mathematics Education, Bergen, Norway.

Herman, J., & Gribbons, B. (2001). *Lessons learned in using data to support school inquiry and continuous improvement: Final report to the Stuart Foundation*. Los Angeles: UCLA Center for the Study of Education.

Levy, R., & Mislevy, R.J. (2004). Specifying and refining a measurement model for a computer-based interaction assessment. *International Journal of Testing, 4*(4), 333–369.

Light, D., Wexler, D., & Heinze, J. (2004, April). *How practitioners interpret and link data to instruction: Research findings on New York City schools' implementation of the Grow Network*. Paper presented at the annual meeting of the American Educational Research Association, New Orleans, LA.

Linn, M.C., Lee, H.S., Tinker, R., Husic, F., & Chiu, J.L. (2006). Supporting online material for teaching and assessing knowledge integration in science. *Science, 313*, 1049–1050.

Lonsdale, P, Baber, C., & Sharples, M. (2004, September). *Engaging learners with everyday technology: A participatory simulation using mobile phones*. Paper presented at the Mobile Human Computer Interaction 2004: 6th International Symposium, Glasgow, UK.

Marsh, J.A., Pane, J.F., & Hamilton, L.S. (2006). *Making sense of data-driven decision making in education: Evidence from recent RAND research*. Santa Monica, CA: RAND Corporation.

Mason, S. (2002, April). *Turning data into knowledge: Lessons from six Milwaukee public schools*. Paper presented at the annual meeting of the American Educational Research Association, New Orleans, LA.

Mazur, E. (1997). *Peer instruction: A user's manual*. Upper Saddle River, NJ: Prentice Hall.

Means, B. (2006). Prospects for transforming schools with technology-supported assessment. In R.K. Sawyer (Ed.), *The Cambridge handbook of the learning sciences* (pp. 505–521). New York: Cambridge University Press.

Means, B., & Haertel, G.D. (Eds.). (2003). *Evaluating educational technology: Effective research designs for improving learning*. New York: Teachers College Press.

Minstrell, J. (2001). Facets of students' thinking: Designing to cross the gap from research to standards-based practice. In K. Crowley, C.D. Schunn, & T. Okada (Eds.), *Designing for science: Implications from everyday, classroom, and professional settings* (pp. 415–443). Mahwah, NJ: Erlbaum.

Minstrell, J. (2003). *Facets of learning*. Seattle, WA: FACETS Innovations.

Mislevy, R., Hamel, L., Fried, R.G., Gaffney, T., Haertel, G., Hafter, A. et al. (2003). *Design patterns for assessing science inquiry* (PADI Technical Report 1). Menlo Park, CA: SRI International.

National Center for Education Statistics (NCES). (2005). *Internet access in U.S. public schools and classrooms: 1994–2003* (NCES 2005-015). Washington, DC: U.S. Department of Education, Institute of Education Sciences.

Paek, P. (2005). *Recent trends in comparability studies* (PEM Research Report 05-05). Iowa City, IA: Pearson Educational Measurement.

Pellegrino, J.W., Chudowsky, N., & Glaser, R. (Eds.). (2001). *Knowing what students know: The science and design of educational assessment*. Washington, DC: National Academy Press.

Penuel, W.R., & Riel, M. (in press). The new science of networks and the challenge of school change. *Phi Delta Kappan*.

Popham, W.J. (1995). *Classroom assessment: What teachers need to know*. Boston: Allyn and Bacon.

Quellmalz, E.S., & Haertel, G.D. (2005). *Use of technology-supported tools for large scale science assessment: Implications for assessment practice and policy at the state level*. Washington, DC: National Research Council.

Quellmalz, E.S., & Kozma, R. (2003). Designing assessments of learning with technology. *Assessment in Education, 10*(3), 389–407.

Quellmalz, E.S., DeBarger, A.H., Haertel, G.D., Schank, P., Buckley, B., Gobert, J. et al. (2005, November). *Exploring the role of technology-based simulations in science assessment: The Calipers Project*. Paper presented at the annual meeting. of the National Science Teachers Association, Chicago, IL.

Roschelle, J., Penuel, W.R., & Abrahamson, A.L. (2004). The networked classroom. *Educational Leadership, 61*(5), 50–54.

Roselli, R.J., & Brophy, S. (2002, June). *Exploring an electronic polling system for the assessment of student progress in two biomedical engineering courses*. Paper presented at the annual conference and exposition of the American Society for Engineering Education, Montreal, Quebec.

Russell, M., Goldberg, A., & O'Connor, K. (2003). Computer-based testing and validity: A look back into the future. *Assessment in Education: Principles Policy & Practice, 10*(3), 279–293.

Salpeter, J. (2004, March). Data: Mining with a mission. *Technology & Learning, 24*(8), p. 30. Retrieved August 27, 2007 from http://www.techlearning.com/showArticle.php?articleID=18311595.

Schmoker, M., & Wilson, R.B. (1995). Results: The key to renewal. *Educational Leadership, 51*(1), 64–65.

Seibert, G., Hamel, L., Haynie, K., Mislevy, R., & Bao, H. (2006). *Mystery powders: An application of the PADI design system using the four-process delivery system* (Draft PADI Technical Report 15). Menlo Park, CA: SRI International.

Shulman, L.S. (2007, January/February). Counting and recounting: Assessment and the quest for accountability. *Change*. Retrieved April 27, 2007, from http://www.carnegiefoundation.org/change/sub.asp?key=97&subkey=2169

Snipes, J., Doolittle, F., & Herlihy, C. (2002). *Foundations for success: Case studies of how urban school systems improve student achievement.* Washington, DC: MDRC and the Council of Great City Schools.

Sokoloff, D.R., & Thornton, R.K. (1997). Using interactive lecture demonstrations to create an active learning environment. In E.F. Redish & J.S. Rigden (Eds.), *The changing role of physics departments in modern universities: Proceedings of ICUPE* (pp. 1061–1074). College Park, MD: The American Institute of Physics.

Thorn, C.A. (2002, April). *Data use in the classroom: The challenges of implementing data-based decision-making at the school level.* Paper presented at the annual meeting of the American Educational Research Association, New Orleans, LA.

U.S. Department of Education (2002, September 24). *Internet access in U.S. public schools up for seventh straight year.* Press release. Retrieved May 27, 2007, from http://www.ed.gov/news/pressreleases/2002/09/09242002b.html

U.S. Department of Education, Office of Educational Technology (2004). *Toward a new golden age in American education: How the Internet, the law and today's students are revolutionizing expectations.* Washington, DC: Author.

Wayman, J.C. (2005). Involving teachers in data-based decision-making: Using computer data systems to support teacher inquiry and reflection. *Journal of Education for Students Placed at Risk, 10*(3), 295–308.

Wayman, J.C., & Stringfield, S. (2006). Technology-supported involvement of entire faculties in examination of student data for instructional improvement. *American Journal of Education, 112*(4), 549–571.

Wayman, J.C., Stringfield, S., & Yakimowski, M. (2004). *Software enabling school improvement through analysis of student data* (Report No. 67). Baltimore: Center for Research on the Education of Students Placed at Risk, Johns Hopkins University.

Wilensky, U., & Stroup, W.M. (2000, June). *Networked gridlock: Students enacting complex dynamic phenomena with the HubNet architecture.* Paper presented at the fourth annual International Conference of the Learning Sciences, Ann Arbor. MI.

Williamson, O.M., Bauer, M., Steinberg, L.S., Mislevy, R.J., & Behrens, J.T. (2004). Design rationale for a complex performance assessment. *International Journal of Testing, 4*(4), 303–332.

Educational Technology Policy: Educators Influencing the Process

HILARY GOLDMANN

How likely is it that most teacher candidates graduate from an institution of higher education and begin their first teaching assignment entering a classroom that is replete with the latest technology tools and digital resources and provided the necessary educational technology mentoring and support they need to master their use of these tools to enhance content and pedagogy? Do the PK-12 schools they arrive at have the infrastructure—both tools and personnel—to ensure their classrooms are places of 21st-century learning? If not—and that is likely—I write this chapter to invite teachers and teacher educators to work together with policymakers for change and to develop a stronger and more effective cadre of education technology advocates.

How do we impact changes? Where are the policy touch points that impact the classroom? When we think about influencing policy, particularly at the federal level, the average citizen usually thinks about direct lobbying and about the "fat cat lobbyists" who "grease politicians' hands." In reality, direct lobbying is just one of a host of tactics that are used by "special interest groups" to influence policymakers' decisions. And I am not using the term "special interest group" in a pejorative manner, but rather in a positive and assertive sense. Every American has the constitutional right to petition his or her government about matters of importance, and those of us in the education technology community should be proud to stand up and be counted; we are a special interest group and we want the president and the Congress to support policies to bring modern digital tools, content, and practices into our nation's classrooms.

A concerted and focused strategic effort to influence policy requires more than just direct lobbying. Other tactics can include:

Hilary Goldmann is Director of Government Affairs for the International Society for Technology in Education, which provides leadership and service to improve teaching, learning, and school leadership by advancing the effective use of technology in PK-12 and teacher education, and is based in Washington, DC.

- *Public policy development and analysis.* This means developing proposals for new programs that can be turned into legislation, or reviewing legislation that has been introduced and analyzing its impact.
- *Writing and sharing success stories with policymakers.* Do you have examples of how students' test scores improve, drop out rates are reduced, or parental involvement increased, as a result of the integration of education technology? If so, sharing these successes in a one-page narrative with your policymakers and national organizations, such as the International Society for Technology in Education (ISTE), can make a difference.
- *Coalition building.* This involves reaching out to others in your community to support education technology programs. Potential partners might include local companies, nonprofit organizations, and parent/teacher organizations. It is important to be creative—the local environmental group may want to work with you to recycle school computers!
- *Grassroots recruitment and mobilization.* Educators and others can join the Education Technology Action Network (www.edtechactionnetwork.org), a free network of education technology advocates, and can encourage colleagues to join as well as become active advocates.
- *Media outreach.* Anyone can write an op-ed for his or her local newspaper and invite the local media (print, radio, and TV) to report on the successes as well as the existing needs in local schools, all in addition to direct lobbying.

Each of these tactics require distinct skill sets, so those of us who are not interested in or comfortable with participating in direct lobbying activities (meeting with members of Congress or their staff) may prefer to play a significant role by drafting success stories, analyzing policy proposals, or galvanizing grassroots efforts.

All of these tactics are employed by the Government Affairs Department of the ISTE (see http://www.iste.org/ for more details). The key to successful lobbying is knowing how to integrate these activities, depending on the issue at hand, in order to achieve success. As ISTE's Director of Government Affairs, I leverage both ISTE's location in Washington, D.C. and the ISTE membership's expertise and shear strength of numbers to influence federal policy. Through ISTE's Board of Directors and Public Policy and Advocacy Committee, we develop an annual *U.S. Public Policies Principles and Federal & State Objectives* document to guide our policy activities for the year. This document states "ISTE's public policy principles and federal and state objectives are founded upon our members' uncompromising commitment to provide students the technology and information skills and tools necessary for success in the 21st century" (ISTE, 2006).

In particular, through the Committee For Education Funding (http://www.cef.org), America's largest education coalition, reflecting the broad spectrum of the education community (PK-20), and the Mission Critical Campaign (http://www.missioncriticalcampaign.org), a national campaign to advance technology as critical for K-12 education, as well as other coalitions, ISTE is able to bring its message to a broad range of education, corporate, and public service organizations. Additionally, I am able to tap the ISTE membership's expertise through formal and informal channels to garner advice, guidance, and timely feedback when developing legislative proposals and monitoring legislation that is moving in the halls of Congress. ISTE members have been an indispensable resource in helping guide our policy positions on E-Rate, No Child Left Behind, and teacher preparation legislation, all discussed further below.

From the Federal Level to the Classroom

Now that we have identified the strategies meant to impact policy at the federal level, we need to ask the question: do decisions made by policymakers at the federal level really have a direct impact on classroom learning? It is true that education policy and funding have historically and continue to be primarily a local/state responsibility. In fact, only about 8% of U.S. education funding comes directly from the federal government. This federal money, however, comes with "strings attached"—certain requirements, assessments, and accountability measures that must be taken into account in exchange for receiving these monies. Most school districts accept these dollars with their requirements rather than forgo these funds, thus providing the federal government with significant influence and direction setting for the nation's education agenda.

Since the No Child Left Behind Act became the law of the land in 2002, we have witnessed how decisions made "inside the beltway" do indeed have a direct impact on local decision making and consequently on the teaching and learning taking place in our nation's classrooms, through mandates such as standardized testing and requirements for adequate yearly progress. More specifically, the impact of federal policy on the infusion of digital tools and content in the classroom and in teacher preparation programs can be illustrated by the E-Rate program, the Enhancing Education Through Technology (EETT) program (Title II—Part D of NCLB), and the Preparing Teachers to Use Technology (PT3) program. Exactly how are these programs affecting our nation's classrooms, and what impact are education technology advocates having on influencing the development, implementation, and continuation of these programs?

E-Rate

The E-Rate program has had the most direct impact of any education technology program on our nation's schools. Congress listened to their constituents in the education and library communities, recognized the growing importance of new technologies and the Internet for improving education via student access to critical information, and voted to create the E-Rate program as part of the Telecommunications Act of 1996. It provides $2.25 billion annually in discounts to schools and libraries for telecommunications services, Internet access, and internal connections.

A recent report (Education & Library Networks Coalition, 2007) celebrating the successes and continued need for the E-Rate program profiles the way ten school districts and libraries from across the country are leveraging their E-Rate funding, noting that as "students and community residents compete for employment in a 21st Century job market that demands technologically adept employees, the E-Rate has played a central role in delivering powerful new communication and information learning technologies to America's schools and libraries . . . helping to spur the deployment of high speed Internet access throughout the nation" (http://www.nctet.org/Documents/NCTET%2010th%20Anniversary%20Report.pdf).

The resounding success of this program is evident in the following comparison: in 1996, 14% of our nation's classrooms were connected to the Internet; today more than 94% of them are connected. The Federal E-Rate program was the catalyst for this significant achievement. Without the E-Rate program, the Internet connection in many of our nation's classrooms, particularly those in underresourced neighborhoods, simply would not exist.

Although most of the nation's classrooms are connected to the Internet, the job of the E-Rate program is not complete. Connectivity is no longer enough if the speed is inadequate for today's technology applications. Schools rely on the E-Rate program to upgrade their connectivity and expand their bandwidth capabilities to keep up with the current and future demands on their networks. Policymakers must be educated about this ongoing need for the program to continue. ISTE is on record as recommending to the Federal Communications Commission (FCC) that schools strive for adequate bandwidth and speed for the following connections over the next three to five years:

- connection speeds between wide-area networks (WANs),
- connection speeds between WANs and district buildings, and
- connection speeds inside the building to the desktop computing device or wireless router.

Maintaining optimal services means that students, teachers, and community members will continue to enjoy access without delay to valuable online materials and resources, such as electronic card catalogs and grade books; interactive whiteboards for classroom lessons; video-streamed content to augment in-classroom lessons; videoconferencing equipment to communicate with schools around the country and across the globe; and collaborative learning technologies such as interactive educational simulations.

Over the last several years there have been congressional efforts to eliminate the E-Rate program and an accounting change that actually forced the program to shut down for several months in 2004. A strong coalition of education, library, community, and industry groups have banded together to thwart attempts to eliminate this vital resource.

No Child Left Behind and EETT

The No Child Left Behind (NCLB) legislation that was signed into law by President Bush in 2001 includes a new education technology program called the Enhancing Education Through Technology Program (also known as EETT or E2T2). Under EETT the U.S. Secretary of Education allocates funds directly to states based on the number of disadvantaged students eligible for federal assistance. After reserving 5% for state activities, the states in turn allocate 50% of this funding to local education agencies (LEAs), based on the number of disadvantaged students in the LEA. The rest of the funding is awarded to LEAs through a competitive grant program administered at the state level. EETT is designed to undergird NCLB's goals by supporting professional development, the implementation of educational software and digital content for use in the curriculum, instruction and classroom/school administration, computer-assisted and online testing, data-driven decision-making systems, and technology-based strategies to improve parental involvement. It also includes the goal that all students be technologically literate by the 8th grade.

EETT successes are being seen across the country. To highlight a few:

- In Utah, Missouri, and Maine, the eMINTS (http://www.emints.org) program provides schools and teachers with educational technology tools, curriculum, and over 200 hours of professional development to change how teachers teach and students learn. In classrooms in the same school (one with eMINTS and one without), the student achievement of students in the eMINTS classroom was consistently over 10% higher than the control classroom.
- In Michigan's Freedom to Learn technology program (http://www.ftlwireless.org/content.cfm?ID=505), 8th-grade math achievement increased from 31% in 2004 to 63% in 2005 in one middle school, and science achievement increased from 68% of students proficient in 2003 to 80% in 2004.
- In Texas, the Technology Immersion Pilot (TIP; http://www.txtip.info/), implemented in middle schools, demonstrated that discipline referrals went down by over half with the changes in teaching and learning; while in one school, 6th-grade standardized math scores increased by 5%, 7th grade by 42%, and 8th grade by 24%.
- In Iowa, after connecting teachers with sustainable professional development and technology-based curriculum interventions, student scores increased by 14 points in 8th-grade math, 16 points in 4th-grade math, and 13 points in 4th-grade reading, compared with control groups (see http://www.setdatapp.org/ for details).

With a $1 billion authorization, this program could have significantly transitioned our schools into 21st-century learning environments. However, an authorization does not automatically turn into funding. "Authorizing legislation" such as NCLB is legislation that creates programs and provides guidelines as to how much funding can potentially be spent on individual programs. The authorizing legislation, however, does not fund the programs. Another legislative track called the "appropriations process" actually funds the programs. The appropriations or funding decisions are made annually, which means each year Congress determines, for example, how much funding each program under NCLB will receive.

To make things more complicated, the appropriations bill that funds all education programs (elementary, secondary, and higher education) is also the same piece of legislation that provides funding for *all* programs at the Departments of Labor and Health & Human Services (including the National Institutes of Health). One can imagine the difficult situation members of Congress are in when faced with making decisions about funding all these important programs. Often there are not enough dollars allocated to a particular funding bill to invest in all of the competing and vitally important programs. And, when Congress and the president set a goal to cut federal spending, there is even less money to direct to these programs. Therefore, we are living in a "zero sum game," in which some programs will get cut just to keep other programs funded.

EETT funding has not fared well in this funding environment. In its first year, EETT was funded at $700 million, close to its $1 billion authorization, but was slashed to $496 million in FY 2005 and then subsequently cut again in FY 2006 to $272 million. This funding cut is a loss of real dollars for schools. It is my sense from discussions with educators that schools have had to cut back on significant education technology initiatives as a result of the funding decline in the EETT program. This funding cut has had a direct impact on local decision making and on the availability of resources, professional development, and tools teachers and administrators and their students need to succeed. The EETT program is an opportunity to provide teachers and administrators with new skills and opportunities, rather than mandates and accountability measures. It is important for us to take the responsibility for communicating the critical importance of these resources to policymakers in order to maintain these programs.

Working with ISTE membership and other organizations in the education and corporate communities, we were able to maintain funding for the EETT program the last few years through a strategic and effective lobbying and grassroots effort, despite strong attempts in Congress to eliminate funding entirely. It was the direct contact of constituents in Senate offices, coupled with "inside the beltway" lobbying efforts, that has repeatedly saved this program. We need to redouble our efforts in support of EETT if we are to maintain a dedicated funding stream for education technology in our nation's primary K-12 law.

To make matters more confusing, most laws have an expiration date, and NCLB is no exception. The bill expires in 2007, and Congress must pass and the president must sign a new law reauthorizing the legislation prior to this date. If a new law is not signed, then Congress must pass and the president must sign legislation to extend the existing law, or else all of these programs disappear. At the time of this writing, neither the House nor the Senate Education Committees have introduced their proposals for NCLB reauthorization. Members of Congress and their staff are working diligently, after listening to their constituents and other groups such as the education and business communities as well as public officials, to craft legislative proposals about possible changes to NCLB. Some members of Congress have already started introducing individual bills that they hope will later be included in the final reauthorization. One of these bills is the Achievement Through Technology and Innovation (ATTAIN) Act, introduced by Representatives Lucille Roybal-Allard (D-California), Ruben Hinojosa (D-Texas), Judy Biggert (R-Illinois), and Ron Kind (D-Wisconsin) in the House and by Senators Jeff Bingaman (D-New Mexico), Patty Murray (D-Washington) and Richard Burr (R-North Carolina) in the Senate. This bill was developed by ISTE, the Consortium for School Networking (CoSN), the Software and Information Industry Association (SIIA), and the State Educational Technology Directors Association (SETDA) as a replacement for EETT.

To combat the diminished congressional support for the EETT program, ISTE, CoSN, SIIA, and SETDA recognized that, if we are to get traction for an education technology program in the next authorization of NCLB, we need to bring to the Congress a proposal that significantly updates and revamps the existing law. Taking what we have learned about the successes of EETT, melding that with the feedback from policymakers, and underscoring ISTE's guiding principle to promote technology as the means to move our schools toward becoming effective digital learning environments, these organizations agreed on a framework for our efforts; namely, that a new program should focus on systemic school redesign and innovation with a strong focus on professional development. Working together as well as with the ISTE membership, we crafted a proposal that became the ATTAIN Act. This act focuses on systemic redesign, innovation, and professional development for both administrators and teachers, and strengthened the existing 8th-grade technology literacy component. Recognizing the importance of building a strong coalition and reaching out to various education interest groups, we shared drafts of the ATTAIN proposal with many of these groups. More than 20 of them, including the American Federation of Teachers, Apple, Intel, the National Education Association, and the National School Boards Association, have signed onto a letter of support.

The ATTAIN Act would revamp and replace the EETT program by building on its successes and focusing resources on those practices known to best leverage technology for educational improvement. The Act recognizes learning technologies as critical for our schools, both to meet No Child Left Behind's goals of raising student achievement and ensuring high quality teaching and to ensure that our nation's students are prepared to compete in the 21st century. Research (such as the EETT program data cited earlier) and experience demonstrate that systemic redesign initiatives and professional development centered on technology show great promise in improving teaching and learning. Yet many schools lack the capacity and training necessary for the 21st-century classroom to meet the needs and expectations of today's "digital native" (Prensky, 2001) students.

There has been very positive feedback from key education committee congressional staff with regard to ATTAIN, and the likelihood of its inclusion in the House and Senate education committee's proposals is promising. This would be a significant victory for the education technology community and a testament to the power of our coalition building, networking, policy development, and member input and lobbying efforts.

Preparing Tomorrow's Teachers to Use Technology (PT3)

This federal grant program provides funds to institutions of higher education to prepare new teachers to use technology in the classroom. It was established by the Clinton administration and enacted into law as part of the Higher Education Act reauthorization in 1998. The PT3 program was created to prepare prospective teachers to use advanced technology to help all students to meet challenging state and local academic achievement standards and to improve the ability of institutions of higher education to carry out such training.

When an administration leaves office, it is not unusual for its priority programs to lose their priority with the succeeding administration, and this is what happened to PT3 when the Bush administration took office. With no leadership from the White House to support PT3, no member of Congress to champion the program, and a lack of a vocal grassroots constituency, the funding for this program languished until it was completely eliminated.

Congress is currently in the process of again reauthorizing the Higher Education Act. Recognizing the opportunity to revamp the PT3 program, ISTE proactively convened the leaders of its Teacher Educator Special Interest Group (SIGTE) and charged them with crafting a pre-service program focused on teacher preparation and the use of technology. The result was the "Preparing Teachers for Digital Age Learners" proposal, which would provide grants to colleges and universities to either:

- develop long-term partnerships with LEAs focused on effective teaching with modern digital tools and content that substantially connects pre-service preparation of teacher candidates with high-needs schools; or
- transform the way schools of education teach classroom technology integration to teacher candidates.

We have had very favorable feedback from the entire SIGTE membership and from key members of Congress on this proposal and are hopeful that the legislation will be introduced during the 110th Congress for inclusion in the reauthorization of the Higher Education Act. This is yet another example of how, in working as a team, we can influence policy decisions at the federal level.

I hope I have made the case that what happens at the federal level of government has a direct impact on local decision making and the resources and policies that directly impact classroom teaching and learning. So what do we do as a community, and how do we work together to continue to impact policy at the federal level?

Making a Difference

ISTE had the foresight to open an office in Washington, D.C., in 2002, which helped to advance one of its top priorities: advocacy at the federal level. As ISTE's Director of Government Affairs I am responsible for raising ISTE's visibility and influence "inside the beltway" and for growing ISTE's grassroots efforts. Influencing policy is a team effort, and having a "lobbyist" in D.C. is just one component of impacting legislation. What really resounds in the halls of Congress are *constituent voices*. Members of Congress must hear from the people who vote for them, or else they will not know that education technology issues (or any other issues) are a priority (or should be) for their district. Policymakers have many competing demands weighing on them, and therefore it is the education technology community's responsibility to make sure they hear our message. The question becomes, how do we influence these policies and make sure they hear our message?

Members of Congress—your senators and representatives—are elected to represent *you* and they need to know how you feel about issues of the day. Each member of Congress relies on staff who in turn handle a large portfolio of policy issues. For instance, the staff person who handles education (this would include PK-higher education) may also handle healthcare, agriculture, housing, and labor issues. So, when I meet with this staff person and share information about education technology, I need to remember that five minutes later there will be someone else in the office meeting with this same staff person who will share vital information about a completely different policy area. Even if I made a compelling presentation, how can I ensure that my message will resonate and land on the list of priorities for this member of Congress? The answer remains: only if the constituents of this senator or representative are contacting the office with a message similar to mine. This is the way an issue gets on the priority list—complementary and multiple messages resonating from the districts.

How do teachers and teacher educators get started and contribute to galvanizing our community to be more vocal advocates for education technology? There are a variety of ways to begin, and I endorse the following first steps.

First, ISTE has affiliate organizations in almost every state (for a list, see http://www.iste.org/Content/NavigationMenu/Membership/ Affiliates/Directory_of_ISTE_Affiliates/ISTE_Affiliates_in_United_ States_of_America1.htm). Many of these state organizations either have an advocacy committee or are in the process of developing one. This is a great way to become involved and have a ready-made network of like-minded advocates who support educational technology expansion in our classrooms. Many of these organizations are becoming more vocal at both the state and federal levels. For example, the Alabama Education Technology Association (AETA), Massachusetts Computer Using Educators (MassCUE), and Michigan Association for Computer Users in Learning (MACUL) affiliates host an advocacy day at their respective state capitols. These statehouse days showcase student projects and are combined with photo opportunities, media and press coverage, and face-to-face meetings with members of the state legislature. The California affiliate, Computer-Using Educators, Inc. (CUE), recently conducted two high-profile interviews with two key California representatives, Congressman George Miller (Chair of the Education and Labor Committee) and Congresswoman Lucille Roybal-Allard (lead sponsor of the ATTAIN legislation). These interviews will be published in CUE's quarterly magazine. The Louisiana Association of

Computer-Using Educators (LACUE) sent a delegation to ISTE's national State Advocacy Capacity Building Conference in the spring of 2007. Attendees returned to the state galvanized and lobbied hard for educational technology funds. Their efforts resulted in the Louisiana State Legislature passing a $25 million education technology funding bill—the most technology funding from the state in the past ten years! Additionally, affiliates all across the country host Education Technology Action Network (ETAN) booths at their annual conferences, where conference attendees are able to make their voices heard by sending emails to their representatives.

There are a number of other strategies for getting involved with advocacy activities; they are listed and several are discussed in more detail:

- Join the Education Technology Action Network (ETAN) at http://www.edtechactionnetwork.org, and volunteer at an ETAN booth.
- Ask superintendents, principals, and college and university leaders to include educational technology in wish lists to legislators.
- Attend a legislator's town hall meeting and ask a question or make a comment about the important role of education technology in schooling.
- Write a letter to the editor about the importance of educational technology in our nation's classrooms.
- Compile success stories describing successes in student achievement based on the successful integration of digital tools and content into the curriculum.
- Meet with congressional staff in the district.
- Invite policymakers to an event or to visit the school and showcase your successes and needs.
- Attend ISTE's Advocacy Training Conferences and the annual Washington Education Technology Policy Summit.

The ETAN network is a free website service that enables users to send email letters to members of Congress in support of education technology initiatives. It is very easy to use. Simply go to the site (http://www.edtechactionnetwork.org) and type in your zip code. A prewritten draft letter will appear and the names of your representatives will be listed as well. Personalize the letter by adding your own thoughts and comments, type your name and address in the area provided, and click to send the letter. It is that easy, and these letters do make a difference. As I meet with congressional staff, I hear from them about the increased communication they are receiving about education technology policy from their constituents, partly as a result of the ease of using the Internet for such communications. You can also check the advocacy section of ISTE's website for news about upcoming advocacy conferences and the latest information from "inside the beltway."

It is vital that K-12 teachers and faculty who educate teachers share their success stories with policy makers. ISTE has developed an advocacy toolkit that includes examples of success stories, a template to follow when drafting success stories, and a starter kit for making your argument to a specific audience—from building and district administrators to school board representatives and state and federal policymakers. This toolkit is available for no charge at http://www.iste.org/Content/NavigationMenu/Advocacy/Advocacy_Toolkit/Advocacy_Toolkit_Making_the_Case_for_Educational_Technology.htm

Members of Congress regularly schedule town hall meetings in their district. Consider attending one of these meetings, bring a group of friends, and ask a question or make a comment about education technology and the importance of continued funding for your district's students. In addition to fielding questions about the war in Iraq and healthcare, it is critical for policymakers to field technology questions and to hear how significant technology is for raising student achievement and ensuring that our students can compete in today's world. Go to http://www.senate.gov and http://www.house.gov and then connect to your senators' and representative's web pages to check out when and where they will be speaking.

In addition to having offices in Washington D.C., representatives have at least one office in their district and senators have offices throughout the state. Staff at these offices are eager to meet with constituents locally, and will meet in the evening or on weekends to accommodate constituent schedules. This is a great opportunity to form a coalition of education technology advocates and hold a meeting with local congressional staff. Your group might include a faculty member of a college or university, a teacher, an administrator, a business representative, and a community representative. These are powerful meetings, and an excellent first step toward building relationships with local congressional offices and getting your message to the policymaker.

I hope this chapter has persuaded readers that federal policy does directly affect the teaching and learning that takes place in our nation's classrooms and that each of us has the opportunity and the responsibility to, in turn, influence those federal policies. Those of us with a passion and commitment for improving teaching and learning by advancing the effective use of technology to transform our nation's schools, increase student achievement, and ensure our students develop the skills they need to succeed in the 21st century must band together and "make our voices heard." The key to success in whichever advocacy activity you embark on is to remember that policymakers are there to serve you and that they want to hear from their constituents. If not us, who? If not now, when? Together we can make a difference.

REFERENCES

Education and Library Networks Coalition (EDLiNC) (2007, February 28). *E-Rate: 10 years of connecting kids and community*. Retrieved August 30, 2007 from http://www.edlinc.org/.

International Society for Technology in Education (2006, April 7). *ISTE's 2006 U.S. public policy principles and federal objectives*. Retrieved September 2, 2007 from http://www.iste.org/Content/NavigationMenu/Advocacy/2006_U_S_Public_Policy_Principles_and_Federal_Objectives.htm.

Prensky, M. (2001). Digital natives, digital immigrants. *On The Horizon, 9*(5), 1–6.

A Teacher's Place in the Digital Divide

MARK WARSCHAUER

Over the last decade, the term *digital divide* has been widely used to indicate unequal access to digital technology. However, there are in fact many forms of social and educational inequality related to technology access and use rather than a single divide (for an overview, see Warschauer, 2003). In this chapter, I first explore five types of digital difference that impact teaching and learning, which I call *school access*, *home access*, *school use*, *gender gap*, and *generation gap*, and then discuss strategies that teachers and schools can use to help overcome these multiple divides. I explore these divides and ways to bridge them from the perspectives of sociocultural learning theory, which emphasizes how learning is shaped by broad social and cultural contexts, and critical literacy theory, which situates reading, writing, learning, and meaning-making within the context of broader power differentials in schools and society.

Types of Digital Difference

School Access

School access refers to the unequal availability of digital technology in schools. Although differences in amounts of computing equipment and Internet access between high- and low-socioeconomic status (SES) schools have diminished, they still exist (see, e.g., Parsad, Jones, & Greene, 2005). In addition, some schools make special use of new technology for enrichment activities for students who are already performing at high levels, thus providing relatively less computer access for at-risk students (Schofield & Davidson, 2004).

Home Access

Home access refers to the availability of computers and Internet access to children in their home environment. Overall, teachers in

Mark Warschauer is a Professor of Education and Informatics at the University of California, Irvine, and Director of the university's Ph.D. in Education program. His most recent book is *Laptops and Literacy: Learning in the Wireless Classroom* (Teachers College Press, 2006).

high-SES schools are reasonably confident that just about all their students have access to a home computer and the Internet (see discussion in Warschauer, 2006; Warschauer, Knobel, & Stone, 2004). However, in low-SES schools, teachers know that many students might lack these resources or might face difficult conditions (slow Internet access, an outdated computer shared by several people, etc.) that prevent the efficient use of the Internet for schoolwork. They also know that many students might lack the basic computer skills that are developed from computer use in home contexts. Facing such a situation, many teachers in low-income communities are reluctant to assign homework involving computer use, and when they carry out school-based instruction with computers feel obligated to spend a good deal of time reviewing computer basics (Warschauer et al., 2004). In contrast, in high-income communities, teachers feel much more comfortable assigning computer- or Internet-based homework, as well as skipping over the basics when computers are used in school (Warschauer et al.).

School Use

The earlier point relates to a more general topic: differential ways that computers are used with high- and low-SES students in school. A number of studies (e.g., Becker, 2000; Schofield & Davidson, 2004; Warschauer, 2000, 2006; Warschauer & Grimes, 2005; Warschauer et al., 2004; Wenglinsky, 1998) provide evidence that student income and race correlate strongly with the type of use students make of computers in schools. Overall, students who are black, Hispanic, or low-income are more likely to use computers for drill and practice, whereas students who are white or high-income are more likely to use computers for simulations or authentic applications (Becker; Wenglinsky).

Of course, at one level, this is not surprising. Students with lower literacy and language skills require more basic levels of instruction to achieve proficiency, whereas students with higher language and literacy skills can leverage those skills to carry out more advanced project work. It would thus be unrealistic to think that all students, regardless of their background knowledge, skills, and abilities, are best served by the exact same instruction. Nevertheless, there are pedagogical approaches that can give *all* students more challenging and exciting experiences with new technology while still meeting their needs for language and literacy scaffolding, as will be discussed later on in this chapter. With the right approach, all students' education can be enhanced through meaningful use of technology.

Gender Gap

While the first three divides listed deal with socioeconomic status and race, this next divide considers differences based on gender. Simply put, do boys and girls access and use computers differently? Some earlier concerns that girls were being shut out of computer access and use have alleviated over time. Today, girls appear to use computers about as much as boys, but in different ways. Girls more frequently use digital technology to communicate and network with friends, whereas boys more often play computer games (Lehnart, Madden, & Hitlin, 2005).

Nevertheless, girls are still failing to enter computer science and other technological careers as much as boys (American Association of University Women [AAUW] Educational Foundation, 2000). One recent study suggested that computer science is seen by girls as being too individualistic for their needs and interests as well as too divorced from most academic content areas (Goode, Estrella, & Margolis, 2006). This suggests that developing technology-based instruction in schools that is more collaborative and more closely tied to academic content may be a successful strategy for increasing girls' comfort level with pursuing computer-based careers. Interestingly, the same approach may also be beneficial to boys, who are too often falling behind girls in academic achievement. A better integration of technology, and, in particular, of collaborative games and simulations with academic content should help boys leverage their interest in computers and gaming to improve their academic achievement.

Generation Gap

This last gap examines differences not among students, but rather between students and teachers. Many youth today have spent much of their lives surrounded by, and multitasking with, computers, video games, cellular phones, digital cameras, digital music players, and the Internet (Lehnart et al., 2005). These youth often feel more at ease in a digital environment than in the world of books, newspapers, and other forms of print (Howe & Strauss, 2000). They want and expect to have easy access to diverse sources of information, learning material in multiple media, and opportunities to network and interact online with peers (Levin & Arafeh, 2002). They are, in Prensky's (2001) words, *digital natives*.

In contrast, today's teachers did not grow up using computers, the Internet, and other digital media on a daily basis. They are thus, continuing Prensky's (2001) analogy, *digital immigrants*. Like all

TABLE 1
21ST-CENTURY SKILLS

Digital-age literacy	• Basic, scientific, economic, and technological literacies
	• Visual and information literacies
	• Multicultural literacy and global awareness
Inventive thinking	• Adaptability, managing complexity, and self-direction
	• Curiosity, creativity, and risk taking
	• Higher order thinking and sound reasoning
Effective communication	• Teaming, collaboration, and interpersonal skills
	• Personal, social, and civic responsibility
	• Interactive communication
High productivity	• Prioritizing, planning, and managing for results
	• Effective use of real-world tools
	• Ability to produce relevant, high-quality products

immigrants, they learn to adapt to their environment, but "they always retain their 'accent,' their foot in the past" (p. 2). Their teaching style, which likely reflects the way they were taught as children, may not match well with the learning styles of their digital native students.

Children today not only have different learning styles; they also face different learning requirements. Youth growing up in this new millennium will require a broad range of understanding, skills, and attitudes suitable to today's knowledge economy and society that go beyond the three Rs required a couple of generations ago. These have been nicely summarized (see Table 1) by one educational coalition as including digital-age literacy, inventive thinking, effective communication, and high productivity (North Central Regional Educational Laboratory & The Metiri Group, 2003). The teaching and learning of these 21st-century skills is greatly facilitated by, and in many cases dependent on, the use of information and communications technology, thus further complicating the role of teachers facing all the other gaps described earlier.

In summary, these five divides pose daunting challenges for teachers seeking to better meet the needs of a new generation through technology-enhanced learning, especially in low-income communities. How these challenges play out functionally was illuminated in our multi-site case study of technology integration and use in eight California secondary schools, including both low- and high-SES populations (Warschauer et al., 2004). We found three overriding themes related to technology use in schools, which we labeled *workability*, *complexity*, and *performativity*.

Workability referred to the challenge of coordinating technology use, including scheduling rooms, arranging appropriate software, and maintaining hardware, software, and network connections in working order. Workability difficulties surfaced more often in low-SES than high-SES schools, in part because of the higher turnover rates of teachers, administrators, and staff in those schools. For example, we encountered a teacher in a low-SES school who in one academic year taught in a room with high-speed Internet access but no computers, and in the following year in a room with several computers but no Internet access.

Even if all the equipment was accessible and working, there was still a good deal of *complexity* in integrating technology into instruction. The emphasis on standardized testing increased this complexity, as teachers often could not figure out how best to prepare students for tests while also emphasizing the kinds of discovery learning that are enhanced by technology use. Again, complexity was heightened in low-SES schools because of the special attention given to raising test scores in those schools as well as the larger numbers of English language learners (ELLs) those schools enrolled. For example, in a number of classrooms, we witnessed ELLs cutting and pasting information from the Internet to complete an assignment, with no evident understanding of the material they were working with. This last example is an illustration of what we called *performativity*, that is, technological performance for its own sake rather than in connection with meaningful learning goals.

Designing technology-enhanced lessons for culturally and linguistically diverse students with limited English literacy is without doubt complicated, but it can yield important rewards when done well (see examples in succeeding discussions and further examples in Brown, Cummins, & Sayers, 2007). In the remainder of this chapter, I examine some approaches for addressing these challenges that have been shown to be effective, using contexts of both limited and extensive technology penetration.

Addressing Challenges

Following my most recent study of learning and literacy development in 10 technology-intensive K-12 schools (Warschauer, 2006), I identified two general categories of how technology can benefit struggling students, which I labeled the *word* and the *world* (Warschauer, 2006). On the one hand, digital technology has proven to be a powerful tool for helping learners understand and manipulate text, that is, to grasp the *word*. Images and video can scaffold texts and provide clues for developing readers. Annotations can offer further scaffolding and encourage appropriate reading strategies. The use of different fonts, colors, and highlighting can draw attention to particular words and phrases and the relationship between them. Graphic organizing software can help students analyze texts or plan their own writing. Word processing software allows students to achieve a more iterative writing process and to carry out the formatting required for a wide variety of genres. Dictionaries, thesauruses, spelling and grammar checkers, and bibliographic software provide additional forms of support for students to improve the quality of their writing. The readability of computer-generated texts, as a result, makes them more suitable for evaluation and feedback from peer, teacher, and machine. Online discussion forums enable students to communicate in written form, thus providing further opportunities for learners to notice others' written language and hone their own writing. While these tools are potentially valuable to all students, they can have a special benefit for those facing literacy challenges such as ELLs, at-risk students, and learners in special education programs, as these groups of learners may have the most need for the kinds of scaffolding and support available via computer.

On the other hand, digital technology is a potent tool for bringing the wider *world* into the classroom and thus both motivating and contextualizing literacy practices. Students can discover authentic reading material on almost any topic and be introduced to up-to-date information and perspectives from peoples and cultures across the globe. They can gather information and resources to address diverse social issues from how to maintain varied ecologies, to weighing the benefits and disadvantages of technological progress, to understanding why and how societies go to war. Students can then develop and publish high-quality products that can be shared with particular audiences or the general public, whether in their community or internationally. And through these products, from book reviews published for Amazon.com to multimedia designs shared with children of other countries, students can not only learn about the world but also leave their mark on it.

Unfortunately, these perspectives of word and world are often separated from each other. Educational leaders and policymakers who are concerned about raising at-risk learners' test scores, as they should be, too often grab onto narrow means to achieve these ends. The resulting scripted literacy programs or drill and practice computer activities attempt to focus students' attention on the *word* without bringing to bear the wider resources of the *world* that make the word meaningful.

Not surprisingly, students view such teaching as disconnected from their lives and their community, and they disengage from school.

At the same time, many technology enthusiasts focus exclusively on the broader *world* and dismiss the *word*. In their excitement about the potential of media production, international communication, and video games for promoting student learning, they sometimes forget that stimulating environments in and of themselves do not magically transform learners. Realistically, sufficient amounts of scaffolding and support are required to help learners make sense of and learn from such environments. And, crucially, the amount of scaffolding and support necessary is inversely proportional to learners' prior expertise (Kalyuga, Ayres, Chandler, & Sweller, 2003). At-risk students, including ELLs, students with learning disabilities, and students reading behind grade level, are least able to cope with unstructured environments because the lack of structure places too heavy a cognitive load on the learner (see discussion in Feldon, 2004). As far as literacy development goes, exposing learners to the world without providing adequate support for them to master the word is a likely way to worsen educational inequity.

Balancing the Word and the World

Fortunately, these two need not be separated. One excellent model of how to link them is provided by Cummins (1996; see also Brown et al., 2007), who first developed a model for promoting students' language and literacy abilities while engaging them in cognitively stimulating environments, and then adapted the model so that it could be applied to technology-enhanced classrooms (Brown et al.). In the model presented in Figure 1, the central sphere represents the interpersonal space created in the communication between teachers and students, both within an individual classroom and in online exchanges. Activities that provide maximum opportunities for both cognitive engagement and identity investment are chosen by teachers, and within these activities, teachers guide students in focusing on three aspects of language: meaning, form, and use.

This model is important for several reasons. First, many educators focus principally on how technology can be *affectively* or *behaviorally* engaging (see Fredricks, Blumenfeld, & Paris, 2004 for a detailed discussion of affective, behavioral, and cognitive engagement). The emphasis on cognitive engagement, again with appropriate scaffolding, helps ensure that activities are designed to maximize opportunities for thinking and learning. Identity investment is crucial for giving diverse

FIGURE 1
A FRAMEWORK FOR THE DEVELOPMENT OF ACADEMIC LANGUAGE LEARNING
Source: Brown, Cummins, and Sayers (2007, p. 215)

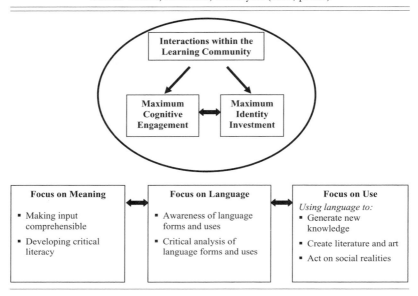

learners a real stake in the learning process and outcome through involvement in activities that reflect their backgrounds, experiences, and interests (see Cummins, 1996; Gee, 2000). And a focus on language meaning, form, and use helps ensure the proper scaffolding for students to handle challenging material and progress toward greater academic language proficiency (Cummins).

Brown et al. (2007) provide several detailed examples illustrating the power of this model for reaching at-risk learners. These include an oral history project by diverse middle school students that explored their own families' and communities' relationship to world events; a long-distance biography project of elementary school students integrating math, science, and language arts; an elementary school project to create a multimedia, multilingual dictionary; and a research project by elementary school students on the conditions of farm workers. I will discuss this latter example at length, drawing on the work of Brown and colleagues as well as on my own earlier discussion of this project following interviews with the two teachers involved (Warschauer, 2003).

FIGURE 2
STUDENTS AT MAR VISTA LOOKING OVER NEIGHBORING STRAWBERRY FIELDS

"Project Fresa": Fostering Critical Thinking With Technology

Mar Vista Elementary School is located in the midst of strawberry plantations in Oxnard, California, a couple of hours drive north of Los Angeles. About 80% of the students in the school are Latino (including Mexicans, Mexican Americans, and Latin Americans), and the majority of them have family members working as laborers in the strawberry fields that surround the school (see Figure 2). Even though most schools in California ended formal bilingual education following a 1998 statewide initiative, Mar Vista continued their bilingual programs thanks to a progressive administration and parental demand. Teachers at Mar Vista became leaders in effective use of new technologies to promote academic skills and critical awareness among traditionally marginalized students. This was accomplished through a theme-based, project-oriented instruction that was sensitive to students' own social concerns while at the same time engaging students in complex and cognitively demanding learning tasks.

Project Fresa, a yearlong project for primary school students, took as its main focus the local strawberry (*fresa*, in Spanish) industry. A summary of the curricular activities is seen in Table 2. The children began by formulating their own research questions about the conditions of strawberry workers. They then used these research questions to

TABLE 2
CURRICULAR ACTIVITIES IN PROJECT FRESA

Activity	Subject Area	New Technologies Used
Formulating interview and survey questions	English Language Arts (ELA), Spanish, social studies	Word processing
Carrying out interviews and surveys	ELA, Spanish	—
Analyzing and graphing data	Math	Spreadsheets
Free writing and poetry	ELA	Word processing
Drawing	Art	Scanners
Searching online for information	Social Studies	Internet browsers
Writing letters to elected officials	Social Studies, ELA	Word processing, e-mail
Writing letters to strawberry growers	Social Studies, English	Word processing, e-mail
Writing letters to children in Puerto Rico	Social Studies, ELA	Word processing, e-mail
Making public presentations	ELA, Social Studies	Presentation software

generate interview and survey questions, enrolling their family members, relatives, and neighbors as respondents (they frequently conducted the interviews in Spanish and then translated responses into English). Afterward, the students learned to record the responses on spreadsheets and to produce graphs of the data in various formats (analyzing, for example, which types of graphs best display what types of information). The graphs were incorporated into slide presentations and web sites together with photos and quotations from the people they interviewed and students' original artwork, journals, and poetry (see Figure 3). With the guidance of the teachers, they then searched for further information about the conditions of strawberry workers on the Internet and also invited guest speakers into their classroom from environmental and workers' rights groups. Based on the information obtained from the Internet and guest speakers, students wrote letters via e-mail to the strawberry growers, expressing the concerns they had about strawberry workers' rights. They also sent e-mails to elected officials, including the governor, with real and informed inquiries about agricultural laborers' rights. Later they began an e-mail exchange with children in Puerto Rico who live in a coffee growing area to compare notes about the two industries and the condition of workers. At the end

FIGURE 3
STUDENT'S ARTWORK AND POETRY FOR PROJECT FRESA

fresa 2.pict

Fields

Seeds, Soil

Growing, Picking, Eating,

Our Fields, Our History

Strawberries

-Victorico

of the year, the students at Mar Vista made a public presentation and their parents and other community members were invited to view the multimedia products they created.

Looking back at the model in Figure 1, we see that Project Fresa involved intense interaction, both within and outside the classroom. The project enabled maximal cognitive engagement, as students were challenged to understand—through art, mathematics, language arts, and social sciences—a series of complex phenomena. Students also heavily invested their own identities in the project because of the importance of the topic to themselves, their families, and their community. As one student wrote in her journal,

I am related to the strawberries because my whole family has worked in the strawberry fields. Every day, my mom used to get up at 4:00 a.m., make her lunch, and go to work. When she got home I would be already asleep. My two aunts also worked in the strawberry fields. When they would get home they were very tired. It was really hard for them because they would have to stand up all day. (Eliana, quoted in Singer & Perez, n.d.)

Another student commented that, working on the project, "I feel nice inside because I know that with all this work some day we will make César Chávez's dream come true" (quoted in Brown et al., 2007, p. 145).

The variety of genres and formats involved, and the intense discussion of these genres and formats, helped students comprehend sophisticated texts and develop critical language awareness. For example, several of the strawberry growers who replied to student e-mails did so with standard disclaimers about unnamed labor contractors being responsible for working conditions. The students worked together to understand the meaning of these texts and to critique both the content of the message and the way it was delivered. They also used language to generate new knowledge (about the conditions of the laborers), to create literature and art (through their poetry and drawings), and to act on social realities (by writing to the governor, for example). Although the project has not been independently evaluated, the teachers believe that it contributed to higher standardized test scores, increased parental participation in their children's education, and enhanced students' academic motivation (see discussion in Lynn, 2000).

As positive as the project appeared to be, it was not continued after the two teachers left the school, one for retirement and one for an administrative position (M. Singer, personal communication, June 23, 2005). The difficulty in sustaining and expanding such projects is partly due to the current political climate, which emphasizes mastery of numerous discrete standards rather than deeper learning, and is partly related to the challenges of organizing technology-based learning in settings with limited computer access. It also stems from the difficulty that many teachers have in learning to teach in ways that are fundamentally different from the kinds of instruction they themselves experienced as both students and student teachers (Cuban, 1993). These obstacles, compounding issues of school access, home access, school use, and generation gaps, create an environment in which promising initiatives are difficult to sustain.

In the remainder of this chapter, I report on initiatives to provide more extensive student access to computers, together with more intensive professional development for teachers, thus making such groundbreaking project work as described earlier easier to organize.

Expanding Student Access

The student–computer ratio in U.S. public schools has fallen from 168.0:1 in 1983 (Anderson & Ronnkvist, 1999) to 3.8:1 in 2005 (Market Data Retrieval, 2005). Yet in spite of this marked improvement in computer access, teachers still have substantial difficulty integrating technology into instruction when multiple students have to share a single computer. In many school districts, only a small handful of pioneers (such as the two teachers involved in Project Fresa) take the time and initiative to implement complex technology-enhanced projects in the classroom.

To facilitate more and better technology-enhanced learning and teaching, some educational reformers have proposed what are known as *one-to-one* programs (see, e.g., Papert, 1996), in which a laptop computer is provided for each child to be used throughout the school day and, in most cases, at home (for a history of such laptop programs, see Johnstone, 2003). Currently, there exists a statewide middle school and a sizable high school laptop program in Maine; a countywide laptop program among middle and high schools in Henrico County, Virginia; and other smaller laptop programs throughout the country. Such programs are relatively expensive and can thus only be offered when there is a shared community investment. They can also represent a challenge for teachers who, as noted earlier, are often not as comfortable with new technologies as are their students. The most successful one-to-one laptop programs, such as Maine's, have a serious ongoing professional development component woven into their design.

I directed a team of researchers that investigated 10 diverse one-to-one laptop programs in California and Maine (Warschauer, 2006) in a mixed-methods multi-site case study. The laptop programs took place in urban, suburban, and rural schools, in high-SES and low-SES neighborhoods, and in regular education, gifted, and alternative education programs, as well as in programs targeted to second language learners. Our research team conducted 650 hours of classroom observations; interviewed about 200 teachers, students, staff, and parents; surveyed 1,000 students and teachers; collected and analyzed the print and digital work from 60 students; and examined state test scores before and after the laptop programs were implemented.

The study confirmed prior research indicating that teaching and learning changes markedly in the laptop classroom (see, e.g., Silvernail & Lane, 2004; Walker, Rockman, & Chessler, 2000). With students having constant access to a computer and the Internet, teachers can much more easily integrate technology into instruction without having to be concerned about when computers may or not be available. Teachers can also move quickly past instructing students on hardware and software operations (because children, with their own laptop, learn these matters quickly) and focus on underlying instructional content. In schools where students are allowed to take laptops home, the laptops become what one student in our study called a "portable study guide," (Warschauer, 2006, p. 135), providing children a place and means to organize all their school work; take, review, and edit their notes; search for, maintain, and incorporate educational resources; and bring all these resources back and forth between school and home.

Our study focused in particular on literacy practices, and we found that the processes, sources, and products of literacy changed substantially in the laptop classroom (see Table 3). Literacy practices in the laptop classroom became more autonomous, with students having greater control over content and pacing. Practices became more public, with greater opportunities for students and teachers to see student work, and were more frequently authentic in purpose and audience, as opposed to being produced for the sake of a grade. They were more frequently collaborative, based on student cooperation, and reflected a more iterative process, based on greater attention to planning and revising work. More scaffolding was provided, for example, through computer-based dictionaries, thesauruses, and spell checkers, and more feedback was provided by peers, teachers, and automated engines.

Students in laptop classrooms made use of a greater variety of published sources, taking advantage of the huge amount of material available online either on the public web or through proprietary information services. Students also made greater use of empirical data, either gathered from the web or collected in the classroom (e.g., using computer-connected scientific probes). They were better able to archive their own prior work and experiences (e.g., via digital video) as a source for analysis and reflection, and they produced a wider variety of textual genres including brochures, newspapers, petitions, posters, and business letters. They also produced considerably more multimedia of diverse genres—not only slide presentations (e.g., PowerPoint, common in

TABLE 3
CHANGES IN LITERACY PRACTICES IN THE LAPTOP CLASSROOM

Typical Classroom	Laptop Classroom
Literacy Processes	
Mostly teacher controlled	More autonomous student control
Mostly private and individual	More often public and collaborative
Mostly for teacher and a grade	More often for an authentic purpose and audience
Limited revision	More iterative process with greater revision
Little feedback provided	More feedback provided
Some scaffolding	More scaffolding
Literacy Sources	
Use of few published sources (mostly from school libraries or textbooks)	Greater use of published sources, with library and textbook material supplemented by a wide range of online material
Limited access to and use of data	Greater access to and use of data from online materials or collected by students in class (using computer-connected probes, etc.)
Limited ability to record and reflect on students' own experiences and prior work	Digitalized audio and video allow better opportunity to record and reflect on students' own experiences and prior work
Literacy Products	
Text products are mostly essays	Essays supplemented by other genres such as brochures, newspapers, and business letters
Multimedia products largely restricted to slide presentations (e.g., PowerPoint)	Greater diversity of multimedia products, including musical composition, videos, animation, and web sites

many classrooms), but also musical compositions, videos, animation, and web sites.

All these changes brought about four main benefits for students. The most important of these was in the teaching and learning of 21st-century learning skills. Students in the schools we visited had constant access to information, resources, and data, and learned to access that information, analyze and critique it, and work it into a wide variety of authentic products. This occurred especially in schools that already had strong information literacy programs, from the classroom to the library, and where critical inquiry was valued.

Second, we noted greater student engagement because of their use of multimedia. Students' ongoing work with texts, images, video, sound, music, and animation both increased their interest in school and heightened their ability to produce and interpret multimodal content, a valuable 21st-century skill in its own right.

Third, we found an increase in the quantity and quality of student writing. Students in laptop schools wrote much more than students in traditional classrooms. They revised their writing more easily and frequently. They took pride in the professional appearance of their writing. And they received more feedback on their writing.

Finally, we found that students engaged in deeper learning. Technology provided students multiple angles to get at the same material. It thus facilitated project-based work that allowed students to dig further and deeper into material. Nearly all the schools we visited reported a greater emphasis on in-depth research than before, and the work we collected from these projects was impressive.

Expeditionary Learning in a Laptop School

The laptop schools that were most effective with at-risk students used approaches consistent with the academic language learning model depicted in Figure 1. An excellent example is seen in Castle Middle School (a pseudonym) in Maine, whose students live in the most destitute housing projects of the eastern seaboard and include large numbers of African refugee immigrants. Castle has eliminated all tracking and also incorporates as many special education students and ELLs into regular classrooms as possible. Students at Castle are grouped into "houses" of about 60 learners and four main teachers, with the teachers having broad autonomy over class scheduling. Most important, almost all academic work in the houses and school is integrated into 8–12 week interdisciplinary research projects called "learning expeditions" (see Expeditionary Learning, 2006). For example, in a 10-week expedition called Four Freedoms, students drew on a 1941 speech by Franklin Roosevelt and a subsequent series of paintings by Norman Rockwell to examine freedom of speech, freedom of worship, freedom from fear, and freedom from want. Using magazine materials, the students produced art collages on one of these four freedoms to explore how the ideas of freedom change over time and how some people's notion of freedoms may conflict with others'. The students then wrote commentaries in which they explained the significance of their collages. Finally, students assembled the commentaries and collages in posters that were exhibited at the Maine College of Art as well as in a hypertext that was published on the Internet.

Similar to Project Fresa, this project was designed to be cognitively engaging, in this case by asking students to relate important historical concepts to social realities today. The topics involved, such as freedom from fear and freedom from want, were highly relevant to the school's students, the majority of whom had experienced both impoverishment and violence in their lives. The combination of artistic and textual response provided students multiple ways to interpret these relationships, and to reflect on their own identities in doing so, and also made the projects appealing to both boys and girls. In creating work for public presentation, online and in a museum, the students became highly motivated to focus on the form and meaning of what they wrote. And in the process, they also developed technological skills such as finding and making use of online information. Overall, this project and a number of other projects we witnessed in the laptop schools showed us how improved access to technology, combined with an appropriate pedagogical approach, can help students access both the word *and* the world.

Additional Technology Resources

Although relatively few schools have laptop computers for all students, falling costs of laptops suggest that this could be a widespread model in the future. In the meantime, districts that cannot afford one-to-one initiatives are finding other ways to enhance student access to technology. Many schools are experimenting with laptops on mobile carts shared by multiple teachers. These carts allow teachers to provide a one-to-one wireless computing environment in their own classroom, but not on a daily basis. In addition, keeping school computers available after school, either in a computer lab or in the school library, can ensure that all students have opportunities to complete computer-based homework assignments. Many neighborhoods in low-income areas also provide computer access in children's afterschool programs or in public libraries, and schools can pass on information about these computer resources to parents and may also work with municipal authorities to try to encourage the provision of free wireless access in their community. Finally, because data suggests that even in low-SES neighborhoods the great majority of families already have at least one computer (see, e.g., Warschauer et al., 2004), schools can build on this by loaning computers to the minority of families that lack them, thus helping ensure that all students have some kind of access to a computer outside of school.

If steps such as these are taken, teachers can then with more confidence assign homework that may require or benefit from the use of a computer. Students in low-SES schools are cheated of important educational opportunities when their teachers shy away from assigning in-depth research projects that may depend on access to technology outside of school. Rather than avoiding these important assignments, teachers and schools should instead work to ensure that all students have at least minimal access to the technologies needed to complete them.

In summary, then, the aforementioned issues of complexity and workability can be addressed by providing students and teachers more consistent and reliable access to computers and the Internet, either through true one-to-one programs or through leveraging other technology resources in schools and communities. Overcoming performativity depends on instructional approaches that focus not only on mastery of technological applications, but also on broad learning goals related to academic content, as seen in the examples of Project Fresa and Expeditionary Learning discussed earlier. A focus on developing both technological skill and academic expertise around topics related to students' life experiences makes such projects engaging and meaningful to both male and female students of diverse cultural backgrounds.

Conclusion

A recent national study commissioned by the U.S. Department of Education (Dynarski et al., 2007) suggests that tutorial software in reading and mathematics is ineffective in raising student test scores. Many will likely respond to such research by questioning the suitability of computers in schools.

However, evidence suggests that it is principally low-income students who are predominately subjected to such drill-and-practice software, while high-SES students have more opportunities to use school technology for broader purposes of research, simulation, data analysis, and creative expression (see, e.g., Becker, 2000). Thus, sadly, the same low-SES students who often lack opportunities to use technology creatively at home—because of lack of computer access, Internet access, or social support (Warschauer, 2003)—also too often lack similar opportunities at school.

If we are going to overcome multiple digital divides, we can neither ban computers from schools nor subject low-SES students to the most narrow uses of such technology. Rather, we must continue to expand student access to technology, either by lowering student–computer ratios or by finding other ways to connect low-income students to school and community technology resources. And we must choose pedagogical approaches that combine cognitive engagement, identity investment, and a focus on language meaning, use, and form. Project Fresa in California and Expeditionary Learning in Maine provide a view of what can be accomplished when good teaching and technology are combined to help diverse students access both the world and the word.

REFERENCES

American Association of University Women (AAUW) Educational Foundation (2000). *Tech-savvy: Educating girls in the new computer age*. Washington, DC: AAUW.

Anderson, R.E., & Ronnkvist, A. (1999). *The presence of computers in American schools. Teaching, learning, and computing: 1998 survey report*. Irvine, CA: Center for Research on Information Technology and Organizations.

Becker, H.J. (2000). Who's wired and who's not? *The Future of Children, 10*(2), 44–75.

Brown, K.R., Cummins, J., & Sayers, D. (2007). *Literacy, technology, and diversity: Teaching for success in changing times*. Boston: Allyn & Bacon.

Cuban, L. (1993). *How teachers taught: Constancy and change in American classrooms 1890–1980*. New York: Longman.

Cummins, J. (1996). *Negotiating identities: Education for empowerment in a diverse society*. Los Angeles: California Association for Bilingual Education.

Dynarski, M., Agodini, R., Heaviside, S., Novak, T., Carey, N., Campuzano, L. et al. (2007). *Effectiveness of reading and mathematics software products: Findings from the first student cohort*. Washington, DC: U.S. Department of Education.

Expeditionary Learning (2006). *Expeditionary learning: It's the way school should be*. Retrieved February 2, 2006, from http://www.elob.org/

Feldon, D. (2004). Dispelling a few myths about learning. *UrbanEd, 1*(4), 37–39.

Fredricks, J.A., Blumenfeld, P.C., & Paris, A.H. (2004). School engagement: Potential of the concept, state of the evidence. *Review of Educational Research, 74*(1), 59–109.

Gee, J.P. (2000). Identity as an analytic lens for research in education. *Review of Research in Education, 25*, 99–125.

Goode, J., Estrella, R., & Margolis, J. (2006). Lost in translation: Gender and high school computer science. In J.M. Cohoon & W. Apray (Eds.), *Women and information technology: Research on reasons for underrepresentation*. Cambridge, MA: MIT Press.

Howe, H., & Strauss, W. (2000). *Millennials rising: The next great generation*. New York: Vintage Books.

Johnstone, B. (2003). *Never mind the laptops: Kids, computers, and the transformation of learning*. Lincoln, NE: iUniverse.

Kalyuga, S., Ayres, P., Chandler, P., & Sweller, J. (2003). Expertise reversal effect. *Educational Psychologist, 38*(1), 23–31.

Lehnart, A., Madden, M., & Hitlin, P. (2005). *Teens and technology*. Washington, DC: PEW Internet & American Life Project.

Levin, D., & Arafeh, S. (2002). *The digital disconnect: The widening gap between Internet-savvy students and their schools*. Washington, DC: Pew Internet & American Life Project.

Lynn, R. (2000, November 13). Oxnard teachers use parents' work in fields to grow students' minds. *The Desert Sun*, p. A3.

Market Data Retrieval (2005). *The K-12 technology review 2005*. Shelton, CT: Market Data Retrieval.

North Central Regional Educational Laboratory & The Metiri Group (2003). *enGauge 21st century skills: Literacy in the digital age*. Naperville, IL, and Los Angeles: Authors.

Papert, S. (1996, October 27). Computers in the classroom: Agents of change. *Washington Post*, p. R1.

Parsad, B., Jones, J., & Greene, B. (2005). *Internet access in U.S. public schools and classrooms: 1994–2003*. Washington, DC: National Center for Educational Statistics.

Prensky, M. (2001). Digital natives, digital immigrants. *On the Horizon, 9*(5), 1–6.

Schofield, J.W., & Davidson, A.L. (2004). Achieving equality of student Internet access within schools. In A. Eagly, R. Baron, & L. Hamilton (Eds.), *The social psychology of group identity and social conflict* (pp. 97–109). Washington, DC: APA Books.

Silvernail, D.L., & Lane, D.M. (2004). *The impact of Maine's one-to-one laptop program on middle school teachers and students*. Gorham, MA: Maine Education Policy Research Institute.

Singer, M., & Perez, A. (n.d.). *Project Fresa*. Retrieved May 8, 2007, from http://eden.clmer.csulb.edu/netshare/cti/%20FOR%20PSRTEC%20WEBSITE/Amada%20and%20Michelle/

Walker, L., Rockman, S., & Chessler, M. (2000). *A more complex picture: Laptop use and impact in the context of changing home and school access*. Retrieved February 2, 2006, from http://www.elob.org/

Warschauer, M. (2000). Technology and school reform: A view from both sides of the track. *Education Policy Analysis Archives, 8*(4). Retrieved October 18, 2007, from http://epaa.asu.edu/epaa/v8n4.html

Warschauer, M. (2003). *Technology and social inclusion: Rethinking the digital divide*. Cambridge, MA: MIT Press.

Warschauer, M. (2006). *Laptops and literacy: Learning in the wireless classroom*. New York: Teachers College Press.

Warschauer, M., & Grimes, D. (2005). *First-year evaluation report: Fullerton school district laptop program*. Retrieved February 2, 2006, from http://www.fsd.k12.ca.us/menus/ltol/evaluation/FSD-laptop-year1-eval.pdf.

Warschauer, M., Knobel, M., & Stone, L.A. (2004). Technology and equity in schooling: Deconstructing the digital divide. *Educational Policy, 18*(4), 562–588.

Wenglinsky, H. (1998). *Does it compute? The relationship between educational technology and student achievement in mathematics*. Retrieved February 2, 2006, from ftp://ftp.ets.org/pub/res/technolog.pdf.

Reconsidering the Digital Divide: Using Online Content to Understand Teaching and Learning

SHARON TETTEGAH, EUN WON WHANG, NAKIA COLLINS, AND
KONA TAYLOR

The key to change is empowering individuals, schools, and communities to believe in themselves, and to adapt technology to their own purposes (Solomon & Allen, 2003, p. xxiv).

In today's web-based society, data can be obtained and sorted in larger quantities than ever before. In this sense, using web-based applications and Internet technology, education can be advanced and tailored to the needs of current society. American society is known for its incredible diversity, which gives it many economic and cultural benefits. Yet in order for this society to continue to succeed, a larger effort must be placed on giving the educators of this nation the necessary tools to cope with such a diverse group of students. Practicing and pre-service teachers are and will be educating the future leaders of this country and must understand the many facets of diversity and the importance of using information communication technology (ICT) to deliver meaningful and relevant content.

In a typical American classroom, students will represent different races, cultures, and ethnicities. Because of this, it would be impossible to create a technology-rich curriculum for educators to address each and every student, but it *would* be helpful if they could at least understand the different perspectives that these students possess. Just as we recognize the vast differences in our students, it would be naïve to think that all educators think the same or share the same perceptions and beliefs; therefore, it is important to study and eventually understand how to handle the enormous task of creating educators who are aware

Sharon Tettegah is a Professor in the Department of Curriculum and Instruction, Math, Science & Technology Division, at the University of Illinois, Urbana-Champaign (UIUC). Eun Won Whang is a graduate student in the Department of Curriculum and Instruction at UIUC. Nakia Collins is a teacher at a Chicago public school. Kona Taylor is a graduate student in the Department of Curriculum and Instruction at UIUC.

and sensitive and understand issues related to our diverse global world, using technology to accomplish the task of understanding differences.

The nexus of diversity and technology as a means to explore areas of teaching and learning is currently emerging as an important phenomenon to deal with a different aspect of the digital divide than the one we commonly understand (Solomon & Allen, 2003). So much talk has emerged on issues related to this divide, but there is little focus on the integration of diversity, multicultural education, and technology in order to address diversity within the classroom. Now that we understand that we need the hardware for teachers and students to acquire technological competence, we also need to understand that once there is access, the next task is to review what it is that teachers and students are getting access *to*. What types of content are they accessing through information communication technologies? Is there appropriate content with sound representation from diverse groups? Is there social justice embedded within the content?

Educators have asserted that it is important to know how to use the tools of information literacy to assess and analyze content while moving from a digital *divide* to a digital *opportunity* environment (Kuttan & Peters, 2003; Solomon & Allen, 2003). Some argue for access to meaningful high-quality material that represents diverse content (Bolt & Crawford, 2000; Fox, 2005; U.S. Department of Commerce, 2004; Wiburg & Butler, 2003). As we continue to explore issues of digital divide and digital equity based on access to hardware and broadband, we must also prepare our leaders to integrate multicultural education and technology (Appelbaum & Enomoto, 1995; Gorski, 2004; Sleeter & Tettegah, 2002; Tettegah, 2002, 2005), though there is little scholarship on this issue (Au, 2006; Sleeter & Tettegah).

Several websites and portals have been developed to address issues of digital divide and digital equity, with a primary focus on multicultural and diverse content.[1] Most focus on multicultural resources and how to deal with the digital divide through engagement of reader voices. Often the portals maintain public discussion forums and offer news reporting as a medium to discuss digital divide and equity issues (see, for example, www.socialjusticenews.net). However, these portals generally do not provide the critical content that offers a stimulus to address or deal with issues directly associated with classroom teaching and learning practices rooted in social justice and equity, and that use technology for engagement. Simply put, there are few representations of technology use as a tool in multicultural, diversity, or social justice teaching.

This chapter will offer a research-based discussion on why it is critical for teacher educators and pre-service and practicing teachers to have the skills and knowledge to engage diversity, multicultural, and social justice activities using technology, and how a web portal designed with this in mind has managed to make a difference.

The Digital Divide Revisited

Issues related to digital divide and equity have been at the forefront of K-12 and higher education since the late 1960s (Kuttan & Peters, 2003; Wiburg & Butler, 2003). Traditional definitions of digital divide refer to a gap between those who have access to hardware and information communications technology and those who do not, as well as the socioeconomic and racial differences between these groups. In this chapter we focus on how technology can be used to address issues of diversity and other differences associated with classroom teaching and learning. The nature of the content on the web portal we discuss is derived directly from the authors' experiences with pre-service and in-service teachers, parents, and students. This portal is unique in its philosophical orientation in that its forums for discussion, resources related to culture, and solid pedagogical approaches to integrating technology are framed by issues of multiculturalism, diversity, and social justice (Tettegah, 2005, 2007).

Teacher educators believe teachers should have a foundation in skills and knowledge so that they become familiar with the basic concepts related to multiculturalism, diversity issues, and social justice education (Au, 2006; Sleeter & Tettegah, 2002; Solomon & Allen, 2003). In addition, teachers should also gain an understanding of how cultural differences influence personal feelings and assumptions as well as interpersonal and intergroup relations. And within the previously discussed context teachers should also be able to define and understand their own cultural identity and how it may influence their ability to perceive differences.

Teacher educators and pre-service and in-service teachers must deal with all of the aforementioned issues in their classrooms. They should be knowledgeable, prepared, and grounded in an understanding of how their beliefs and attitudes affect student achievement, self-esteem, and academic performance. With all of these challenges teachers face, how can we better understand what they themselves think would help them to confront and overcome these hurdles? One important way to get to know what pre-service and in-service teachers need is by leveraging technology to get teachers to confront uncomfortable or unpleasant dilemmas as a means to explore social injustices experienced in classrooms. Technology affords us the opportunity to examine presumptions about teaching and learning in ways that do not put the students or teachers at risk of public humiliation or retribution. For example, a teacher may not handle a situation equitably when she perceives an African American male student as acting aggressively toward a Latina classmate. In addition, the student or parent perspectives are frequently absent from discussions involving classroom teaching and learning. Current technologies can encourage teachers to confront the digital divide and explore potential dilemmas among parents, teachers, and students, by presenting realistic classroom situations to pre-service and in-service teachers.

The Inter/IntraCultural and Cross-Cultural Teaching Portal

The advancements of technology and the growth of global societies place educators in the position of needing to prepare students to understand the many different aspects of America's multicultural and technologically oriented society. To meet this goal, the Inter/Intra Cultural and Cross-Cultural Teaching Portal (ICCTP; http://www.icctp.net, see Figure 1) was designed, based on Tettegah's (2005) belief that it was important to provide abundant cultural information for educators utilizing current technology:

I believe that preparing tomorrow's diverse educators to better communicate, understand, and respect each other must start with helping educators provide quality multicultural teaching and learning competencies, modeling prosocial behaviors and conflict resolution in today's classrooms using the vast number of information technology tools available. (p. 372)

To accomplish these goals, Tettegah created the ICCTP with a network of links to useful online diversity, equity, and multicultural resources; surveys; discussion forums; an "ask a professional" resource; and an ANV storytelling tool (Clover), as well as options for interacting with Animated Narrative Vignettes (ANVs) to gather information on educators' beliefs about multicultural issues.

Information about Events and Resources

The information page of the ICCTP portal provides important information, such as links to events and conferences and to grant

FIGURE 1

HOME PAGE OF INTER/INTRA CULTURAL AND CROSS-CULTURAL TEACHING
PORTAL

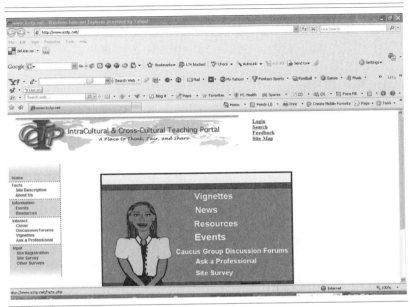

funding agencies with a specific focus on math, science, and technology and multicultural education integration. ICCTP also provides links to resources that explore social justice issues associated with teaching and learning, and links to literary resources for educators and students with specific focuses on literacy. There are also links to online courses, lesson plans, research articles, technology, and culture with reports and funding information, and relevant games, simulations, and virtual reality environments.

Input: Surveys

The input section maintains a site registration, site survey, and other surveys that assess teaching and learning. The site survey specifically focuses on understanding the teacher in relation to diversity, social justice, and multicultural classroom school interactions. Visitors are asked to take the survey to help us better understand their multicultural interests. General survey results ($n = 408$) from pre-service teachers who were given the opportunity to engage with ICCTP indicate that 91% of them found the site useful.[2] Respondents suggested it was useful for three main purposes: resource gathering, dialoguing, and rehearsing classroom situations.

Resource gathering. As a tool for resource gathering, the convenience and the usefulness of keeping current information linked and available, reducing the amount of work teachers needed to invest in finding online resources, were the main attractions. One respondent wrote, "I think this site is very useful especially since the Internet is so broad it's hard to search for specific sites that focus on multiculturalism/diversity." The resource section appears to be a draw for future traffic, with some respondents suggesting they will check back for updated information: "The resource page looks very interesting and helpful. I feel like I will be visiting that page often."

Dialoguing. Dialoguing with other teachers was an important draw for many pre-service teachers who expressed a desire to learn more about bridging differences through multiculturalism in the classroom. "I think it is important to have a place to dialogue one's feelings about touchy issues like race, language, religion, special needs, etc. It is good to think in a deeper way about these subjects" wrote one visitor. One goal of the site is to help practicing and pre-service teachers realize that discussing "touchy issues" may lead to the discovery of solutions that many might not be aware of otherwise. The site is also a place teachers can turn to for some exposure to cultural norms and beliefs that they might not otherwise have an opportunity to be exposed to, and to consider concerns they might not realize can develop into more serious issues if neglected. Another visitor commented, "This site is very useful, especially for teachers who may not have been exposed to different cultures, students with special needs, social classes, etc. This is important because teachers need to be aware of these issues in the classroom."

Respondents also seem to appreciate that the site offers some professional information on how to understand and better deal with problematic classroom situations if and when they do arise: "This site gives information as to how to deal with these issues which is a good thing because some teachers may feel that they cannot address certain issues without hurting someone's feelings." Collegiality is thus nicely preserved and supported by maintaining a professional standard while at the same time facilitating difficult and challenging dialogue related to diversity.

However, while this is obviously a commendable goal, a critical analysis of respondents' answers reveals a significant "color-blind" mentality is at play. This comes through in respondents' reflections, which presumes the absence of racial and ethnic considerations in teaching until these considerations are pointed out. That is, the discourse of respondents in their expressed desires to dialogue with other teachers reveals that, for the most part, race and ethnicity are not something they consider as a factor in their classrooms until it is called into existence through an incident which makes it impossible to ignore. For example, one respondent stated, "I thought this site was very useful because as educators you don't think of running into situations of students discriminating against others because they are different. This website gives good resources and it makes you think about what you would do in certain situations."

Rehearsing classroom situations. In addition to providing a space for dialogue, the site also provides a space in which to rehearse more desirable responses to difficult situations. Since the situations depicted on the site would very likely be highly uncomfortable should they actually happen, it can be difficult for a teacher to adequately assess the incident and respond appropriately. Of course, the option to rehearse challenging situations is one strategy in helping prepare for such occurrences. One respondent writes, "It brings to mind some of the possible situations that teachers may experience in the classroom and offers them a chance to think about various situations before they may actually be involved in them." Another commented "In a sense this site is a tool to prepare people for specific things that may come or happen." The format in which the site invites participation is also a positive aspect for visitors: "It introduces scenarios in real time format . . . This is better than simply reading from a book because it is more engaging."

For the most part, many respondents failed to acknowledge, in their responses, any awareness that racial or gendered discrimination happens in classrooms. This ignorance preserves the status quo with its silent assumptions. Roughly 75% of respondents describe the classroom as a lake of social calm, prone to isolated spontaneous eruptions from under the surface, rather than a space that is already full of racial, ethnic, and gender dynamics. Despite this, it is encouraging that many respondents are interested in learning about other people's points of view: "I am going to appreciate reading the views that fellow educators have on certain teaching issues and learn about how they would handle a problem differently than I would. Hopefully I receive some great advice on how to handle these situations."

Universities that prepare teachers continually grapple with the questions of what their students "should" know about diversity and social justice and how to teach them the skills to recognize and appreciate these differences. Despite the last 40 years of multicultural, intercultural, cross-cultural, social justice, and diversity scholarship, we still have not gotten it right. We still have not figured out what is best for teachers and students in regard to diversity issues, and we are a long way from helping them with this through technology. One possible avenue, though, is *social simulation technology*.

Interacting with the ICCTP Site

The ICCTP Interact section focuses on activities or resources that are interactive for users. This section provides access to discussion forums, an "ask a professional" page, downloadable software, and the Clover program (Bailey, Tettegah, & Bradley, 2006; Tettegah, Bailey, & Taylor, 2007) for users to create their own social simulations.

Animated Narrative Vignettes (ANVs)

Simulation technology has already been extensively used for a variety of educational purposes. In medical schools, students use simulations as a way to practice and train prior to performing a real-life procedure (Chau, Chang, Lee, Ip, Lee, & Wootton, 2001; Regan de Bere & Petersen, 2006; Schachter, 2006). The United States Air Force uses flight simulators to train pilots, and the Air Force as well as commercial airlines require their students to use flight simulators prior to piloting airplanes in real-time flight (Dy, 2006; Jones & Laird, 1999). There is a great deal of information available on the use of simulations in science for teaching a specific skill; however, up until recently there has been a dearth of research on social simulations in education.

Social simulations are now being studied more frequently (Tettegah & Anderson, 2007; Tettegah, 2007). They are useful in that they can be based on relevant concerns for teachers and grounded in content taken directly from teacher, student, and parent narratives. ICCTP's simulations are not games, which are often pedagogically irrelevant, flashy, and reinforced by a positivist reward system. Instead, they depict real-life experiences developed completely from parents, students, and practicing and pre-service teachers.

Of all the resources available on ICCTP, one of the most important is Clover, a software application for developing animated narrative vignettes (ANVs) that is available free for download. Clover differs from traditional filmmaking applications because it is an application that enables those who use it to draw, animate, and add sound to animated vignettes—in ICCTP's case, simulations designed to engage educators in problematic situations that can occur in a typical classroom, based on real-life stories. Tettegah (2005) explained that the idea of using ANVs to engage educators in such situations originated from the use of vignettes, noting "observations of the vignettes involve reflection on [teachers'] own individual identities as social beings in our gendered, racialized, and class-originated society" (p. 379).

To come up with the stories for the ANV simulations available for viewing on the site, real-life examples from different people have been collected in narratives.[3] Stories can be collected in many different representations, such as texts, images, animations, sound, dance, movies, and so on. Close analysis of the collected narratives may surface other important variables that are not as obvious as easily recognizable examples of discrimination; for example, lowered expectations from teachers for minority students. With this contextualization, real-life stories can be transformed into animations that allow practicing and pre-service teachers to share perspectives and opinions about challenging situations with others from around the world.

With this in mind, the ICCTP site contains a number of ANVs that illustrate such problematic situations, and then collects the reactions of pre-service teachers to the question "What would you do if you were a teacher in this situation?"

"*What would I do?*" This question allows a teacher a place to "rehearse" what they might do in an uncomfortable situation. Interestingly, ANVs have a particular benefit in that the use of animation reduces extraneous variable affects. Many times when video vignettes featuring real people are used for instruction, those watching tend to focus on details such as what people are wearing or their size and less on the interactions and problems presented (Sleed, Durrheim, Kriel, Solomon, & Baker, 2002). Also, the situations depicted in the ANVs on the site might be disturbing in a real classroom, and it can often be difficult for a teacher to act or react to the classroom incident synchronously. Comments on the ICCTP site reveal that 85% of participants were able to immerse themselves in a given situation and to think about related diversity issues as they affect classroom teaching and learning.

FIGURE 2

S<small>CREEN SHOT FROM THE</small> *B<small>ROWN VERSUS</small> B<small>OARD OF</small> E<small>DUCATION</small>* <small>VIGNETTE.</small> T<small>HIS</small>
<small>SCENE IS OF THE PARENT,</small> M<small>RS.</small> S<small>ORENSON, AND THE TEACHER,</small> M<small>RS.</small> P<small>AYSEN</small>

ANVs seem to work almost like a virtual reality (VR) environment for participants. VR, also referred to as simulation, is a powerful way to project one's self into a realistic situation electronically. According to Riva et al. (2004), virtual reality is "a communication interface based on interactive 3D visualization, able to collect and integrate different inputs and data sets in a single real-life experience" (p. 3). ANVs shown on ICCTP were able to collect a wide variety of outputs (feedback) from users, thus providing information on teacher assumptions and beliefs. Theoretically, ANV simulations could be used in classes with diversity and equity content, as frameworks to provide lifelike experiences for students who are willing to learn from vivid imagery situations.

The ANVs on the ICCTP site deal with issues of gender, race and ethnicity, and physical appearance. One study's focus, based on responses from data collected at the ICCTP site, was on understanding how teachers might respond to a parent–teacher interaction over a student who believes she experienced racial discrimination from her middle school math teacher (see Figure 2) (Tettegah, 2007; Tettegah & Anderson, 2007). We wanted to learn more about whether pre-service and practicing teachers felt empathy for a student who felt discriminated against; to whom in the interaction they expressed concern; and what other type of reactions they displayed toward the participants in the interaction (as portrayed in the ANV).

While doing critical analysis on the responses,[4] it became apparent that as many as 60% of the respondents did not clearly identify the perceived discrimination in the simulation (see Tettegah & Anderson, 2007, for details regarding coding). Only 24.4% of responses indicated empathy for the student. One example of empathy read:

I think that the teacher obviously is treating Jennifer different because of her race. Because of the teacher's racism, Jennifer is not able to perform at her full potential. I think that it is a shame that a teacher's ignorance and racism has a negative impact on a student's performance. In the education system, we need to make sure that all teachers are accepting of all minorities, and that no student is treated in a different manner simply because of race. The parent was very efficient in the way she approached the teacher.

More than 80% of the respondents focused on the parent of the student or the teacher. A comment that targeted the teacher in the ANV (40% of respondents) read:

I am flabbergasted at this situation, particularly the way in which the teacher responded to very polite, non-aggressive questioning from Mrs. Sorenson [the parent]. I was especially shocked at the conference and at the teacher's obvious lack of comfort at being in the room alone with two African-American people.

Another respondent wrote:

I think that the teacher is definitely racist and she has issues of her own. She seems uncomfortable even carrying on a conversation with a black woman and her black child. I think that it was interesting that the teacher brought in other teachers at one point because she could not handle herself. I have not heard or seen a situation like this before but I'm sure it occurs often among some teachers.

These proportions of responses are similar to results from previous studies conducted by Tettegah (Tettegah, 2005, 2007; Tettegah & Anderson, 2007), which reported that teachers seldom expressed "empathic concern" for students who felt victimized in some fashion, as demonstrated by any direct reactions to or about the students themselves.

Empathy for students, regardless of their background, is important, especially for student–teacher relationships, and this study is one of only a few to explore teacher empathy as a variable using ANVs (Bailey,

Tettegah, & Bradley, 2006; Tettegah, 2005, 2006; Tettegah & Anderson, 2007). Perhaps because of the lack of direct response to the student in the ANV, participants in the simulation generally failed to express a sense of concern and display empathy toward the student. ANVs have the potential to provide pre-service teachers with significant experiences in which they can gain self-knowledge to use when dealing with school conflicts, especially those that have a relation to a student's academic well-being. However, that does not mean that an ANV will directly change the attitude of teachers. Encouraging dialogue, discussion, and feedback can help pre-service and in-service teachers examine their responses and reflect on how they might appear to others in interactions. Responses can be used for a deeper discussion of classroom management as well as for developing powerful pedagogies. Using ANVs as social simulations can contribute to personal development for teachers, enabling them to become more responsive, patient, and self-aware educators; foster a deeper and richer conversation with other educators; and enhance multicultural consciousness in our classrooms, with the goal of eliminating disparities and bridging this digital divide (Tettegah & Anderson, 2007; Tettegah, 2005, 2007).

Conclusions

Pandharipande (n.d.) once said, "The most crucial aspect of diversity is not mere co-existence with others; it is the acceptance of the value of their 'otherness' and the willingness to change oneself in the pursuit of truth." Unfortunately, some teachers' exposure to equity, diversity, and multicultural topics manifest as celebrations or festivities a few times a year or as looking up resources on the Internet without engaging in any type of reflection. This distance prevents educators from truly valuing "otherness," especially when the exploration is defined primarily by small group discussions or writing papers. Through web-based technologies like ANVs, participants are able to reflect on issues from different and more challenging perspectives. Our data indicate that it is critical to engage teachers-as-students meaningfully when developing curriculum, using current technologies for both course content and instructional methods.

The purpose of the ICCTP site and its Clover and ANV simulations is to prepare pre-service and practicing teachers to experience, through a variety of web-based technologies, unexpected classroom situations which would provide the opportunity to consider issues related to diversity and equity in their classrooms. More ANV simulations are being developed and added to the site, based on our continued examination of the feedback from participants. It seems that the issues deemed "unimportant" by participants may raise red flags and lead us to examine our biases around diversity and classroom teaching. Recognizing these red flags, exploring them further, and bringing them to users' attention are ongoing tasks of the ICCTP site.

Ladson-Billings (2001) viewed multicultural education as "a composite" (p. 50), arguing that multicultural education can no longer be separated into discrete components. Correspondingly, the three main strengths of using a cultural portal like ICCTP—as an ICT resource tool, a space to dialogue, and a space to rehearse—must be viewed in their entirety. In particular, the complexities of dialogue and rehearsal show that sites such as these move far beyond the traditional role of a web portal, doing much more than simply providing information—instead provoking a sophisticated engagement from visitors that we hope will ultimately lead to shared perspectives and to empathic individuals who value "otherness" and who maximize the capabilities of information communication technologies for fostering these purposes.

NOTES

1. Websites and portals that provide further information on digital equity and the digital divide include The Digital Divide Network (http://www.digitaldivide.net/) and Digital Divide.org (http://www.digitaldivide.org/dd/index.html). Websites and portals that address multicultural education include the Multicultural Pavilion (http://www.edchange.org/multicultural/index.html); New Horizons for Learning (http://www.newhorizonsorg/strategies/multicultural/front_multicultural.htm); Tolerance.org (http://www.tolerance.org/index.jsp); Children L.E.A.D. (http://www.childrenlead.org/); and Understanding Prejudice (http://www.understandingprejudice.org/).

2. Of the 408 respondents, 75% identified themselves as white, 24% stated they were from underrepresented groups, and 1% identified themselves as Asian American. Feedback from surveys is being collected and will eventually be disseminated to teachers and teacher educators; in addition, we hope to use survey data in the long term to inform practice and training.

3. Stories are collected from pre-service teachers (as a course assignment) and practicing teachers (largely from workshops) after they have written them up. Student stories have been collected from students in Chicago (Tettegah & Neville, forthcoming).

4. Research assistants coded responses to vignettes using a grounded theory approach, organizing, coding, generating categories, testing the categories, and searching for hypotheses and explanations from the vignette responses. During the analysis, we noticed that a significant number of responses made no mention of the student. As a result, a coding format was developed that took close consideration of who respondents responded to, and how, and included the following response categories: 1) empathic target (i.e., did the participant direct any empathy towards the student?); 2) problem-solving strategies (i.e., in which ways did the participant express that they would address the problem?); 3) direction of focus of change (i.e., who did the participant express needed to change?); and 4) who if anyone was viewed as a victim.

REFERENCES

Appelbaum, P.M., & Enomoto, E.K. (1995). Computer-mediated communications for a multicultural experience. *Educational Technology, 35,* 49–58.

Au, K. (2006). Diversity, technology, and the literacy achievement. In M. McKenna, L.D. Labbo, R.D. Kieffer, & D. Reinking (Eds.), *International handbook of literacy and technology, Vol. 11* (pp. 363–368). Mahwah, NJ: Lawrence Erlbaum Associates Publishers.

Bailey, B.P., Tettegah, S., & Bradley, T. (2006). Clover: Connecting technology and character education using personally-constructed animated vignettes. *Interacting With Computers, 18*(4), 793–819.

Bolt, D., & Crawford, R. (2000). *Digital divide: Computers and our children's future.* New York: TV Books.

Chau, J., Chang, A., Lee, I., Ip, W., Lee, D., & Wootton, Y. (2001). Effects of using videotaped vignettes on enhancing students' critical thinking ability in a baccalaureate nursing programme. *Journal of Advanced Nursing, 36*(1), 112–119.

Dy, B. (2006). Airware. *Aviation History, 16*(6), 64–70.

Fox, S. (2005, October 5). *Digital divisions.* Pew/Internet, Pew Internet & American Life Project. Retrieved October 2, 2007, from http://www.ntia.doc.gov/reports/anol/NationOnlineBroadband04.pdf

Gorski, P.C. (2004). Multicultural education and progressive pedagogy in the online information age [Electronic Version]. *Multicultural Perspectives, 6*(4), 37–48.

Jones, R.M., & Laird, J.E. (1999). Automated intelligent pilots from combat flight simulation. *AI Magazine, 20*(1), 77.

Kuttan, A., & Peters, L. (2003). *From digital divide to digital opportunity.* Lanham, MD: Scarecrow Press, Inc.

Ladson-Billings, G. (2001). New directions in multicultural education: Complexities, boundaries, and critical race. In J.A. Banks & C.A.M. Banks (Eds.), *Handbook of research on multicultural education* (pp. 265–290). San Francisco: Jossey-Bass.

Pandharipande, R.V. (n.d.). Statement from the Office of Vice Chancellor for Student Affairs. Unpublished.

Regan de Bere, S., & Petersen, A. (2006). Out of the dissecting room: News media coverage of anatomy teaching and research. *Social Science and Medicine, 63,* 76–88.

Riva, G., Botella, C., Castelnuovo, G., Gaggioli, A., Mantovani, F., & Molinari, E. (2004). Cybertherapy in practice: The VEPSY updated project [Electronic version]. In G. Riva, C. Botella, P. Legeron, & G. Optale (Eds.), *Cybertherapy: Internet and virtual reality as assessment and rehabilitation tools for clinical psychology and neurosciences.* Amsterdam: IOS Press.

Schachter, A.D. (2006). Computational simulation of renal biopsy accuracy in focal segmental glomerulosclerosis. *Pediatric Nephrology, 21*(7), 953–957.

Sleed, M., Durrheim, K., Kriel, A., Solomon, V., & Baker, V. (2002). The effectiveness of the vignette methodology: A comparison of written and video vignettes in eliciting responses about date rape. *South African Journal of Psychology, 32*(3), 21–25.

Sleeter, C., & Tettegah, S. (2002). Technology as a tool in multicultural teaching. *Multicultural Education, 10,* 3–9.

Solomon, G., & Allen, N.J. (2003). Introduction: Educational technology and equity. In G. Solomon, N.J. Allen, & P. Resta (Eds.), *Toward digital equity: Bridging the divide in education* (pp. xvii–xxiv). Boston: Allyn Bacon.

Tettegah, S. (2002). Computer mediated social justice: A new model for educators. *Technology Trends, 46,* 27–33.

Tettegah, S. (2005). Technology, narratives, vignettes, and the intercultural and cross-cultural teaching portal. *Urban Education, 40*(4), 368–393.

Tettegah, S., & Anderson C. (2007). Preservice teachers' empathy and cognitions: Statistical analysis of text data by graphical models. *Contemporary Educational Psychology, 32*(1), 48–82.

Tettegah, S., Bailey, B.P., & Taylor, K. (2007). Clover: Narratives and simulations in virtual environments. *Journal of Negro Education, 76*(1), 43–56.

Tettegah, S. (2007). Preservice teachers, victim empathy, and problem solving using animated narrative vignettes. *Technology, Instruction, Cognition and Learning, 5*, 41–68.

Tettegah, S., & Whang, E.W. (2006). Building your own social simulations. In M. Grabe & C. Grabe (Eds.), *Integrating technology for meaningful learning* (5th ed., pp. C1–C42). Boston: Houghton-Mifflin.

Tettegah, S., & Neville, H. (forthcoming). Empathy among black youth: Simulating race-related aggression in the classroom. *Scientia Paedagogica Experimentalis. Special issue on bullying at school: Current trends for definition and prevention.*

Wiburg, K., & Butler, J.F. (2003). Creating educational access. In G. Solomon, N.J. Allen, & P. Resta (Eds.), *Toward digital equity: Bridging the divide in education* (pp. 1–13). Boston: Allyn Bacon.

U.S. Department of Commerce. (2004, September). *A nation online: Entering the broadband age.* National Telecommunications and Information Administration Access. Retrieved October 1, 2007, from http://www.ntia.doc.gov/reports/anol/NationOnlineBroadband04.pdf.

Technology Out of School: What Schools Can Learn From Community-Based Technology

OLGA A. VÁSQUEZ

Teaching and learning in out-of-school contexts has a long history of successfully adapting pedagogy to local and current needs of student participants. The innovative uses of technology, the flexible social organization, and the everyday relevance of out-of-school activities make these learning contexts ideal for innovation. Almost two decades of studying the benefits and challenges of creating innovative technology-based learning environments in after-school settings ostensibly demonstrates their cognitive and social benefits (Martinez & Vásquez, 2006; Vásquez, 2003). In this chapter, I draw on this work to theorize the feasibility of transporting the lessons learned about teaching and learning in this kind of context to the classroom setting. I begin with a brief sketch of the social conditions in contemporary America that call for the imaginative use of information and communication technologies (ICT) as critical tools for learning, then describe a technology-based intervention called *La Clase Mágica* that has shown tremendous promise for addressing the social and academic needs of language minority youth (Vásquez). I follow with a discussion of two types of valuable lessons that could be incorporated into classroom teaching and learning: those that easily fit with traditional modes of pedagogy and others that would require a "new paradigm of thought" for their implementation.[1]

Contexts for Change

At the onset of the 21st century, the reality was that most schools had the technology and the connectivity to explore teaching and learning in creative and unconventional ways. The spread of Internet access had been unprecedented, growing exponentially into every aspect of the human experience. In the 1990s, President Bill Clinton's "Technology

---

Olga A. Vásquez is an Associate Professor in the Department of Communication at the University of California, San Diego.

Literacy Challenge" addressed the issues of access and connectivity in schools across the United States. Today, nearly every school is equipped with computers and most families have a computer at home. The prediction that digital literacy would be a prerequisite for full participation in an information-based, global society is clearly evident in the social world, if not in the classroom of today (Pachon, Macias, & Bagasao, 2000). In the labor force, the uses of information technology are growing faster than the number of individuals with the knowledge and skills required to advance that technology. Even attitudes toward computers have shifted from an initial distrust and annoyance to a common belief that computers improve the quality of both education and life. Families who have traditionally not been in the forefront of technological advancement are increasingly using the Internet as a way of maintaining family ties, through email, instant messaging, and web postings.

In this new social reality, the most critical problem facing teachers is how technology can be used to "define educational visions, prepare and support teachers, design curriculum, address issues of equity, and respond to the rapidly changing world" (Gordon, 2000, p. 14). Schools and teachers face three critical challenges in adapting education to meet the social and economic realities of this technology-based globalized world: (1) boosting the slow pace of incorporating new technologies into the core of the instructional program; (2) shifting the notion of technologies as a learning tool or enrichment activity to that of a "functional prothesis" that extends the power of the brain for learning (Battro, 2004); and (3) bridging not only the digital but also the cognitive gap that underserved populations suffer around the world (Warschauer, 2003). In short, ICT have yet to form the basis of the instructional program, exceed the traditional pedagogy in fundamentally new ways, or be applied uniformly across income and racial groups. The innovative use of technologies is the exception rather than the rule, happening in select classrooms where individual teachers have both the vision and the skills (Cuban, 2001).

The Slow Pace of Incorporation

By all indications, a great majority of teachers do not take advantage of the available access and connectivity to the Internet and do not use information technology to achieve new ways of enhancing the intellectual capacity of learners, relying instead on the customary acquisition of bits of knowledge that are disconnected from the learning context. In spite of the pervasiveness of advanced technologies and their growing significance in peoples' daily lives, teachers continue to use computers sparingly, as enrichment activities, and/or to "sustain patterns of teaching rather than to innovate" (Cuban, 2001, p. 135). Paradoxically, this pattern does not change even in places where the local context is technologically advanced, such as the Silicon Valley in the San Francisco Bay Area, the acclaimed hotbed of the information revolution. Cuban, for example, found that among the teachers he studied, 85% of them rarely used computers, if at all. Teachers considered "serious users" (10% of them) used computers only once a week and less than 5% of teachers integrated computers into the regular curriculum and instructional routines. In short, very few teachers used computers as a central component of the instructional program.

The entrenchment of the culture of schooling is the likely source of this reticence (Gallego, Cole, & LCHC, 2001; Vásquez, 2005). As Elmore (1996) has found, the core of schooling—i.e., the teaching and learning—is resistant to change. In fact, the organizational structure of the classroom has not changed for the past 2,000 years. The teacher continues to stand in front of a group of learners, seated neatly in a series of rows, as the only authority in the room. It is exactly this hierarchical structure, the strict adherence to a Western canon, and the singular focus on the individual that the new vision of a technology-based education threatens to disrupt with the availability of alternative sources of knowledge outside the classroom and the facility for collaborative engagement in the generation of new knowledge.

Impediments to New Forms of Transformative Pedagogy

The application of innovative and cognitively enhancing technology-mediated learning is indeed a tall order for overworked teachers and overstressed schools. High-stakes testing fueled by the accountability craze (McNeil, 2000; Valenzuela, 1999) and underpreparation of teachers does not allow teachers the time or the energy to develop new forms of teaching and learning. As Linda McNeil points out, the accountability craze of the last decade has stripped teachers of their creativity and their expertise. According to the California Teachers Association (n.d.), schools are spending more time on a narrow curriculum and filling out forms in order to comply with the government's demands for data and higher scores. These demands provide little time for experimentation and cross-discipline collaboration, critical foundational elements of technology-based curriculum. Under the specter of a reclassification to "Program Improvement Schools"—i.e., schools that have failed to demonstrate Adequate Yearly Progress—teachers and schools are hard-pressed to demonstrate progress. They have little or no energy for the risk-taking that is needed to explore and discover new avenues for developing technology-mediated instruction. To complicate matters, accountability measures do not serve as diagnostic tools that can generate more strategic instruction, but rather focus on program evaluation. Thus, the "opportunity costs," the time teaching to the tests that could otherwise be used for instruction, are especially high and fall particularly on English learners and students with disabilities (Zellmer, Frontier, & Pheifer, 2006).

Cognitive and Digital Divides

The unevenness of the material access and the prevalence of the cognitive and digital divide along socioeconomic and racial lines are vexing problems for technology-based reformers. Poor schools, for example, are less likely to provide Internet access than wealthy schools (DeBell & Chapman, 2006), preventing minority youth from immersing themselves in "an ocean of possibilities" afforded by the Internet (Battro, 2004, p. 82). Charron (2005) found that 38% of Spanish-dominant learners and low-income students respectively rely solely on schools for Internet access. Teachers who do not want to single out students often do not assign homework requiring information technologies, handicapping them even more.

Warschauer (2003) notes that the intellectual quality and literacy building power of computer activities are unevenly distributed along ethnic and economic lines. Students from higher income backgrounds receive greater access to cognitive enhancing activities, while minority youth from low-income communities are differentially relegated to repetitive, uninspiring activities. One group is provided with a motivating and enlightening mechanism for learning (Schofield, 1995) that research is beginning to link to academic achievement (Pastor-Relaño & Vásquez, 2005) and the other is relegated to the realm of irrelevance (Vásquez, in press), managed through "drill and kill" activities. The result is what Warschauer calls "social and economic stratification or exclusion" (p. 29), which is compounded by the likelihood of these students also attending underfunded schools with a high proportion of unqualified teachers (Vásquez, in press).

The problem of computer use in education is not limited to minorities; it is more complex than that. The slow pace of the incorporation of advanced technology-based pedagogy and the entrenchment of out-of-date pedagogy limits the development of what Ulmer (2002) calls "electracy"—the skill and facility necessary to exploit the full communicative potential of new electronic media—as well as cognitive development, visual intelligence, and access to information skills that potentially facilitate communication, improve education and labor market prospects, and accomplish everyday tasks quicker and better (DeBell & Chapman, 2006). In an age in which *information* rather than money or goods is the valued commodity, where creativity and flexibility are privileged, and multiple languages and cultures are assets rather than liabilities, the absence of these skills is debilitating. It is critical that the educational system of the United States produce workers and citizens for a world saturated with electronic media. To maintain its prominence in the international community, education must make a significant and aggressive shift from an industrial model of education to one that is based on knowledge and information, and it must be done within a very short time to catch up with a future that is already here (Vásquez, 2006a).

After-School Technology Intervention

This crisis in education makes after-school programming an attractive intersection to examine technology-based pedagogy. Outside the school's field of ideological production (Bourdieu, 1977), away from the accountability forces and the top-down administrative structures, researchers and practitioners who focus on after-school have much more flexibility to imagine and institute ideal worlds where learners can achieve optimal possibilities with the use of technology (Vásquez, in press). Out-of-school technology, that is, technology used in community-based and educationally oriented after-school programs, shows much promise for providing valuable lessons about creating innovative learning environments for all students and for facilitating the academic and social integration of a growing number of minority youth (Cummins, in press). These new technology interventions can more flexibly encourage the requisite skills needed for a knowledge- and information-based society than the traditional school curriculum, which is tied to a prearranged scope and sequence regime. Suárez-Orozco and Qin-Hilliard (2004) admonish us that the skills privileged in a globalized world are very different from those being promoted by the schools:

Taking multiple perspectives, reversing mental routines, and articulating multiple hypotheses from a common set of facts and working through the logical and rational vectors that would best explain those preexisting facts are crucial features of human intelligence. (p. 5)

The malleability of after-school contexts make them ideal venues for testing the viability of innovative technology-supported learning environments, nonstandard sources of knowledge, and futuristic visions of a new world order with its corresponding vision of education, the learner, and the citizen (Vásquez, in press). The loose power structure provides the flexibility to tweak the system according to newfound knowledge or the availability of new technological advances and allows for the discarding of methods and technology that do not fit the ever-changing goals and objectives of the respective contexts. The scope and sequence regiment of school is sidestepped for a flexible pace and progression determined by individual interest and ability.

The Benefits of After-School

With the kind of freedom to diverge from the formality of school, what can after-school teach traditional school about creative technology-based pedagogy? Extant research and almost 2 decades of work in after-school settings leads me to the conclusion that there is much promising practice in after-school programs that could be useful during regular school hours. Nationwide, research on after-school programs repeatedly shows the positive impact it has on participants' safety, behavior, social skills, and self-confidence (Gayl, 2004; Heath & McLaughlin, 1994). The After School Corporation (TASC) of New York; the 21st Century Community Learning Centers (21st CCLC); the Extended-Service Schools (ESS) initiative; and San Francisco Beacons Initiative (SFBI) show that participation in after-school programs has a positive effect on grades and work habits, behavior in school, and emotional adjustment and peer relations, and promotes a greater sense of belonging to the community.[2] The National Institute on Out-of-School Time (NIOST) and the Forum for Youth Investment (2002) identify the following connections between participation in quality after-school programs and traditional school:

- In supporting the development of a range of non-academic competencies—i.e., social and critical thinking skills—after-school programs support young people's academic learning.
- The frequent and close contact with caring and encouraging adults provides young people with critical developmental input that helps to ensure academic success and promotes full engagement and preparation to succeed in school.

- After-school programs offer rich alternatives that often are not available during the regular school day, providing further opportunities for development and enrichment.
- After-school programs eliminate the consistent barriers to learning faced by young people who may otherwise have been unreachable because of disruptive behavior, lack of interest, poor sense of self, or repeated failure in more structured contexts.
- After-school programming is part of a larger "developmental space" that intentionally links to other settings in which young people grow and develop—e.g., counseling, health, and recreation services (p. 6).

The Fifth Dimension

One of the foremost after-school initiatives that has attempted to address the cognitive, academic, and social needs of children has been sponsored by the Laboratory of Comparative Human Cognition (LCHC) at the University of California, San Diego (UCSD) (Cole & The Distributed Literacy Consortium, 2006; Vásquez, 2003). Much of this work has centered on an activity system called the Fifth Dimension, which is designed to link the resources of the university with community institutions to both study and promote the learning potential of children using a computer-based pedagogy. Collaborators at LCHC began by trying to address the educational needs of learning disabled children within the school structure, but found the after-school hours more flexible for manipulating both the curriculum and the relations of power to achieve maximum interaction between children and adult participants (LCHC, 1982). With support from undergraduate students enrolled in a university course, researchers created a fictional world in which the power of adults was diminished in direct proportion to the increases in the power of the participating children. The model system evolved into a university and community partnership held together by an after-school computer-based activity founded on play and education and an undergraduate course that applied theory to practice as a means for creating and studying innovative learning environments (Cole, 1997).

Within these conditions, researchers and practitioners have continually tweaked the ecological learning system in response to the emergent needs and interests of the participants and the learning contexts. In pursuit of both promoting and studying learning, this approach aims at opening zones of possibilities for young participants who attend the after-school sites (Moll & Greenberg, 1990). Adult–child collaborations are organized to create an opportunity structure in which the learner collaborates with a more experienced peer (Vygotsky, 1978). This approach has provided researchers and participants alike the opportunity to test the potential of ICT to create innovative learning environments and to study its effect on language, literacy, and cultural development. As Lucy Friedman, president of TASC, says in the foreword to the book written about the Fifth Dimension program (Cole & The Distributed Literacy Consortium, 2006):

The philosophy that undergirds the Fifth Dimension—that children will benefit from a learning environment that is not simply "more school" but that does support what is learned during the school day—is reflected in the computer activities, which are less structured and more fun than those in school and yet are not just games. (p. xiv)

After-school programs modeled after the Fifth Dimension have sprung up around the world and seek to study culture and cognitive development in nonhierarchical, computer-based learning environments that are based on play and education. One of these variations is *La Clase Mágica*, a bilingual/bicultural adaptation focused on the academic achievement of language minority youth and their representation in higher education. In 1996, when the University of California dismantled affirmative action, a combination of the *La Clase Mágica* and Fifth Dimension models was adopted at all of the university's nine campuses under the umbrella of a multicampus, intersegmental faculty initiative called UC Links. At the height of state funding, UC Links sponsored up to 40 after-school programs in low-income, minority communities (see http://www.uclinks.org for more information).

Today, researchers worldwide have appropriated this methodology and constructed after-school activity systems to study local issues relating to language and literacy practices (Gutiérrez, Asato, Santos, & Gotanda, 2002; Moll, 1992), the relationship of school to the social integration of minority groups (Mijandos & Romero, 2006; Vásquez, 2003) and the linking of important contexts to human development (González, Moll, & Amanti, 2005).

La Clase Mágica

Building on the Fifth Dimension's protean character, *La Clase Mágica* added bilingualism and biculturalism to the original curriculum, an extended "developmental space" to its organizational structure, and a strategic focus on the melding of old and new knowledge to its computer-based pedagogy (Vásquez, 2006b, in press). Using Vygotsky's interventionist methodology, *La Clase Mágica* made the study of the academic achievement of minority youth and their representation in higher education key components of its research agenda (Vásquez, 1996). It sought to link important contexts for human development through a cross-system infrastructure of collaboration for sharing costs, expertise, and newly generated knowledge. Examples of the developmental spaces making up this system include the Head Start Program, the recreation room at two housing projects, the education center at an American Indian reservation, the university and community college classrooms, the enrichment hour at school, and the research staff meetings. Aligning these learning contexts has allowed us to metaphorically conceive the proverbial "educational ladder," and thus, study the developmentally driven changes in pedagogy and uses of technology that take place at each level of the system.

In 2007, *La Clase Mágica* encompassed a federation of six community-based programs spread across San Diego County. Jointly, UCSD, Palomar Community College, and the Center for Academic and Social Advancement (a non-profit organization that grew out of the community effort at the original site) provide the intellectual resources and institutional support to carry out the daily activities of the after-school sites. Every year, the two higher education institutions together provide the sites with approximately 90 undergraduate students to work closely with the child participants. Almost 25 community and education units across San Diego County constitute the functional system that serves the educational needs of approximately 300 children and 25 parents each year.

A three-quarter practicum course on Child Development at UCSD offers one quarter that focuses specifically on the viability of information and computer technology for making the difference in bridging the cognitive and digital divide that minority learners face.[3] Applying theory to practice—i.e., mobilizing sociohistorical theories of learning and development—undergraduate students create opportunities for learners to achieve their optimal potential as they move through a series of computer-based activities involving Internet searches, educationally-oriented computer games, and online chats with an electronic entity called *El Maga* (see Vásquez, 2003 for details). Over the years, student analyses have questioned whether the capacity of computer technology can bring about substantive change on its own power or whether it requires a specific type of technology-based pedagogy to accomplish the goals of enhancing learning and development in innovative ways. These deliberations have been instrumental in driving the continuous change and reflection that characterizes *La Clase Mágica*.

Much of the attraction of the children to *La Clase Mágica* has been the series of computer games that are organized in a maze format, setting the stage for collaborative dialogue between the learners and their undergraduate *amiga/os*. Importantly, the maze also sets up the context for creative imaginings about their capabilities vis-à-vis the endless possibilities that the games afford them for learning. As the children move from imaginary room to imaginary room, solving problems and accomplishing tasks, they master new information skills connected to the games in a natural and uneven manner. The learner not only practices everyday skills and language embedded in the activities; he or she also acquires the norms and expectations of an acculturated member of the system. From the very first step—when the child is asked to choose one of four possible points from which to enter the maze—the journey demands active and deliberate participation. At the end, having made hundreds of other decisions about which direction to take, what game and level to play, and what language and culture to use, the child exits the maze as a transformed being—one with expert knowledge of how things work at *La Clase Mágica*. At that point, the first-level participant assumes the role of Wizard Assistant, the highest rank of expert in the system (apart from *El Maga*) (see Vásquez, 2003 for details).

The changes in social conditions as a result of the economic and cultural processes taking place worldwide have increasingly pressed *La Clase Mágica* to alter its theoretical foundation and research lens to reflect the new realities of the 21st century (Vásquez, 2006a, in press). In particular, its focus on the affordances of technology-supported environments has intensified to include the new competencies that are privileged in a globalized world—e.g., financial literacy, entrepreneurship, health and nutrition, environmental studies, and digital literacy. At the beginning of its 19th year—the fall of 2007—*La Clase Mágica* opened with multiple Internet and computer activities that fostered the development of global citizenship skills and sensibilities, global awareness, cultural understanding, environmental concern, and health awareness.

What Can Schools Learn From After-School Education-Oriented Programs?

Much of the work that examines the impact of after-school on children's learning makes claims about the benefits of participation in after-school programs on classroom learning. For example, Blanton,

Moorman, Hayes, and Warner (1997) make the case that the special experience in Fifth Dimension after-school programs is transferable to the school. Penuel and Kim (2000) and Martinez and Vásquez (2006) also point out the positive effects of after-school programs on participants' learning and community engagement. However, it is not the transferability of learning from one context to another that is addressed in this chapter; rather it is the pedagogical insights that have been gained from almost 2 decades of continuous tweaking of a particular kind of after-school computer-based pedagogy. Many of these lessons can be transported to the classroom, but only under two separate conditions: (1) that these lessons can be applied within a traditional pedagogy; and (2) that the instructional program welcomes a new "paradigm of thought," much like Luke's (2000) notion of "cyber-school" (p. 81), that incorporates a new cultural perspective, a new language, and new forms of interrelating with both people and media.

What Is Readily Transportable?

Hundreds of course studies that my "Practicum in Child Development" undergraduate students have carried out in after-school programs, situated in both schools and community-based institutions, reveal four key lessons that teachers can readily adopt within the classroom or during innovative playtime activities:[4]

1. The importance of the social aspect of computer-mediated learning.
2. The essential value of collaborative inquiry activities in learning and development.
3. The social and cognitive value of mixing play and education.
4. The advantages of building partnerships with families, community, and business.

Rich social context. Our research consistently confirms extant research that claims that the computer alone cannot enhance cognitive development or modify social behavior (Crook, 1994; Schofield, 1995). Learning is highly dependent on a dialogically rich social environment (Cummins, in press; Vásquez, 2003, in press; Wells, 2000), however, around the computer, it is ever more crucial. Warschauer (2003), for example, shows this quite clearly in his study of several contexts in which computers were made available without the technical assistance and support of the community. He showcases an Irish town and the "hole in the wall" experiment in New Delhi, India as examples of "people's ability to make use of that device and line to engage in *meaningful social practices*" (p. 38, emphasis in the original). These same findings are confirmed by the studies of novice anthropologists—the undergraduate students enrolled in the course linked to *La Clase Mágica* field sites.

Students have repeatedly noted that when children are placed in front of the latest in advanced computers, the use of headphones and computer programs such as "SuccessMaker" deprive them of critical elements for learning and development—i.e., social cues, expert assistance, and the opportunity to explore. The difference between the nature of *La Clase Mágica's* nonhierarchical and self-directive structure in which goals are achieved collectively in a free flow manner and the more structured individually centered classroom was noted in many of the field notes written by students who carried out their practicum at two sites that were situated in schools (Vásquez, 2005). The "culture clash" was even more pronounced when the activity was held in the classroom during prep time and within earshot of the teacher. The students documented in their field notes that although teachers did not take part in the program activities themselves, they insisted on a turn-taking structure in adult–child interactions and often intervened from across the room to discipline children for not following school rules, telling them "not to talk, goof off, or speak without raising their hands" (student field notes, February 1, 2007). At the other within-school application of *La Clase Mágica*, the school opted to use only SuccessMaker, a computer-based learning software based on a behaviorist learning theory of drill and practice.[5] The undergraduate students who attended the site reported that the computer had become a form of "computerized ditto sheets" leading to boredom and disengagement (student field notes, January 18, 2007). This same student further documents the obstacles to innovative uses of the technology that children encounter playing SuccessMaker:

If the subject gets a certain number of questions correct, the questions will start getting more difficult, if the child is not doing so well with problems, he or she stays at the same level. If they pass 20 or more problems with 80% or more problems correct, they are free to use the program to access the Internet. On the Internet, they are *only* allowed to go to PBSkids.com which has games, coloring activities, and stories based on the different children's TV shows (including Barney and Teletubbies). A majority of the students do not receive 80% or better on their section and therefore do not get to use the Internet.

Play and collaboration. Two constituent elements of the technology-based pedagogy of *La Clase Mágica*—collaboration and the mixture of play and education—are critical aspects of cognitive and social development (Cole, 1996; Rogoff, 1998; Vásquez, 2003; Vygotsky, 1987), particularly around the computer. Vygotsky, for example, claims "with collaboration, direction, or some kind of help, the child is able to do more and solve more difficult tasks than he can independently" (p. 209). Rogoff goes further to say that collaboration is a cognitive process. This central focus on collaboration, in particular between expert and novice participants, has been foundational to the development of the culture of collaborative learning on which the Fifth Dimension model is based (Nicolopoulou & Cole, 1993). Thus, one of the goals of technology-based after-school programs based on socio-historical theories of learning and development has been to provide opportunities for novice learners to reach their optimal potential in collaboration with those with more expert knowledge and skills. The undergraduate assistants, called *amiga/os* at *La Clase Mágica*, are charged with scaffolding the children's progress in socially rich collaborative relations of exchange that make enhanced social, academic, and technical skills possible.

Although programs differ significantly in terms of their structure and goals, it is safe to say that after-school programs promote positive youth development across multiple domains (Eccles & Gootman, 2002), particularly when they incorporate play and collaboration as central features of their activities. Around the computer, we have found that the invaluable experience of expert peers facilitates the development of the child's attention span, his or her orientation to the task, longer and more meaningful engagement, and the fine-tuning of social skills. Undergraduate researchers frequently focus their course research on the difference in collaboration around homework and computer activities and invariably confirm Schofield's (1995) finding that collaboration around computer use is richer, longer, and more engaging and enjoyable than other classroom activities. The following segment of a longer field note written by one of the undergraduate students illustrates the unexpected but valuable learning that can emerge from computer-mediated collaboration:

Gina was coloring a picture on the computer of a boy looking into a pond, and she made this boy's hair black and his face pink. The *amigo* asked Gina what nationality she thought the boy in the picture was. At first the child said, "I dunno," but then the *amigo* explained what nationality meant and gave an example of a nationality like European. This inspired a conversation about Gina's nationality as well as what she thought people of other nationalities looked like. (Student field notes, February 7, 2007)

In the classroom or the lunchroom, this type of goal-directed interaction with peers is often not permitted. Instead, as our research in two schools reveals, teachers admonished children for talking to their peers, limiting their abilities to develop their social and academic skills (Vásquez, 2005). If, as Schofield (1995) points out, computers in the classroom make it difficult for teachers because they "put new and different demands on teachers and can change classroom process and structure" (p. 191), then they can try to incorporate computer activities outside the instructional program—during free play, recess, homeroom, or in-class play-stations when the teacher can get extra help in the classroom from parents, aides, volunteers, or mentors.

Developmental spaces. Another important lesson from after-school that can easily be taken up by the schools without challenging the integrity of the traditional pedagogy is the inclusion of important contexts for human development as mechanisms for bringing about effective change in the individual as well as the society. The latest reports of the Policy Studies Associates in Washington (Reisner, 2007) has found that "when all parties with responsibilities for and interests in the welfare of youth, especially disadvantaged youth, unite to engage young people in high-quality after-school experiences, communities are more likely to succeed in promoting positive development for the largest number of youth at risk" (p. 1). Thus, the social milieu—i.e., relevant cultural systems (i.e., the family, community, and educational systems) and multiple institutional contexts (i.e., the individual schools, research units, funding organizations, and various learning sites such as the classroom, after-school learning settings, and staff meetings)—influence child development in multiple ways (Bronfenbrenner, 1977; Rogoff, 1994; Wells, 2000; Wertsch, 1985) and must be taken into consideration in planning a technological intervention (Warschauer, 2003). Building an elaborate cross-system collaborative provides a socializing system for the developing learner, citizen, and worker (Martinez & Vásquez, 2006).

This cross-system collaborative effort supports the mission and development of each of its integral components, creating the opportunity for systemic change. Structurally, these social and electronic linkages help bridge distances, social groups, and education levels to communication and coordination frameworks that correspond effectively with the K–16+ educational pipeline initiatives being mobilized in universities across the country. The outcomes of such relationships create new pathways to circulate accumulated knowledge throughout the system (Vásquez, 2003). Thus, each part of this multilevel system contributes to the formation of new visions of learners and the institutions that serve them. As more of these types of partnerships spring up all over the country in an effort to work together in supporting children's learning in school, even sharing sensitive data such as children's test scores (CNN, 2006), the classroom is bound to change.[6]

Other valuable lessons can, of course, be garnered from after-school research and practice. However, as I argue elsewhere (Vásquez, in press), their transportability to the classroom is contingent on the kind of learning environment that is available, goals and objectives that are delineated for the individual, and a concern for learning that is collaborative, dialogic, and literacy enhancing as well as deep, active, and community-based (Cummins, in press; Vásquez). The technology-based pedagogy that I propose grows out of years of testing the viability of innovative technology-supported learning environments, exploring nonstandard sources of knowledge, and imagining new visions of education from a position of flexibility and relative freedom (Vásquez). Given the right combinations of conditions, I believe that it is not only possible but also essential for this kind of pedagogy to flourish in the classroom.

While this may seem straightforward for typical classroom instruction, the experience of our two after-school programs in schools reflects a complex tension between the ideals of the technology-based pedagogy that I propose and more conventional education systems. Problems such as technological, institutional, and theoretical boundaries, experienced in all kinds of technology-based programs as Yagelski and Powley (1996) noted, are amplified in the schools where we worked. Although our activities were set apart from the instructional program, at times these boundaries seemed insurmountable obstacles to our theoretically informed pedagogy. Our programs faced technical standards—i.e., firewalls and platforms—and official guidelines—i.e., time schedules, procedures, acceptable images—and theoretical and practical approaches to the learner, content, and instruction that strained insider–outsider relations, thwarted the project's culture of optimal learning, and intensified disciplinary issues (Vásquez, 2005). These experiences highlight the tensions that an "outsider" agency has within the structure of the school, as well as the difficulty that a new way of thinking encounters vis-à-vis the school culture (Gallego, Cole, & LCHC, 2001)

The toughest obstacle for an "after school" pedagogy is the issue of what type of learning is acceptable in the classroom. Learning in after-school programs as reported by Penuel and Kim (2000), Miller (2003), and others seems readily transportable; however, it is the kind of learning that goes beyond what is possible with pencil-and-paper tasks—learning which may be emergent, unplanned, or unidentifiable and will face the greatest scrutiny and lack of acceptance (Vásquez, in press). Cross-disciplinary research advocated by Gardner (2004) and by Gee's (2003) theories about the 36 learning principles he believes are designed into video games (and by extension into the surrounding social context) have received little uptake by reformers in spite of the fact that they "fit better with the modern, high-tech, global world today's children and teenagers live in than the theories (and practices) of learning that they see in school" (Gee, p. 7).

A New Paradigm of Thought

In spite of this apparent reticence, it is critical to carve out and experiment with the possibilities of a new paradigm of thought. We must envision what it would be like if education were truly about providing optimal and relevant opportunities for learners to be pre-pared for the social, technical, and economic realities of the 21st century. Such a vision calls for a technology-based pedagogy that embodies transformative goals for the use of technology (Schofield, 1995, p. 224). In sociocultural terms, this means that the goals of technology should be the transformation of both the classroom culture and the learner's developmental trajectory from novice to expert at whatever level they find themselves in. Using Cole's (1995) notion of culture-as-medium, this calls for organizing, a priori, the right combination of conditions to help children learn and develop in new and emergent ways. Our research and practice over the years offers three insights that lays down the foundation for a new paradigm of thought for technology-based education:

1. Seeing the learner, learning context, and content in new and emergent ways.
2. Working within a culture of optimal learning.
3. Positing the computer as a mindtool rather than a "ditto machine."

New Ways of Seeing

One of the major lessons we learned from working within the context of the school is that our project staff had different ways of seeing the learner, the role of the teacher, the learning context, and the content than school personnel did (Vásquez, 2005). Outside of the material and philosophical motivations for enhancing children's achievement and the social development both the school and *La Clase Mágica* hoped to encourage, we each held divergent theoretical understandings regarding the abilities of the learner and the proper course of action. We saw the learner in a state of readiness, willing and able to move to the next level of development with expert support. The school personnel, on the other hand, labeled the learners who were referred to the program as "at-risk" and in need of remedial treatment. In the classroom, children's learning was guided toward a specific skill by the didactic guidance of the teacher. At *La Clase Mágica*, children were guided by movement inscribed in the representation of a 20-room maze printed on an 8 × 11 sheet of paper (see Vásquez, 2003 for details). In the classroom, children were motivated by the individual evaluation of their performance; at the after-school program, by the movement to another computer activity that resulted from collaborative engagement with peers and/or undergraduate pals. In the classroom, fear of failure and teacher disapproval motivated children to stay on task. At *La Clase Mágica*, the *amiga/os'* gentle prodding and their own driven motivation to "win" kept them engaged.

The vision of the "new classroom" that I propose posits the teacher as *collaborator*. The adults—both the undergraduate students and the site staff—are theoretically informed to build on the child participants' multiple knowledge sources and their variety of capabilities. Their goal is to scaffold the learners' optimal potential by providing guiding questions, mnemonic devices, personal experiences, and Internet search engine demonstrations. Our experiences in the two in-school sites confirmed Luke's (2000) assertion that once teachers (authority figures) are free from "the 'batch processing' of students through a 'mass-market basic curriculum' they will 'manage the pace of their [students'] online learning'" (p. 91). That is, when undergraduates and adult staff concentrate on extending the learning potential of their child collaborators at the child's own pace and direction, behavioral issues are infrequent. When hierarchical, rule-oriented relations and designated content are imposed on the children, behavioral problems increase.

Misbehavior grew out of the tensions between the culture of *La Clase Mágica* and the culture of school—e.g., talking without raising hands, getting too excited about completing an electronic activity, and speaking too loudly with co-collaborators. This seeming "free-for all" ran counter to expectations of the classroom (Gallego, Cole, & LCHC, 2001; Vásquez 2005), and many times, it was I who ended up in the principal's office explaining the need for children to speak freely in collaborative engagements around the activities. I explained that, instead of focusing on managing social and personal behavior, the role of adults was to dialogically scaffold the progress of the learner through a continuous series of what Griffin and Cole (1984) call "leading activities" leading to the learner's proximal development.

Our studies found the content of our activities as open and emergent as the role of the teacher and the abilities of the learner previously described. Content is not scripted by one monolithic culture, but is open to new sources of knowledge that frequently go outside the learning context and the adult's experience—moving beyond earlier notions of a *culturally* relevant curriculum to one that is *globally* relevant. Our data from the after-school site located at a local American Indian reservation, for example, teach us that conceptions of multiculturalism and culturally relevant curriculum were appropriate for one particular target group—in our case, Mexican origin children—and not applicable to another. We learned that it is possible and desirable to make connections to the children's own lives and to the lives of those outside of their local communities through a variety of literacies—media literacy, print literacy, and electrecy. The learners' multitude of understandings of the world was easily juxtaposed with those of others' experiences near and far. We found that computer and information technology provided excellent opportunities for these kinds of activities, and provided the vehicle for maintaining a living history, reinforcing and/or acquiring the local language or second language, and learning about learners' similarities and differences vis-a-vis other cultural groups.

A Culture of Optimal Learning

The new paradigm of thought that I propose builds on Nicolopoulou's and Cole's (1993) notion of the *culture of collaborative learning* in which adults and children negotiate meaning as equal and collaborative partners. In nonhierarchical relations of exchange, the adult and child draw on multiple worlds to solve problems or co-construct new knowledge. Our research lens has increasingly zoomed in on the significance that optimal goals play in the culture of the six after-school sites we have studied for years. Participation and collaboration, of course, continue to play a critical role in cognitive development; however, what I argue is that optimal learning is foundational to the goals and objectives of the learning context. We found that the right combination of conditions that help the learner grow and develop to his or her optimal potential included intent collaboration, a cognitively rich environment, and the validation of the learner's cultural and linguistic resources. These conditions made it possible for the learner to engage actively and dialogically in activities in which he or she could draw from multiple resources to achieve new understandings of the self and the world.

To achieve a new paradigm of thought in which we can meet these kinds of goals, the culture of optimal learning has to be written into the very fabric of the system of artifacts that make up the learning context. At *La Clase Mágica*, this included the instructional guides (task-cards), adult–child interactions and the computer games and activities that constituted the learning context. Every interaction, every activity must be structured to open zones of possibilities for learners to develop their interests and their emergent skills. Learners must be afforded their complete linguistic, sociocultural, and academic repertoire as intellectual tools, along with access to alternative ways of knowing that are available in and outside the learning context (Gutiérrez et al., 2002). The facility of ICT to access, store, and create knowledge is integral to this type of learning ecology. Thus, "the power to know what others know" is put in the hands of the child participants (Papert, 1993). At an early age, child participants will be able to mobilize their intellectual resources to access the technical and cultural capital they need to prepare for higher education and a global community of learners.

Mind Tools

Typically, activities in after-school programs encourage participants to search the Internet for information that is purposeful, timely, and outside the learning context. They search for information that will help them move through a game after they complete their homework or complete a photographic journal on such topics as low riders, the latest hip hop stars, or their family's history. Alone or in collaboration with a peer or adult, they seek knowledge that leads them to new ways of thinking, doing, and seeing themselves (Gee, 2003). According to Gardner (2004, p. 254), this is a contrast to the measurable bits of "information, concepts, [and] definitions" that are called for in the classroom. Rather than simply managing or entertaining, the computer can provide endless opportunities for child-generated inquiries that lead to discovery, creation, and management of new knowledge. Its feedback capabilities allow the learner to make an imagined situation visible, explore its infinite possibilities, and uncover some of one's own inherent potentialities. Achieving such a level of engagement with computers and information technology heightens the possibility for developing creativity, a skill highly regarded in the global economy. As the "power to know" shifts from the teacher to the learner, learners learn a new way to organize experience. They encounter a set of expectations about what it means to know and understand (Turkle, 2004, p. 97) and they become critically aware of the role they play in the world.

Playing computer games and exploring the Internet are some of the ways in which computer and information technology spurs the flight of the imagination. Learners can take a task, collaboratively develop it, change it completely, or reject it and start something altogether new. It is critically important to emphasize the difference of these technology-enhanced environments in particular—computer games have cognitive value, in contrast to what many people may believe (Gee, 2003). Learning is both the process and the product of good computer games, not only because of "the theory of learning" inherent in their design (Gee), but because they also lend themselves to a rich dialogic context for language and literacy development. Our research and on-the-ground experiences at *La Clase Mágica* demonstrate that the use of computer games not only facilitates learning but also encourages it. As Hopkins (2005) points out, "Technology can be used to engage students in ways that other tools cannot," in particular with students who have little access in the home—students from low-income minority backgrounds who can greatly benefit from a deeper engagement in cognitively enhancing activities.

These three foundational components of a new paradigm of thought are critical to an education of the future. Of course, they can be adapted to classroom technology-based instruction in varying degrees but the ideas of a new learner in a new context with technology-supported content and instruction are irreducible. The teacher-coach, for example, could reject commercial games for activities that free the student to actively and critically explore the boundaries, meanings, and (inter)relationships of self, the task, and the learning environment and/or that include any other learning principles that Gee (2003) identifies. He or she could very well set aside the notion that students must first complete a prescribed level of competence before introducing new material and allow students of different abilities to collaborate on unfamiliar material. And, most importantly, teachers could refuse to use ICT for "drill and kill" activities and instead use them for mind-extending explorations.

An Alternative Vision

The new model of education that I propose marks a shift from privileging select groups, content, and theoretical perspectives to a more open type of education that I call an "education of the future" (Vásquez, 2006a)—a future that the recurring innovations in technology remind us is already here. Far-reaching, complex, and interactive change is the catalyst for a system that must be responsive to a world marked by a new emphasis on globalization. It is an education that prepares individuals to be citizens as well as workers in a world that is in constant flux at every level of our social experience. At no other time in history has it been more evident that there is a blaring disconnect between technology-based instruction in the classroom and what students are able to do with technology outside the classroom. They come to the classroom versed in the social and technical possibilities afforded by iPods, virtual worlds like Second Life and My Space, and the ubiquitous cell phone. They know how to seek, store, replay, share, and construct knowledge in ways that counters the unilinear, unifocal knowledge transmission of the classroom.

The aim of this chapter has been to offer lessons we consider valuable for optimizing children's learning potential, in hopes of helping teachers crack open the core of schooling that has been so resistant to change (Elmore, 1996). Although these lessons were acquired in contexts with a relative amount of freedom to tweak the system according to emergent needs and interests, they can still provide a window for what is possible and necessary if schools are truly to attend to achieving the optimal potential of their students while preparing them at the same time for a world that privileges critical and reflective skills related to collaboration, cooperation, problem solving, systems thinking, and technological literacies.

NOTES

1. I wish to thank my students in my course, "Education and Global Citizenship," offered through the Department of Communication at UCSD; especially Kyle Samia, for suggesting that in order to conceptualize an education that prepares global citizens it was necessary to shift into a new paradigm of thought.

2. For more information, see these organizations' websites: TASC of New York (http://www.tascorp.org/); the 21st CCLC (http://www.ed.gov/programs/21stcclc/

index.html); the ESS initiative (http://www.education.ky.gov/KDE/Instructional+
Resources/Student+and+Family+Support/Extended+School+Services); and SFBI (http://
www.sfbeacon.org/).

3. The other two quarters focus on the ways that gender, language, and culture intersect with access to educational resources, particularly for language minority youth.

4. At least one academic quarter a year for the last 15 years, undergraduates enrolled in the "Practicum in Child Development" course offered through the Department of Communication and Human Development Program at UCSD focus their ethnographic studies on the intersection of technology and learning and development at after-school computer-based field sites where they serve as collaborators with children from Mexican origin and American Indian communities.

5. The school bought the math version of SuccessMaker and cycled grades 1–3 through it during the sessions that had been arranged for the *La Clase Mágica* activity.

6. For 3 years, *La Clase Mágica* and the Neighborhood House Corporation (NHC) shared blind STAR scores of children attending both *La Clase Mágica* and the local Head Start Program that NHC oversaw. The two schools also shared blind scores of the STAR scores of participants and nonparticipants for within and across school comparisons.

REFERENCES

Battro, A.M. (2004). Digital skills, globalization and education. In M.M. Suárez-Orozco & D.B. Qin-Hilliard (Eds.), *Globalization, culture and education in the new millennium* (pp. 78–96). Berkeley: University of California Press.

Blanton, W.E., Moorman, G.B., Hayes, B.A., & Warner, M.L. (1997). Effects of participation in the Fifth Dimension on far transfer. *Journal of Educational Computing Research, 16*, 371–396.

Bourdieu, P. (1977). *Outline of a theory of practice*. Cambridge: Cambridge University Press.

Bronfenbrenner, U. (1977). Toward an experimental ecology of human development. *American Psychologist, 32*, 513–530.

California Teachers Association (n.d.). Erase, rewrite and reauthorize! Reauthorizing ESEA/NCLB: Seven myths of No Child Left Behind. Retrieved August 31, 2007, from www.cta.org/.../0/4ESEANCLBEraseRewriteandReauthorizeSevenMythsof NoChildLeftBehind41907.doc.

Charron, C.-Y. (2005). *From the digital guide to digital opportunities: Measuring infostates for development*. Montreal: Orbicom.

CNN (2006, July 13). Afterschools tap school records to get to know students. *CNN Reports*. Retrieved August 30, 2007, from CNN.com%20%20Afterschools%20tap %20school%20records%20to%20get%20to%20know%20students%20-%20Jul %2013,%202006.html

Cole, M. (1995). Culture and cognitive development: From cross-cultural research to creating systems of cultural mediation. *Culture & Psychology, 1*, 25–54.

Cole, M. (1996). *Cultural psychology: A once and future discipline*. Cambridge, MA: The Belknap Press of Harvard University Press.

Cole, M. (1997). A model system for sustainable university-community collaboration. In N.H. Gabelko (Ed.), *Cornerstones of collaboration: A publication of the Berkeley National Writing Project Corporation* (pp. 113–119). Berkeley: University of California Printing Services.

Cole, M., & The Distributed Literacy Consortium (2006). *The Fifth Dimension: An after-school program built on diversity*. New York: Russell Sage.

Crook, C. (1994). *Computers and the collaborative experience of learning*. London: Routledge.

Cuban, L. (2001). *Oversold and underused: Computers in the classroom*. Cambridge, MA: Harvard University Press.

Cummins, J. (in press). Technology, literacy, and young second language learners: Design-
    ing educational futures. In L.L. Parker (Ed.), *Technology-mediated learning environ-
    ments for young English learners: Connections in and out of school*. New York: Taylor &
    Francis Group.
DeBell, M., & Chapman, C. (2006). *Computer and Internet use by students in 2003* (NCES
    2006-065). U.S. Department of Education. Washington, DC: National Center for
    Education Statistics.
Eccles, J., & Gootman, J.A. (Eds.). (2002, November). *Community programs to promote
    youth development. Policy Brief*. Washington, DC: National Academy Press.
Elmore, R. (1996). Getting to scale with good educational practice. *Harvard Educational
    Review, 66*(1), 1–2.
Gallego, M.A., Cole, M., & The Laboratory of Comparative Human Cognition (LCHC).
    (2001). Classroom cultures and cultures in the classroom. In V. Richardson (Ed.),
    Handbook of research on teaching (4th ed., pp. 951–997). Washington, DC: American
    Educational Research Association.
Gardner, H. (2004). How education changes: Considerations of history, science and
    values. In M. Suárez-Orozco and D. Qin-Hilliard (Eds.), *Globalization: Culture and
    education in the new millennium* (pp. 235–258). Berkeley: University of California
    Press.
Gayl, C.L. (2004). *Afterschool programs: Expanding access and ensuring quality*. Retrieved
    August 3, 2006, from http://www.ppionline.org/documents/afterschool_0704.pdf
Gee, J.P. (2003). *What video games have to teach us about learning and literacy*. New York:
    Palgrave/Macmillan.
González, N., Moll, L.C., & Amanti, C. (Eds.) (2005). *Funds of knowledge: Theorizing
    practices in households, communities, and classrooms*. Mahwah, NJ: Erlbaum.
Gordon, D.T. (Ed.). (2000). *The digital classroom: How technology is changing the way we teach
    and learn*. Cambridge, MA: The Harvard Education Letter.
Griffin, P., & Cole, M. (1984). Current activity for the future: The zo-ped. In B. Rogoff
    & J.V. Wertsch (Eds.), *Children's learning in the zone of proximal development:
    New directions for child development* (No. 23, pp. 45–64). San Francisco: Jossey-
    Bass.
Gutiérrez, K., Asato, J., Santos, M., & Gotanda, N. (2002). Backlash pedagogy: Language
    and culture and the politics of reform. *The Review of Education, Pedagogy, and Cultural
    Studies, 24*(4), 335–351.
Heath, S.B., & McLaughlin, M.W. (1994). Learning for anything everyday. *Curriculum
    Studies, 26*, 471–489.
Hopkins, G. (2005, January). Tech & teaching: Principals share best uses of classroom
    technology. *Education World*. Retrieved August 12, 2007, from http://www.
    educationworld.com/a_admin/admin/admin387.shtml
Laboratory of Comparative Human Cognition (LCHC). (1982). A model system for the
    study of learning difficulties. *Quarterly Newsletter of the Laboratory of Comparative
    Human Cognition, 4*(3), 39–66.
Luke, C. (2000). Cyber-schooling and technological change: Multiliteracies for new
    times. In M. Kalantzis & B. Cope (Eds.), *Multiliteracies: Literacy learning and the design
    of social futures*, (pp. 69–91). New York: Routledge.
Martinez, M., & Vásquez, O.A. (2006). *Sustainability: La Clase Mágica beyond its boundaries*.
    Unpublished manuscript.
McNeil, L.M. (2000). *Contradictions of school reform: Educational costs of standardized testing*.
    New York: Rutledge.
Mijandos, J.C., & Romero, F. (2006). *Mundos encontrados/Táantanil Yo'okol Kaabil. Análisis
    de la educación primaria indígena en una comunidad del sur de Yucatán*. México: Ediciones
    Pomares.
Miller, B. (2003). *Critical hours: Afterschool programs and educational success*. Dorchester,
    MA: Nellie Mae Education Foundation.

Moll, L., & Greenberg, J. (1990). Creating zones of possibilities: Combining social contexts for instruction. In L. Moll (Ed.), *Vygotsky and education: Instructional implications and applications of sociohistorical psychology* (pp. 319–348). Cambridge, MA: Cambridge University Press.

Moll, L.C. (1992). Literacy research in community and classrooms: A sociocultural approach. In R. Beach, J. Green, M. Kamil, & T. Shanahan (Eds.), *Multidiciplinary perspectives in literacy research* (pp. 211–244). Urbana, IL: National Conference on Research in English.

Nicolopoulou, A., & Cole, M. (1993). The Fifth Dimension, its play world, and its institutional context: Generation and transmission of shared knowledge in the culture of collaborative learning. In E.A. Foreman, N. Minick, & C. Addison Stone (Eds.), *Contexts for learning: Sociocultural dynamics in children's development* (pp. 283–314). New York: Oxford University Press.

National Institute on Out-of-School Time and the Forum for Youth Investment (2002). After school issues. Retrieved August 24, 2007, from http://www.niost.org/publications.html.

Pachon, H., Macias, E., & Bagasao, P. (2000, October). Minority access to information technology: Lessons learned. *Occasional Paper No. 67 Latino Studies Series*. Michigan State University: Julian Samora Research Institute. Retrieved August 20, 2006, from http://www.jsri.msu.edu/RandS/research/ops/oc67.pdf

Papert, S. (1993). *The children's machine: Rethinking school in the age of the computer*. New York: Basic Books.

Pastor-Relaño, A.M., & Vásquez, O.A. (2005). *Accountability of the informal: Challenges and new directions*. Unpublished manuscript.

Penuel, W., & Kim, D. (2000). *Promising practices and organizational challenges in community technology centers*. Menlo Park, CA: V Streets Research Group, SRI International. Retrieved June 14, 2006, from http://www.sri.com/policy/ctl/assets/images/vStreets_Promising_Practices.pdf

Reisner, E.R. (2007, March). *Charting the benefits of high-quality after-school program experiences: Evidence from new research on improving after school opportunities for disadvantaged youth*. Washington, DC: Policy Studies Associates, Inc.

Rogoff, B. (1994). Developing understanding of the idea of communities of learners. *Mind, Culture, and Activity, 1*(4), 209–229.

Rogoff, B. (1998). Cognition as a collaborative process. In D. Kuhn & R. Siegler (Eds.), *Handbook of child psychology: Fifth edition. Vol. 2, Cognition, perception and language* (pp. 679–744). New York: John Wiley & Sons.

Schofield, J.W. (1995). *Computers and classroom culture*. New York: Cambridge University Press.

Suárez-Orozco, M.M., & Qin-Hilliard, D.B. (Eds.). (2004). *Globalization: Culture and education in the new millennium*. Berkeley: University of California Press.

Turkle, S. (2004). The fellowship of the microchip: Global technologies as evocative objectives. In M.M. Suárez-Orozco and D.B. Qin-Hilliard (Eds.), *Globalization: Culture and education in the new millennium* (pp. 97–113). Berkeley: University of California Press.

Ulmer, G.L. (2002). *Internet invention: From literacy to electracy*. New York: Longman.

Vásquez, O.A. (1996). Model systems of institutional linkages: Transforming the educational pipeline. In A. Hurtado, R. Figueroa, & E. Garcia (Eds.), *Strategic interventions in education: Expanding the Latina/Latino pipeline* (pp. 137–166). Santa Cruz, CA: University of Santa Cruz.

Vásquez, O.A. (2003). *La Clase Mágica: Imagining optimal possibilities in a bilingual community of learners*. Mahwah, NJ: Lawrence Erlbaum.

Vásquez, O.A. (2005). Social action and the politics of collaboration. In P. Pedraza & M. Rivera (Eds.), *Educating Latino youth: An agenda for transcending myths and unveiling possibilities* (pp. 321–343). Mahwah, NJ: Lawrence Erlbaum.

Vásquez, O.A. (2006a, April). A pedagogy of the future. *Pedagogies: An International Journal, 1*(1), 43–48.

Vásquez, O.A. (2006b, October). *Technology and culture: Taming the complexity of diversity.* Paper presented at the International Conference, Cultural-Historical Psychology: Current Situation and Perspectives, Moscow State University of Psychology and Education. Moscow, Russia,

Vásquez, O.A. (in press). Reflection: Rules of engagement for achieving educational futures. In L.L. Parker (Ed.), *Technology-mediated learning environments for young English learners: Connections in and out of school.* New York: Taylor & Francis Group.

Valenzuela, A. (1999). *Subtractive schooling: U.S.–Mexican youth and the politics of caring.* Albany: State University of New York Press.

Vygotsky, L.S. (1978). *Mind in society.* Cambridge, MA: Harvard University Press.

Vygotsky, L.S. (1987). Problems of general psychology. In R.W. Rieber & A.S. Carton (Eds.), *The collected works of L. S. Vygotsky.* Volume One. New York: Plenum. (Orig. pub. in 1934)

Warschauer, M. (2003). *Technology and social inclusion: Rethinking the digital divide.* Cambridge, MA: MIT Press.

Wells, G. (2000). Dialogic inquiry in education: Building on the legacy of Vygotsky. In C. Lee & P. Smagorinsky (Eds.), *Vygotskian perspectives on literacy research: Constructing meaning through collaborative inquiry,* (pp. 51–85). Cambridge: Cambridge University Press.

Wertsch, J.V. (1985). *Vygotsky and the social formation of mind.* Cambridge, MA: Harvard University Press.

Yagelski, R.P., & Powley, S. (1996). Virtual connections and real boundaries: Teaching writing and preparing writing teachers on the Internet. *Computers and Composition, 12,* 25–36.

Zellmer, M.B., Frontier, A., & Pheifer, D. (2006). What are NCLB's instructional costs? *Educational Leadership, 64*(3), 43–46.

E-Lessons Learned

NICHOLAS C. BURBULES

The value of this National Society for the Study of Education collection is to bring together different disciplines, different genres of writing, and different perspectives focused upon a shared question: how new e-learning technologies can have a transformative effect on the classroom, but why, for various reasons, they have yet to do so.

I want to take as my keynote a quote from Chris Dede's (this volume) opening essay:

> We must consider that the primary barriers to altering curricular, pedagogical, and assessment practices towards any ICT-based transformative vision are not conceptual, technical, or economic, but instead psychological, political, and cultural. The largest challenges in changing schooling are people's emotions and their almost unconscious beliefs, assumptions, and values. To be achieved, a transformative vision must generate the professional commitment and political will to realize a major shift in education. (p. 11)

Dede captures both the scope of rethinking that is needed for transformation and the barriers to achieving it. As I will discuss here, much of this rethinking does not involve the affordances of new learning technologies per se—although they remain widely misunderstood and underused. It has just as much to do with an unwillingness to rethink or change (or give up) other aspects of the institutional practices and norms of education as carried out in most school settings. Questions of teacher authority, "coverage" of material, and the isolation of school activities from learning that takes place in other contexts (and vice versa) are all impediments to realizing the transformative potential presented by new learning technologies. The essays in this collection challenge us because they represent the problem as a systemic one: schools, higher education and professional

Nicholas C. Burbules is Grayce Wicall Gauthier Professor in the Department of Educational Policy Studies at the University of Illinois. His research focuses on philosophy of education, teaching and dialogue, critical social and political theory, and technology and education.

development programs, national policy, all reinforce in each other a resistance to change. Each feels constrained by the actions of the others. No one knows where to start.

Ubiquitous Learning[1]

My own view is that we need to turn the very complexity and interdependence of these seemingly disparate domains into an advantage. Technological and cultural changes have accelerated the emergence of a highly mobile, networked society. We live in a world of ubiquitous technology, and education needs to be understood in this context. Ubiquitous learning is often equated with the expression "anytime, anywhere" learning. In contemporary markets, the instantaneous and highly customizable availability of services and information is becoming a standard branding device. This ranges from being able to send and receive text messages from your cell phone to 24/7 customer service hotlines. I want to press the idea of ubiquitous learning beyond an "anytime, anywhere" marketing slogan and suggest five interrelated dimensions along which its meaning can be fruitfully extended.

First, there is a spatial sense of ubiquity (the "anywhere" half of the previous slogan). In developed societies, digital technologies are always around: not only in computers and other overt computing devices, but in cars, in public kiosks, and so on. Regional wi-fi means that Internet access is only a click away, wherever you are. From a learning standpoint, spatial ubiquity means continual access to information to an extent that we have never witnessed before. The traditional distinction of formal and informal education is blurred once we recognize that physical location is no longer a constraint on where and how people learn; the processes of learning and memory themselves may be changing as people are less required to carry around in their heads all that they need to know to get through a day effectively—instead, if you need something, you can always look it up. I will return to this theme later.

Second, there is a portability aspect to ubiquity: handheld computing devices, even "wearable" devices, are becoming more commonplace. Portable devices *can* always be with you—which tends to establish and reinforce a social expectation that they *should* always be with you. The portability of these devices, in turn, creates new kinds of social practices—young people who no longer wear watches but use their phones to keep track of time; the many uses and conventions of text messaging that are created simply by virtue of the expectation that others will be constantly online and available. A program in Ireland, sponsored by the National Centre for Technology in Education, was intended to help young people learn and preserve the Celtic language. The program gave them free mobile phones with grammar and vocabulary software already loaded; the instructors wanted to be sure that wherever participants were they could immediately access linguistic information, and it made more sense to use a device that young people would always have with them, knew how to use, and was already seamlessly integrated into their daily social and linguistic practices. (Of course, they were constantly using the phones as phones too.) I cannot think of a better, simpler encapsulation of the principles of ubiquitous learning—in this case, learning reinforced by portability and practical integration into the activities of daily life.

Third, there is ubiquity in the sense of interconnectedness. Automobiles now come equipped with global positioning systems (GPS) and dashboard devices that can tell you where the next gas station or hospital is. Driving on the highway, you can find a hotel, estimate your arrival time, and book your reservation while you are still 500 miles away. For the learner, this interconnectedness creates an "extensible intelligence," extensible in two related senses. Technologically, one's knowledge, memory, and processing power are enhanced by constantly available devices that can supplement and support what we are able to do in our own heads. Socially, one is perpetually in contact with others who may know things or who may be able to do things that we cannot do ourselves. In a real sense a person can be smarter because he or she has access to networked intelligence, whether it is technologically or socially distributed, or both. Educational agencies, for all age levels, have yet to come to grips with the question of what knowledge, skills, and capacities people *do* still need to carry around in their heads, and which ones may be less necessary than they used to be. What is necessary knowledge for the future, and what does this portend for standard views of curriculum?

Fourth, there is ubiquity in a practical sense: how new technologies blur sharp divisions between activities or spheres of life that we have traditionally viewed as separate. Work/play, learning/entertainment, accessing/creating information, public/private are distinctions that conceptually might never have been as clear-cut as our usage suggested them to be; but for a host of social and cultural reasons they are becoming increasingly untenable as sharp distinctions today. These changes are not all technological in nature, at least not directly so; changes in popular culture, in the nature of work, in the structure and activities of home or family life, and so on, have brought with them a host of different expectations and ways of thinking about where, how, when, and why learning takes place. It is not just that the traditional monopoly of those places we call schools and those times we call "class periods" as the sole or even primary sources of learning is being challenged. More substantively, the entire economy of attention, engagement, and motivation to learn needs to be rethought. Learning as a practical human activity, which is always embedded in a wider network of social and institutional contexts, needs to be seen in relation to a new set of genres and practices.

Fifth, there is ubiquity in a temporal sense; the "anytime" dimension of anytime, anywhere (which is of course closely linked with spatial ubiquity and constant interconnectedness). But this temporal shift goes beyond the simple language of "24/7" availability; it reflects a *changed* sense of time. The use of recording devices to "time-shift" television shows and the growing prevalence of asynchronous modes of communication (e.g., in online education programs) reflect a certain customization of scheduling. This yields different expectations and practices that change one's subjective relation to time—of trying to conform the timing of events to one's habits and preferences, and not only vice versa. These new and varied rhythms suggest a different relation, in turn, to learning opportunities—easy availability and convenience, but also a pacing and flow that are more continuous, that allow "stopping in" and "stopping out" at different intervals. Every moment is potentially a learning moment, not only in the quotidian way in which that was always true—but in the sense of structured, intentional learning opportunities, more seamlessly integrated into the routine practices of home, work, and entertainment.

Another, related sense of temporal ubiquity involves the idea of "lifelong learning," but now instantiated in a new way. Generally this term refers to principles of adult and continuing education; but in the present context it expands to mean the truly perpetual availability of learning opportunities and a changed set of expectations about *continual* growth and development of skills and knowledge. It is almost a cliché now to talk about frequent career changes, the need to upgrade skills and knowledge even within an ongoing career, and the shifting demands of a knowledge economy. But "lifelong learning" here means something more: it means that learning is not relegated to a certain age or time, a certain institutional setting, or a certain set of externally oriented motivational structures. Rather, in this changed worldview, *to be is to learn.*

The School as a Knowledge Enterprise

In the picture of education I am sketching here, the nature and activities of schooling will have to change. This means that traditional boundaries need to be broken down in both directions: not only sending new and different kinds of "homework" home with students, but bringing *into* the classroom activities involving other learning tools and resources that have not typically been seen as elements of schooling. Schools, and teachers in schools, need to think of themselves not as the sole (and perhaps not even the primary) source of learning for many of their students—especially students above a certain age—but as *brokers* of a certain sort.

The school, in this model, is a kind of hub: a place that brings together, coordinates, and synthesizes disparate learning resources. The "spokes" radiating out from this hub are the connections to other learning places and activities; many of them largely if not entirely separate from the control or influence of educators. Where educators do still have a crucial influence is in helping young people evaluate and integrate the varied learning experiences they have in these other, less planned environments. Educators also have an important role to play as equalizers between those students who have a tremendous range and number of such opportunities outside school, because of their family situation or location, and those who have far fewer opportunities. In a system of mandatory education, the school is still the one common learning place students share, and that gives it a unique and important responsibility compared with other learning places. But starting from this premise yields a different basis for planning about what needs to take place there, one that links school aims and activities much more fundamentally to learning that is taking place elsewhere.

We see this same perspective in Olga Vásquez's claim, here, that schools can learn important principles of e-learning from after-school programs, including:

- The importance of the social aspect of computer-mediated learning
- The essential value of collaborative inquiry activities in learning and development
- The social and cognitive value of mixing play and education
- The advantages of building partnerships with families, community, and business

In addition, Vásquez points to the failings of teacher education and professional development to realize this transformed vision of learning and the interdependence of learning contexts. Charalambos Vrasidas and Gene Glass echo this theme in their chapter, calling for new models of professional development that, among other things, require teachers to engage in ICT activities based on real-world, authentic contexts; encourage the use of ICT for collaboration; and provide opportunities for informal learning and support.

James Pellegrino and his co-authors document similar failures in pre-service teacher education:

No clear vision about the role of technology in transforming the teaching and learning process was apparent in the rhetoric or execution of the IHE [Institutions of Higher Education] programs. Furthermore, the data on instructional episodes reveal remarkably limited evidence of deep and powerful integration of technology into the learning environments experienced by prospective teachers. Most of that integration was restricted to the use of technology as an information-presentation and content-delivery tool. (p. 82)

Steve Jones and his coauthors make clear that this is not a unique aspect of teacher education programs but a characteristic of higher education more generally; the Pew survey data show that, outside of learners in online programs, student uses of the Internet are almost entirely limited to information gathering, communication with professors, and communication with each other—valuable activities, but activities that are basically *supplements* to the classroom curriculum, and in no way transformations of their modes of learning. Ironically, perhaps, this is taking place during a time when in extracurricular contexts young people are using technology in a wide range of productive ways: from producing YouTube videos to reading and creating blogs. But these activities have little relevance or impact on their learning, or vice versa.

How might we explain the lost opportunity to take advantage of new e-learning technologies to change the practices of teaching and learning in formal, institutional settings? The chapters in this collection indicate some of the answers.

Hilary Goldmann's chapter points to a shortfall at the national policy level. While the E-Rate program has effectively channeled resources into purchasing hardware and equipment, companion programs such as E2T2 and PT3 have failed to keep pace with training and professional development. Geneva Haertel and her coauthors, and James Pellegrino and his, document both a lack of planning and a lack of systematic research to assess what is being done in schools, what is not being done, and what needs to be done differently if the potential of these new technologies is to be more fully exploited.

One way to think about this problem is that education, ironically, has yet to see itself fully integrated into the ethos of a knowledge society, compared with many other institutions. What do I mean by this? A knowledge enterprise is not just concerned with the transmission of knowledge, but with the continual generation of new knowledge, as well as the reflective production of knowledge about its own activities and processes. These new technologies make possible not only communicative and productive activities; they also allow the collection and analysis of information about those activities, in a process that Haertel and her coauthors call "technology-supported formative assessment" (p. 103). Pellegrino and his coauthors call for building a stronger knowledge base about technology availability, use, and impact. A fully integrated knowledge enterprise would planfully design these processes for generating self-knowledge into the ways technologies are used, and then use that knowledge for further redesign and improvement. Educational institutions, whether K-12 or higher education, ought to be leading in this area—but they are trailing. Ironically, such a path of innovation would provide a much better answer to the demands for accountability being leveled against educational institutions, but within a framework that they design and control for their own purposes.

Another aspect of rethinking education as a fully integrated knowledge enterprise is to see a much closer connection between the processes of teaching and learning in pre-service and professional development contexts and the kinds of teaching and learning we want to happen in schools. Pellegrino and his coauthors make these concluding observations:

> ... one implication of contemporary approaches to learning is that teacher candidates need to experience, and not just listen to lectures about, different ways of teaching. . . . As Grossman wisely noted, research on how prospective teachers are taught is of critical importance, because most research on teacher education focuses on the structure of programs rather than on issues of instruction. In teacher education, she argues, "*how* one is taught is part and parcel of *what* one teaches." (p. 60)

Our current understanding of technology's role in teaching and learning goes well beyond the benefits of using general technology tools; it now incorporates specific materials and instructional programs that have been shown to dramatically change what is learned and how well student mastery of the content can be monitored and supported through intelligent, content-based assessment practices. For example, technology tools can provide access to simulations, visualizations, video-based problem-solving environments, concept mapping, graphing applications, and computational aids such as calculators and spreadsheets. (p. 60)

Yet one must also ask, given this argument, how widely used these technology tools are in the teacher education process itself. Until we reconsider the generation of knowledge *about* teaching and *within* teaching through the same transformative lens we say we want to apply to student learning, we will be squandering an historic opportunity. Dede adds:

Little time is spent on building capabilities in group interpretation, negotiation of shared meaning, and co-construction of problem resolutions, particularly in behaviorist and cognitivist instructional strategies. The communication skills stressed are those of simple presentation, rather than the capacity to engage in richly structured interactions that articulate perspectives unfamiliar to the audience . . . [T]o prepare students for 21st century work and citizenship, the usage of sophisticated ICT based on a complementary pedagogical theory, situated learning, is a vital supplement to current educational technologies. In particular, situated forms of instructional design are better suited than behaviorist, cognitivist, or constructivist approaches to teaching sophisticated "problem finding" as the front-end of the inquiry process for making meaning out of complexity. . . . In essence, situated learning requires authentic contexts, activities, and assessment coupled with guidance from expert modeling, situated mentoring, and legitimate peripheral participation . . . (pp. 21, 22, 23)

Dede then goes on to describe three kinds of immersive and collaborative environments that can foster the benefits of situated learning in the classroom: the "world-to-the-desktop" interface; multi-user virtual environments (MUVEs); and augmented reality (AR).

It may seem paradoxical to talk about simulated and virtual environments in this way. In several of these chapters we see the familiar ideas of "authentic context" and "situated learning" invoked to talk about e-learning possibilities. But for the casual observer anything technology-based in this way cannot be "real." This is another way in which our thinking needs to be challenged. Elsewhere I have argued that the "virtual" should not be thought of in contradistinction to the "real," but as a more commonplace experience that is not necessarily technology-based. At the same time, for the learners of this generation, a host of online experiences and interactions are very "real" to them

(Burbules, 2005). The issues are complex here, and simple dualities no longer suffice, I believe. But the key point for this discussion is that these *online* contexts are very much "situated" and "authentic"—and they have all the same characteristics that make them salient for learning. They are domains of complex practice; they are highly social; they are personally and collectively important; they have significant emotional and cognitive impact. Learning *is* taking place there, and indeed some of the *most* important learning is taking place there.

These new spaces for learning, ubiquitous and virtual, represent tremendously exciting possibilities and the chapters in this collection show the way toward a transformed teaching and learning environment. Yet they also reveal one other impediment to achieving this reality for all learners. The "digital divide" literature is now widely familiar; but in ordinary usage it still is thought about primarily in the context of unequal access to the *means* of technologically enhanced learning. More recent studies have shown that the *content* of e-learning environments can also be an impediment—and unless we are mindful of the ways in which "the same" content is perceived and reacted to by different learners, we will simply be providing "equal access" to a profoundly unequal learning experience (Burbules, Callister, & Taaffe, 2006). Mark Warschauer's chapter describes not just one divide, but five, which need to be addressed, each challenging and difficult in its own way; solving one does not mean solving the others. He also asks us to go "beyond access," to recognize also the importance of providing opportunities for what he calls "deeper learning" of the sort described here. Sharon Tettegah et al.'s chapter *shows* how this can be made possible by integrating the themes of multicultural education and difference in the classroom into the teacher education and professional development process. Her means of doing so exemplify the possibilities of incorporating the same technology innovations (simulations, virtual narratives, and critical case-study analysis) into the teacher learning process that we are expecting teachers to incorporate into the student learning process. The pedagogy of teacher education, she argues, needs to be changed if we expect teachers to change their own pedagogy.

In a ubiquitous learning environment, I have been arguing, learning is not just "anytime, anyplace"—the nature of learning itself is changed. It is changed across certain spatial, temporal, practical divides that we take for granted, as these divides become increasingly blurred, if not even erased. The chapters in this collection challenge many of these divides, and ask us to see the domains of policy, research, assessment, and changing professional practice in closer relation to each other—as, indeed, themselves learning environments, properly conceived. Once viewed as such, many other questions become more clear: why the adoption and diffusion of new e-learning methods have been so slow in education at all levels; why the age-old truth that "we teach as we were taught" (as Pellegrino et al. remind us) represents such a severe constraint on imagining truly different educational possibilities; and why current approaches to national accountability *restrict*, rather than *encourage*, significant experimentation and innovation in the classroom. A learning orientation reframes these domains as knowledge-generating opportunities that can mutually inform and support one another in an ongoing, continual process of inquiry, development, and growth. This is not a new idea; you can find variations of it throughout John Dewey's writings and those of others. But in the present context, this wisdom about the interdependence of multiple learning domains is reinforced by the increased use of portable, networked, and mutually supporting learning technologies. The real revolution still lies ahead of us.

NOTE

1. This section is abbreviated and adapted from Burbules (forthcoming).

REFERENCES

Burbules N.C. (forthcoming). The meanings of ubiquitous learning. In B. Cope & M. Kalantzis (Eds.), *Ubiquitous learning*. Urbana, IL: University of Illinois Press.

Burbules, N.C. (2005). Rethinking the virtual. In J. Weiss, J. Nolan, & P. Trifonas (Eds.), *The international handbook of virtual learning environments* (pp. 3–24). Dordrecht, The Netherlands: Kluwer Publishers.

Burbules, N.C., Callister, Jr., T.A., & Taaffe, C. (2006). Beyond the digital divide. In S.Y. Tettegah & R.C. Hunter (Eds.), *Technology and education: Issues in administration, policy and applications in K-12 schools* (pp. 85–99). New York: Elsevier.

Subject and Name Index 106.2

217